— evenness

The range of styles & quality is wide
but there are a
# of fine papers
in this collection, and
their themes harmonize
to create ~~content~~
in subtle but ~~ways/~~ these ~~short~~
~~revre~~ make small effort
to ~~demonstrate~~
sugg.

ANTHROPOLOGY IN THE HIGH VALLEYS:

ESSAYS ON
THE NEW GUINEA HIGHLANDS
IN HONOR OF
KENNETH E. READ

KENNETH E. READ

ANTHROPOLOGY IN THE HIGH VALLEYS:

ESSAYS ON
THE NEW GUINEA HIGHLANDS
IN HONOR OF
KENNETH E. READ

L. L. Langness and Terence E. Hays, Editors

Chandler & Sharp Publishers Inc.
11A Commercial Boulevard, Novato, CA 94947

CHANDLER & SHARP PUBLICATIONS IN ANTHROPOLOGY
AND RELATED FIELDS

GENERAL EDITORS: L.L. LANGNESS AND ROBERT B. EDGERTON

Library of Congress Cataloging-in-Publication Data

Anthropology in the high valleys.

(Chandler & Sharp publications in anthropology and
related fields)
Includes bibliographies.
Contents: A day for stealing : A deviance in a
New Guinea society / L.L. Langness—Semen, spittle,
blood, and sweat : a New Guinea theory of nutrition /
Anna Meigs—"Taboos" and statements about taboos :
issues in the taxonomic analysis of behavioral
restrictions among the New Guinea Kafe / Harold G.
Levine—[etc.]
1. Ethnology—Papua New Guinea. 2. Papua New
Guinea—Social life and customs. 3. Read, Kenneth E.
I. Langness, L.L. (Lewis L.) 1929-
II. Hays, Terence E. III. Series.
DU740.42.A57 1987 306'.0995 86-26415
ISBN 0-88316-555-4

International Standard Book Number: 0-88316-555-4
Library of Congress Catalog Card Number: 86-26415
Printed in the United States of America

Jacket Art & Design: Jacki Gallagher

Contents

Preface

The mid 1950's was a period of rapid growth for the profession of anthropology. This was true for the University of Washington just as it was elsewhere in the United States. Professor James B. Watson was hired to replace Professor Erna Gunther as chairman and to recruit additional faculty. Among the first to be recruited by Watson was Kenneth E. ("Mick") Read who, as the story was told, was on his way to Europe for a sabbatical leave when offered a visiting associate professorship in 1957. I first encountered him upon entering the graduate school at that time. I believe I was his first graduate student. He has remained in Seattle ever since with time out, of course, now and then, to visit New Guinea and other parts of the world. Along with Watson he generated much student interest in New Guinea so that a substantial number of graduate students pursued their fieldwork in that at that time remote and relatively still untouched place. Those students, along with students from other universities who worked in the New Guinea Highlands, were all stimulated by his work, most particularly three classic papers, "Nama Cult of the Central Highlands" (1952), "Cultures of the Central Higlands" (1954), and "Morality and the Concept of the Person Among the Gahuku-Gama" (1955). His book, *The High Valley* (1965) has also become an anthropological classic. *Other Voices* (1980), while very different from the *The High Valley*, does share the same original, literary and innovative style that has come to identify his work.

Mick Read, now retired in Seattle, was an unusual presence in the University of Washington anthropology department. An Australian by birth, trained at the University of Sydney and later at the University of London (LSE), Read never made a fetish

of social anthropology as such. Perhaps this was the
influence of S. F. Nadel with whom he had worked in
Sydney or that of Sir Raymond Firth whom he
encountered at London. In any case Read's work
cannot be characterized as rigid in its orientation,
but, rather, as eclectic and to the point of his own
interest at the time. Naturally one sees the
influence of Durkheim and others of that tradition
but never in the dogmatic or narrow-minded form it
was found in the work of Radcliffe-Brown himself or
the true believer, Max Gluckman. Although Mick never
became caught up in the culture and personality
orientation of his close friend and colleague,
Melford Spiro, he has always been sensitive to
personality and has much insight into human
psychology.

As a teacher Kenneth Read is a bit formal in his
classroom presentation, lecturing from prepared notes
and not always responding well to questions from the
class. Out of class, however, he is quite different,
friendly and concerned and willing to give endlessly
of his time, answering questions with pleasure. It
is this faculty of caring for students and others
that has endeared him to so many. He has always been
generous with students, often with financial aid as
well as with his time.

There was considerable espirit de corps among
the students and faculty in the 1950's. Although the
department was growing there were still few enough of
us that there were parties as well as lectures and
events that could be and usually were attended by
all. Mick was very active in bringing this about and
with his remarkable sense of humor could entertain us
endlessly with tales of his experiences in the
Australian horse cavalry and marvelous anecdotes from
the New Guinea Highlands. When Herbert Passin left
the University of Washington Mick presided at his
going away banquet, reading with a perfectly straight
face his take off on Northwest Coast ethnography,
"The Skittish and the Squeamish." Subsequently the
graduate students, with Mick in a leading role, put
on his play entitled "Schubert's Unfinished

Chimpanzee," a commentary on the trials and
tribulations of graduate students trying to get
through the department at that time. As chairman of
the department for ten years (1960 - 70) his sense of
humor may have been sorely tried but it never
disappeared and, happily, is with him now.

Hays' experience of Mick a decade later was much
the same. As he reports it:

"In the spring of 1969 I received a telegram
from K. E. Read, who was then chairman of the
Department of Anthropology, offering me a fellowship
to complete my graduate training at the University of
Washington. After three years of graduate work
elsewhere, my commitment to New Guinea studies was
firm and the University of Washington then provided
the best such program in the country. Being able to
study under K. E. Read, James B. Watson, and L. L.
Langness was a privilege, and they were actually
proposing to pay me to enjoy it!

"I had read all of Read's work, of course, and
The High Valley had prepared me to some extent for
the man I would come to know better over the next
four years. In those days before 'reflective
anthropology,' his book stood out almost alone and in
Savery Hall (where the Department was then located),
he was almost a legend. He had influenced --
'trained' is not really the right word -- many
students, some of whom were almost legends
themselves. It is not easy to specify the ways in
which his influence was felt at that time. Most of
his published papers could be considered in the
tradition of British Social Anthropology, but I was
personally never reminded of that dimension of his
view of the world. What sticks in my mind is the
remarkably human *tone* of encounters with the man.

"Conversations with Mick were always rewarding,
leaving one with a sense that scholarship and
sensitivity to human concerns were not only mutually
compatible but necessary complements of each other.
For a graduate student, faced with the daily
anxieties of papers, comprehensive exams, and

research grant proposals, such lessons were deeply
appreciated.

"In 1970 few of us in the department had as much
access to Mick Read the man as we wanted, but
Professor Read was very much the same person, and
opportunities to learn from him in that role abounded
for those who attended his undergraduate courses. At
that time, his course called 'Comparative Morals and
Values' was considered the most concentrated and
systematic exposure one could obtain to what he had
to teach. I formally enrolled in the course as a way
of disciplining myself to 'hear the man out,' even
when all of his ideas were not welcome ones. In the
late 1960s and early 1970s, there were many with
willing ears for a view of morality as the
encouragement of the full development of individual
potential. Far fewer were those who were ready to
consider *evaluating* societies in terms of the degree
to which they accomplished that end. Anthropology
was supposed to preach 'relativity,' we thought, but
here was an anthropologist who wanted us to consider
the implications, both scholarly and personal, of
positions casually asserted with regard to what he
considered the most important issues of all.

"As with the *The High Valley*, it was not
immediately apparent whether Mick Read was 'ahead of
his time' (as the current fashion for studies of
'selfhood' and 'personhood' might suggest), or simply
'out of his time.' In any event, he founded no
'school' and was more inspirational than quotable.
Indeed, in the eyes of some he had dropped out of
academic anthropology by then. They have been
surprised by his recent resurgence as a scholar in
Other Voices and additional papers in recent years.

"At least as much as in these latest writings,
Mick's influence and effects can be seen clearly in
the present collection of essays, written by
anthropologists who have had to come to personal
terms, as did he, with aggressive flamboyant New
Guinea Highlanders. The peoples we discuss in these
papers could not be less like Mick Read in their
personalities and values, but they and he have

forever affected us all, in our lives and in our
work."

When the idea for this volume first surfaced we
considered asking all of Mick's many students and
colleagues to contribute. As we could think of so
many we soon concluded the volume might well get out
of hand both in terms of the breadth of interest that
would be represented as well as the length. As his
own interest has been so much in New Guinea we
decided to put together a volume of papers only on
the New Guinea Highlands. While this represents only
a small part of his influence it still represents our
heartfelt affection, appreciation and admiration.

L. L. Langness, Stuttgart
Terence E. Hays, Canberra

A Day for Stealing : Deviance in a New Guinea Society

L. L. Langness

In his "Morality and the Concept of the Person
Among the Gahuku Gama" (1955), an article in some
ways remarkably ahead of its time in view of the
recent interest in the "Anthropology of Self"
(Heelas and Lock 1981; Shweder and Bourne 1984),
Kenneth Read made a series of insightful
generalizations dealing with New Guinea Highlanders'
beliefs about morality and human nature. In the
space of that one article he was unable to offer
specific examples. In this paper I would like to
examine the case of one deviant personality in the
New Guinea Highlands that illustrates many of the
points made in Read's pioneering paper and also
raises further questions about the relationship of
individuals to their cultural context. The Bena
Bena speaking peoples of the Eastern Highlands were
neighbors of the Gahuku-Gama and while not
culturally identical are in most respects very
similar. Like all groups of people they have
occasional troublemakers which, while unfortunate
for them, provides the social scientist with
valuable data:

> There are people in all societies who
> steal, murder, rape, cheat, lie, betray,
> bully, blaspheme, or otherwise offend.

Such people make trouble for other people who then react with indignation, outrage, horror, or direct punitive action. People who make trouble for others by breaking socially accepted rules are known in the social sciences as *deviants*. In everyday life, deviance is a practical problem influenced by law or custom or decency and it requires practical solutions. For social scientists, the problems raised by deviance are theoretical. Why do some people, and not others, break rules and cause trouble? What happens to them when they do? In seeking the answers to these important yet unanswered questions, we shall find that the most fundamental issues about man and society must also be raised (Edgerton 1976:1).

I first heard of Malo,* "a man who steals," in the third month of my original 16 months of fieldwork with the Bena Bena of the New Guinea Highlands (Langness 1963, 1964, 1965, 1967, 1968, 1974, 1976). He was said to be in jail in Goroka, the District Headquarters, some 20 miles to the west. I paid little attention until I saw him for the first time late in the same month and kept an account of his behavior which I either saw or was told about for the next year. Much of the following is from an account I sketched later which I have elaborated upon for inclusion in this volume:

Suddenly, silently, Malo appeared, standing rigidly erect with one hand on the fence enclosing my grassless bare yard.

"It's Malo, back from jail again," murmured Katano, my interpreter, and, as he spoke, I noticed that the normally raucous children were hushed. All eyes were on the strange man who had appeared bringing with him such utter silence.

Malo was not a tall man even by local

* A fictional name as are all others in this paper.

standards. But he was a large man, with a huge barrel chest, powerful arms and hands, and an immense head from which peered two unblinking deep-set and remarkably brown eyes. The impression was one of enormous strength as he stood there rock-like and dignified, staring in at us with no outward trace of curiosity. Most of the men of the village still wore their traditional dress but Malo, in contrast, wore an incredibly dirty lap lap of faded black, topped by a cheap trade store undershirt which was, amazingly it seemed, even filthier. He stood and continued to stare for what I felt was an uncomfortably long time. Perspiration in heavy drops glittered on his forehead or hung suspended from the base of the thick hair above. He turned and walked slowly down the path towards the men's house, looking neither to the right nor the left. Our own eyes continued to be fastened on him, however, as he walked leisurely, carefully, deliberately placing one foot in front of the other it seemed, down the path. Finally he disappeared into the thick clumps of bamboo which hid the men's house from our view.

"Who is Malo?" I asked. I could not help whispering.

After a short pause Katano answered, "He is a man who steals."

"Why didn't you tell me about him when I did the census?" I demanded. I was irritated as I thought I had thoroughly recorded everyone in the village.

"He is my brother and I am ashamed." Katano looked down at this feet as he spoke.

"A true brother?" I asked, knowing that in American terms he might be some form of cousin.

"He is the son of my father's elder brother. But he is a man who steals and brings us shame."

The following morning, when all of the people had assembled, the village counselor (Langness 1963) said, "Malo has returned from jail. He has no wife, no gardens, no pigs. But he is our brother and we must look after him. If he takes things from your

gardens that is nothing . . . you must not be cross
with him. But if he steals your pigs you can bring
him to me and I will decide what we can do. Malo
has been in jail many times. If your are cross with
him he may use his knife. He may cut you."

No one else spoke. Malo was not present at the
meeting. The people left quickly for their weekly
but distasteful road maintenance which the counselor
demanded of them. I was fascinated by the
counselor's benevolent attitude and the fact that no
one had objected. I was even more fascinated by
Malo and determined to learn as much as possible
about him.

"Why was Malo put in jail?" I asked Katano
later.

"He killed one of Sosola's pigs and ate it," he
answered simply.

"Why was he in jail before?" I persisted.

"He is a man who steals, that's all," said
Katano. From his tone it was obvious he did not
wish to discuss it further. I temporarily dropped
the subject.

I found that observing Malo was a difficult
task. He had a habit of disappearing early in the
morning and returning after dark. He did not attend
the morning meetings nor did he, except very rarely,
work with the other men. No one seemed to know just
where he spent his time. They claimed he just sat
out in the *kunai* (grasslands) by himself which
seemed to me most unlikely. On those occasions when
I did see Malo he usually sat to one side alone. He
spoke only occasionally, and always briefly. He was
a good worker when, for some mysterious reason, he
seemed motivated to help. He carried heavier loads
than anyone else with no signs of discomfort and he
handled the heavy twelve-foot-tubes of water-filled
bamboo with an ease that made most others look
awkward. When he helped with housebuilding he knew
what needed to be done and performed his tasks
skillfully and with no hesitation. After a time I
came to the conclusion that Malo was, perhaps,
slightly dull-witted but obviously competent to

perform all the actions necessary to assure his material survival.

"Why does Malo steal?" I asked Katano on another occasion. "Is he *negi negi*" (insane [Langness 1965]).

Katano laughed, "No, he is not insane. He has always stolen things, that is just his way. When he was small he did the same thing."

"But all the children steal," I countered.

"Yes, but the rest of us gave up stealing when we grew bigger. Malo has never given it up. He is just a man who steals. Our fathers used to beat him for it all the time but still he has never given it up."

Questioning further, I learned that Malo's father had died when he was about sixteen and his mother shortly thereafter. The cause of both deaths was attributed to sorcery but no revenge had been taken. There was nothing much one could make of that as orphans were unknown and Malo had been well cared for by Katano's father. What appeared to be of more significance was the fact that Malo alone, of all the youths of his age grade, had refused to be initiated. When the men held him and attempted to force the bent lengths of strong supple cane down his throat he simply refused to open his mouth. It was a dangerous custom and the boys had been warned to be careful lest the ends of the cane come out their noses and kill them, but even so, it was unheard of that a boy could be so cowardly. The men had beaten him severely; they threatened, cajoled, made fun of him, shamed him, but still Malo had kept his mouth tightly fastened and refused to participate. Finally, they had been forced to give up, but he had never been forgiven. Because of this, and perhaps because he already had a reputation for stealing and deviance, the older men did not buy a bride for him when his age-mates married. This, too, was a shameful experience, but everyone agreed that he would never be able to properly look after a wife. It was shortly after this that Malo had gone to jail for the first time.

He had gone to the coast to work on a copra
plantation and while there had stolen a pair of
shorts. When he had been questioned about it he
refused to answer, and he had seldom spoken since
that time. He received a two-month sentence for the
theft.

Much later, in a casual conversation with
Vilolo, I learned the circumstances of Malo's second
sentence.

"Malo and Paloli were out walking about in the
kunai," Vilolo reported, "they were not working or
doing anything. They were just walking about with
their bows and arrows. They picked some tanket
(cordyline) leaves and hung them from their waists
and were singing and pretending to dance. A woman
from Nagamitobo came by. I don't know what she was
doing out in the kunai alone but anyway, she was
there. Paloli said, 'Malo, if you are a real man
you will have intercourse with that woman.' Malo
didn't want to do it but Paloli . . . ah, Paloli . .
. he was a man who liked to play . . . kept telling
him, 'Malo, you are not a real man unless you have
intercourse with her. If you were a real man you
would do it. You are just like a woman.' The woman
was frightened and tried to run away but Paloli
caught her and held her, all the time talking strong
to Malo. Finally Malo did it. He put an arrow to
his bow and threated to kill her. She was afraid
and submitted to him. But later she told her
husband and he came with the Kiap (Patrol Officer)
and took Malo to jail. They kept him there for
three months."

Vilolo laughed heartily as he recounted this to
me. He thought it was very funny indeed. He and
Paloli had been close friends before the latter had
died. Vilolo never tired of relating anecdotes
about him.

Still later, I found out from Katano that Malo
had subsequently molested Fomalini, a little girl
who had been brought to our village as a bride but
who had not yet menstruated. Momosafa's wife had

seen and reported him. Again, he had been sentenced
to three months.

Then there had been a long period during which
Malo had behaved himself and caused no trouble. He
had actually tried to settle down with a wife. He
found a woman who liked him and coaxed her into
running away with him. He had brought her home and
left her with Katano's wife. Malo had wanted to be
married, to have a garden and raise pigs. But after
a few days, for whatever reasons, he stopped coming
to help Katano with the garden fence they had
started for his new "wife" and, naturally enough,
Katano stopped working on it also. Malo just
wandered aimlessly about paying no further attention
to the woman and finally she ran away.

"Why do you let Malo stay here?" I asked
Katano after he had related all this to me. "If he
steals and bothers little girls why do you let him
stay?"

"He is our brother," he said, "where would he
go? Who would look after him? He doesn't always
steal, sometimes he goes a long time without doing
anything troublesome. It is just sometimes that he
steals and does things that cause trouble."

Somehow I doubted that this was quite true.
Malo had been stealing constantly since I had first
encountered him. But it was mostly petty thievery.
He would steal tobacco from Katano's house, sweet
potatoes from the gardens, and once he had stolen
two mirrors and a comb from somewhere and hidden
them in the men's house. They were found and taken
to the counselor but, as no one claimed them, he
finally returned them to Malo. Indeed, there were
moments when I thought the situation was ludicrous
as, for example, when I saw Kenaro one morning
walking around carrying three bows and an enormous
bundle of arrows.

"Why are you carrying three bows and all those
arrows?" I inquired.

"If I leave them in the men's house Malo will
steal them," he replied matter-of-factly.

After a long time and much intensive questioning I began to understand some of the reasons for their remarkable tolerance. Although he was virtually unique in the village because he was lefthanded, Malo was an excellent bowman. Many of the days when he was mysteriously absent in the kunai, he was actually prowling about in other places, shooting and stealing pigs which he invariably shared with the others. Malo would shoot someone's pig, carry it home with his enormous strength, and secretly cook it nearby. Then he would offer it to other men, women and children -- saying grandly, "I don't like this pig, here, you take it," or, "I eat pig all the time, here, you take this piece."

Being chronically meat hungry, everyone appreciated these unexpected gifts of pork. As long as it was not their own pigs that were disappearing they considered it quite a windfall. But Malo occasionally got caught while on these forays. Once he and a young boy, Sipo, had gone to Katagu, a neighboring group an hour's walk away. Malo had just shot a huge pig with one clean shot behind a foreleg when two of the Katagu men caught him, took him by the arms, and asked him what he was doing. Malo said innocently that he was "looking for fire" and when they temporarily released their grip he shook free, turned, and threatened to kill them with his bow which he still held. He was so strong and fierce that the Katagu men were frightened and ran away. Sipo, who had been hiding on a sharp ridge behind some rocks, laughed so hard at their cowardice that he lost his balance and rolled hysterically to the bottom of the ravine. At least that was Sipo's story, and he delighted in repeating it over and over again, denigrating Katagu, and adding to Malo's peculiar reputation.

Malo was old enough to have fought in battle before warfare had been effectively suppressed. He had apparently distinguished himself as an able, even talented warrior. His bravery and competence in battle was well known and respected. Thus, so long as he did not steal blatantly, consequentially, from his own group, they were perfectly willing to tolerate him and he was, it appeared, an asset.

But Malo, it seemed, could last only so long before doing something that would result in his being jailed. The fourth time was for killing a pig that belonged to Kenaro. Even though Kenaro was of Malo's own lineage he could not tolerate the theft. Kenaro had been looking after the pig for a special purpose. His adopted daughter was to have her first menstruation soon and he had wanted to kill the pig in honor of that important occasion. Malo's theft completely disrupted his plans. Kenaro was so angry he immediately had Malo tried in front of the Kiap and, of course, Malo was found guilty and incarcerated again. As always, Malo refused to speak in his own defense, not that he had any defense, and he made no excuse whatsoever. He went as silently to jail as he came out.

Upon his return from this particular sentence, in one of his rare moments of almost jocularity, Malo told some of the younger men that now he "understood" the jail. "I will not die there," he said. "If I steal and they put me in jail I will just come back. I can stay in jail and get good food and I will come back. If I cut someone with my knife they will put me in jail but I will come back. I am not afraid of the jail."

Strangely however, Malo was not a violent man. He had never actually hurt anyone from the village. Nonetheless, he had a reputation and people talked of him and were afraid. His clansmen took care of him, gave him food, and tried to make him understand that they did not want to put him in jail. Malo did well for quite a long time. He pilfered only insignificant items and began to participate more and more in everyday village life. He cajoled another woman into running away with him and this one he left with Kenaro's wife. But the same thing happened as had happened previously; Malo tired of her, ignored her, and she eventually returned to where he had found her. People laughed at his

attempts to get married but he did not seem to mind.
He had an unusual tolerance for being the butt of
jokes and seemed never to become angry. The small
children teased him, poked at him with sticks, made
fun of him, mocked him, but through it all he merely
sat placidly, expressionless, and said nothing. He
was fond of the children in his strange quiet way
and he often gave them gifts of things he had
stolen. Once, for example, he was walking
stealthily through a grove of casuarina trees with
two small pigs, still alive, with their legs trussed
tightly together. He carried one suspended under
each armpit from a bark string around his neck.
Numukola, a young girl, saw him and jokingly asked
for one of the pigs. To her surprise and delight he
casually gave her one without a word and he then
went off to cook the other one which he shared with
some of the other children. He was generous,
humble, even meek; a pleasant but disturbingly
idiosyncratic character. It was just that
occasionally he did something the others simply
could not tolerate. He apparently could not help
himself. His fifth trip to jail was for molesting a
little girl, one of the counselor's daughters. Malo
had meant no harm, he simply could not resist
touching and fondling the little girl who had come
so trustingly to lie in his lap. The people said,
"That is no good! She is too small! She is of our
own clan. She is the same as his own child."

The counselor had him put in jail. Malo,
again, said nothing.

On the rare occasions when I could observe Malo
I could not help but like him. He had a simple,
shy, winning, and timid smile. Sometimes, when he
saw me watching and studying him he would grin as if
he knew I would never understand. He never looked
angry or took offense. I watched him at every
opportunity, trying to understand just what it was
that made him the deviant he so obviously was. I
became obsessed with being able to understand his
aberrant behavior and the exceedingly nurturant
behavior of the others towards him. I felt certain

that they must have an explanation of their own for Malo's behavior and sought desperately for it, questioning everyone. There was no point in questioning Malo himself, I had tried it several times and was met, without exception, with a smile and silence. No one could explain Malo any better than I could. They would simply repeat, "He is a man who steals, that is his way."

There were further incidents in which I looked for clues. There was at that time a man, Kala, living in our village. Kala, unlike the majority of the male residents, did not belong there by virtue of birth. Long before, a man of our village had fled to take refuge in Kala's natal village and had, for reasons which are not clear, looked after Kala. As a consequence of this, Kala was considered his son and had come here to take up residence. Kala was a man of truly violent temper. He had recently spent three years in jail for brutally murdering and dismembering his wife with a bush knife. Malo had been helping himself to sweet potatoes from all the gardens for a long time and no one had admonished him for it. But, one day he took some food from Kala's garden, and Kala became enraged. Early the following morning he attacked Malo with a hatchet. He had surprised him in the men's house and, with no warning, inflicted a very clean, deep, nasty gash behind his left ear. Malo did not retaliate, nor did he say anything. Kala was quickly restrained by other men who were present at the time. Katano, Kenaro and Waru, who were Malo's cousins and closest relatives, were very angry, and for a time it appeared as though there might be a serious large scale altercation. At first they insisted on taking Kala directly to the Kiap but then, realizing that Malo had, in fact, stolen from his garden, they were in a quandary. While they were arguing back and forth, cursing Kala and telling him repeatedly that he did not really belong there, Malo sat unashamed, holding a dirty leaf to his cut, saying, as usual, nothing at all. Kala was so upset that at one point he attempted to set fire to his house, threatening to leave the village, but was quickly restrained by some of the uninvolved spectators.

After the tumult had quieted, Katano angrily explained to me, "Malo is always like that. He never says anything. If he would just open his mouth and talk when these things happen he would not have to go to jail. If he would just tell the Kiap that he can't help it . . . If he would just tell him that he is a man who steals and can't help it . . . then he would not have to go to jail. If he would just tell that to the Kiap he would understand. But he never says anything at all. He just sits there with his mouth shut. Malo has always stolen. That is his way. He can't help it."

I pondered silently to myself Katano's naivete about whatever sympathy Malo might expect from the Kiap, and I watched horrified as they dry shaved around Malo's ear with a dull trade store razor. Malo showed no sign of emotion whatsoever. I put a crude bandage over the gaping naked wound which stayed attached, as I remember, approximately ten minutes before being discarded in the mud.

For quite a long while after this incident Malo avoided further trouble. He stayed in the village although he still did not work. He began to live with one very old woman who looked after him, cooked his food, and talked with him at great length. She was the only one to whom he would talk freely but she would never tell anyone, including myself, what he said to her. She was very old and very feeble. Malo brought her firewood every day without fail and sometimes he helped her with her garden. He stopped sleeping in the men's house and began sleeping on the floor of her decrepit, falling-down old house. When Vilolo and Solo were buying a bride for one of the boys, Malo accompanied them, at their invitation, as they walked for miles in all directions offering the bride price at scattered villages. Malo became less withdrawn, less taciturn, and he began to smile more often. But he still would talk only if just one person were with him. When there were more he remained silent. I asked Vilolo why the old woman looked after Malo. He replied, "He has no wife. Every morning he waits until the other men leave the men's house and then he cooks his own food. She was sorry for him so she looks after him now." He added, as an afterthought, "Malo steals all the time. He takes tobacco and newspaper to make cigarettes mostly. But we don't forget him. We look after him. He walks around together with us."

Malo's stealing did cause certain minor problems from time to time. Once some stick tobacco disappeared from Katano's house. Katano was angry with his wife, thinking she had taken it, and had beaten her. When she denied it he became angry at his daughter, Numuhola. The three of them did not speak to each other for several days, until someone reported to Katano that they had seen Malo sneaking out of his house and running away. Then Katano was sorry he had beaten his wife.

Other people, too, were constantly missing minor items. They usually just shrugged it off, knowing that Malo had probably taken them, never making an issue of it, although they would sometimes shout angrily to everyone that something was missing.

It was almost exactly eleven months from the day I first saw Malo until his stealing broke out again in an important and troublesome way within the village itself. First, Malo and a boy from another place joined forces and shot a pig belonging to one of the other nearby clans. As they were trussing it to carry it away to a hidden spot, some men from there caught them. Malo and the boy were locked overnight in a house after first being severely beaten. The following morning their captors wanted to take them before the Kiap but Katano and several other men, who had heard what had happened, went there and convinced them that it would not be right. They said, "You can't both beat them like that and send them to jail too, that would not be right." So they let Malo go but instructed him never to trespass on their territory again. They threatened

to kill him on sight. Undaunted, Malo returned to
our village and immediately killed a pig belonging
to Gio. Gio was livid! He brought the matter up
before the counselor and threatened to send Malo to
jail for the sixth time. But Katano and the others
again came to his defense saying, "Malo can't help
stealing. You know that. It is just his way. He
was like that when he was small, his mother gave
birth to him like that and he can't help it." They
knew Malo would say nothing and he did not. Gio,
unmollified, left to report to the Kiap.

It should have been obvious to me by this time
that the locals could not explain Malo's behavior,
just as I could not, in spite of their remarkable
tolerance for it. Malo was a puzzle, partly
admired, part legend, part clown, the subject of
innumerable anecdotes, and the butt of many jokes.
I was still unwilling to give up without trying at
least once more for a better explanation. I turned
to Katano, my interpreter for more than a year, one
of those rare interpreters who was genuinely
interested in understanding his own culture and in
trying to explain it to me.

"Katano," I said seriously, "you must think
hard, and tell me, why does Malo steal all the time?
What is wrong with him that he is not like other
people? What do you think about it?"

Running through my mind were all sorts of
explanations for Malo's deviant behavior. There was
the possible trauma of his parent's death, the
failure to go through with the initiation, the fact
that he had never married, his relationship with
others who sometimes encouraged him to steal pigs,
his possible mild retardation, or the fact that he
was caught up in a rapidly changing situation with
its attendant role conflicts. I wanted, I guess,
some similar explanation from the people themselves.
I wanted, at least, a more reasonable explanation
from them than they had given me in the past.

Katano turned very solemn. He looked at his
feet, which was his usual custom when thinking very
hard. He fidgeted, facing one way and then the

other on the camp stool he always sat on when in my
house. Finally, after much deliberation, he slowly,
and with much loving care, rolled a cigarette of
native tobacco and newspaper. He crossed his legs
and then uncrossed them. I waited.

Through the open window I saw Keno, lying
across his mother's crossed legs like a boy floating
in an inner tube, swinging his chubby legs and
sucking greedily on one long, withered dry breast
while pulling on the other with his hands. Bored,
he stood up, held his mother's chin with his left
hand, her nose with his right, forced her mouth open
and peered inside. Satisfied, he pulled the bilum
off her partially bald head and hit down hard on it
with his fist. I still waited.

Katano was concentrating. At last, leaning
down and putting his elbows on his knees, he said
with finality, "I have thought about it a lot. I
have wondered for a long time. Now I know. You see
. . . Malo has a day for stealing, and, when that
day comes, he steals."

I cannot claim to fully understand Malo's
deviance; but his case does illustrate clearly many
of the aspects of New Guinea behavior and morality
that were of concern to Read. It is certainly "a
tribal morality as distinct from the universal
morality of Christian teaching" (Read 1955:256).

No one, for example, ever suggested to me that
Malo's rape of a woman from another clan was morally
wrong. Indeed, the men of Malo's clan recounted the
incident with relative glee and obviously thought it
was more humorous then criminal. In the pre-contact
New Guinea Highlands lone women simply expected to
be raped and did not ordinarily travel without
companions. Whether women themselves felt this was
either universally or morally wrong I do not know.
The information I gathered from women leads me to
believe only that they felt women should not allow
themselves to be found alone. Similarly, no one
ever expressed to me in any way that Malo's penchant
for stealing pigs was wrong -- provided it was not
their pigs that were at issue. It was not uncommon

for most men to occasionally hunt "wild pigs" which,
I eventually learned, was more of a euphemism than a
reality. Rape, pig stealing, and the luring away of
women from other groups as Malo also attempted, were
all expected and even encouraged behaviors. The
rules of morality that pertained to the clan did not
extend much further than that.

As Read also indicated, there is a
"distributive" feature to the moral system
(1955:257). The members of Malo's own subclan felt
more of an obligation to him than did other clansmen
of other subclans, although how clearly Malo himself
felt similar obligations is not entirely clear to
me. Certainly he did not hesitate to steal from his
subclansmen as well as others. Here, however, the
distinction between theft and "borrowing without
permission" becomes difficult to distinguish. Malo
truly was a nuisance. Hardly a week went by without
someone accusing him of having pilfered something.
Whether he was guilty or not, people believed he was
guilty. But although they complained loudly and
sometimes bitterly they rarely tried to do anything
about it. The incident involving Kala is
instructive here. Although Malo was quite clearly
guilty it was felt that Kala had overreacted by
attacking him with a hatchet. Kala's peripheral
status in the village, not usually a matter of
importance, was brought up by Malo's close kinsmen
who suggested that Kala "did not really belong
there." Kala's dramatic attempt to burn his house
brought those in other subclans to his defense.
Eventually the incident played itself out, but not
without a residue of ill feeling that probably
survives even now. In any case it was obvious that
Malo's closest kinsmen defended him while those more
distantly related were better able to mediate or at
least remain neutral.

Malo's fondling of little girls is a much more
difficult issue than any of the above. It was
rarely mentioned by anyone and then only when it
became necessary. Although I have little
information about it, I believe that in the eyes of

my informants it was an unprecedented situation of
which they were genuinely ashamed. As people
commented to the effect that the girls involved were
clan children, "the same as his own child," it might
be inferred that if they were children from other
places it would have been permissible. I cannot
believe this is so. I suspect that describing the
problem in that particular way is the result of
having no previous experience with such a form of
behavior. This is not to say they would have
necessarily condemned it had it occurred otherwise,
but I am certain they would not have defended it.
This could be seen as an example of "curious
possibilities, neither intrinsically right nor
wrong, which they themselves would not consider
correct" (Read 1955:261), but I fear this may be an
oversimplification. As far as I know, the Bena
Bena, like the Gahuku-Gama, believe that
homosexuality is "foolish rather than immoral"
(1955:261), but I am not certain they feel quite the
same way about child molestation. They abhor
incest, for example, and say that it is animal-like,
but the same analogy does not hold well for fondling
small girls. Similarly, it could not have been
"fondling," as such, that caused the problem for
Malo, as small children are almost constantly
"fondled" in some sense. Thus, at the very least,
Malo's particular fondling was regarded as
inappropriate and it obviously offended people in a
way that transcended mere "foolishness." It would
seem to me to have been regarded as "wrong" in at
least some sense of that term. And, as children are
highly valued throughout the Highlands, I find it
difficult to believe that molesting a little girl
from elsewhere would have been seen as any more
acceptable, even though it might have happened, and
even though it might have been difficult or
impossible to actually have done anything about it.
Another case involving children that I have
discussed elsewhere (1981:28) is of relevance here.
Two boys about six years old were locked in a house
as punishment for pulling feathers from chickens

that belonged to a local policeman. The villagers
were outraged at this totally unprecedented act and,
after some time and much discussion, broke into the
house and released them. It was the restraint of
individual freedom that was at issue, not the
question of their guilt or innocence. What is
critical here, however, is that the act of
incarceration was clearly and unequivocally regarded
as wrong. Again, even though this could have
happened had the boys not been locals, I believe it
would not have been defended, philosophically, as
merely a "curiosity." The fact is, in the latter
case, whether it was regarded as wrong or not, it
would have been unlikely that anyone either could
have or would have interfered short of outright
warfare. It might be argued that it is not so much
the absence of broadly and potentially generalizable
moral prescriptions at issue as much as it is the
absence of machinery for insuring compliance, along,
perhaps, with a relative lack of interest in
philosophizing about such matters. We have to agree
with Read "that there is a certain minimum of
behavior which is considered appropriate to human
beings." Whether or not these standards are
universalized is still open to question. What Read
described for the New Guinea case is not
fundamentally so different from the Western-European
case:

> My own point is that human life
> (among the Gahuku-Gama) is given a
> variable value, depending on the social
> positioning of different individuals. It
> is unthinkable to kill in certain
> contexts, wrong in others, right in
> others, and a matter of indifference in
> others. In each case, the moral nature of
> particular social bonds is the important
> factor rather than anything intrinsic to
> man as such. To sum up: morality is
> primarily contextual. The moral judgement
> does not operate from the fixed
> perspective of universal obligation for

the moral assessment of behaviour varies
in different social contexts, according,
that is, to the different values placed on
different   individuals   in   different
contexts (1955:263).

A cynic might well observe that the only real
difference between this case and the Christian one
is in the lip service paid to a supposed universal
commandment by the latter which is conspicuously
lacking in the former. But does the absence of a
specifically verbalized universal moral rule mean
that no such sentiment can exist? In this
particular instance does it mean that it is
permissable to abuse small children at will provided
they are not members of one's own group? I think
not. Even in a society where personal and group
strength makes most things possible it does not
necessarily make them right. People are often
offended by the acts of "big men," but they can
usually do little about it. If Malo had molested
children in a different clan I have no doubt that
his own clansmen would have attempted to defend him.
But they would not have felt that what he did was
either right or even neutral. They would have said,
"that is his way," which leads us to the related
question of human nature.

While I see no reason to assert that the
concept of "person" is necessarily a "higher" self
and that of the idiosyncratic "me" a "lower" (Read
1955:249), the distinction is a useful one even
without the evolutionary implications. I concede
that the New Guinea Highlanders do not employ the
concept of the person as it is defined by Read
following Judeo-Christian tradition. Certainly they
do not believe that "the person is ordained directly
to God" or that "we are obliged, as men, to seek the
good," or etc. (1955:250). So let us turn our
attention to the "highly developed feeling and
regard for the ("lower") psycho-physical self, the
idiosyncratic "me" (Read 1955:273), and accept
Read's summing up of desired characteristics:

Modesty is not a virtue: the respected and successful are those who are most loud in their own praise and most positive in their expressions of self-importance. Pride is something to be worn like a banner, and though he may be loved, considered good and shown some esteem, the unassuming and retiring person is never a major influence in the life of the community, for unwillingness to wrangle and to boast is tantamount to an admission that one is a nonentity (1955:274).

By these standards, which are characteristic throughout the Highlands, Malo was most certainly a nonentity. Far from boasting, he virtually never spoke at all and certainly not in public. Similarly, he did not participate in group affairs, such as weddings, funerals, and the elaborate exchanges of pork, as he had no resources to contribute. In turn, no one was obligated to him, so his name was never mentioned during such affairs. Obviously he could never become "a man with a name," a *gipina* (Langness 1968; Read 1959), nor could he sing his own praises or demonstrate his pride. He was the closest thing to a genuine loner that it was possible to be in spite of the periodic attempts of his clansmen to integrate him more successfully into their activities.

Malo was virtually impossible to label. He was not considered to be *negi negi* (insane), although he was sometimes referred to by that term. He was also referred to at times as *guminalobo* (thief) and, more frequently, as *numuyabe*. *Numuyabe*, as near as I could tell, refers to a person who "does not understand." One difference between *negi negi* and *numu* is that the former have episodes but subsequently recover whereas the latter are permanently impaired. *Numu* are also considered to be wanderers. That is, they travel about indiscriminately and are regarded as harmless and thus are not themselves harmed. However, as Malo

was said to "talk straight," and also was capable of
performing most everyday tasks, he was apparently
not properly or completely any of the above, nor was
he regarded as completely harmless. There is no
term for a child molester and, indeed, the people
claimed that before Malo such a thing had never
occurred. The term *numu* also refers to a man who
was not initiated, who did not swallow the *kata*
(bent cane), and this obviously has a broad symbolic
connotation as well as the more precise meaning.
The only explanation I ever heard for Malo's
deviance other than Katano's "day for stealing" was
volunteered to me one day by Solo. Solo observed
that the trouble with Malo was that he did not like
and indulge in the *kata* or in nose bleeding. That
is, he had not been initiated and did not
periodically cleanse himself through cane swallowing
and nose bleeding as he should have. Hence, he did
not get rid of blood and was as a consequence,
"heavy." Thus he was also "rubbish" and could not
be a good fighter (I am aware of the contradiction
here). Solo also indicated that men sometimes
brought this up to Malo and told him to "go and stay
with the women." Interestingly, there was an older,
very successful man, Patani, who was sometimes
jokingly referred to as *numu*. The reason for this
was that Patani, also, had not swallowed the *kata*
during his initiation. In his case, however, he had
actually tried and failed and then subsequently
learned how to do it and actually engaged in it as
men were supposed to do. The only explanation I was
ever given for why some men became *numu* was *nalisa*
(sorcery), but no one seemed very clear about what
particular variety of *nalisa* might be involved (and
several varieties were otherwise distinguished).

Malo's case, on the one hand, is an example of
social control through self-regulation (Nadel 1953)
and on the other, perhaps, an example of a
self-fulfilling prophesy. As Malo did not marry he
could not participate in the normal and expectable
patterns of conduct. As he had no wife, and
therefore no gardens, he also had no pigs. Without

such resources he simply could not participate in
the various activities that would have assured him a
good name and a respectable position in the
community, even had he chosen to do so. Without a
wife he had no in-laws to whom he could turn for
help, no possibility of refuge, and, of course, no
children. Such a person inevitably was "rubbish," a
"weak" man without "strength," as Read discussed
such stereotypes, and one without the ability to
achieve, maintain or deny "equivalence" (Read
1959:428). But in this sense Malo was, as Nadel put
it, being *penalized* rather than *punished* (1953:268).
Indeed, without the introduction of a court system
with its attendant judges and jails it is difficult
to imagine that Malo could have been punished.
Quite likely he would have at some point simply been
killed.

Even though Malo was considered a "rubbishman"
and as such ommitted from most activities, he was
not out of peoples' minds and conversations. The
Bena Bena, like the Gahuku-Gama, "give full
recognition to the idiosyncracies of others, noting
the manner in which they characteristically behave,
their foibles and their typical reactions" (Read
1955:274). The people I talked with and questioned
about Malo's behavior were no more successful than I
was in explaining why he was as he was. Generally,
they merely said over and over again, "that is his
way," "he is just a man who steals," "he has a day
for stealing," and so on. Having not read Freud,
Piaget, or any other developmental psychologists,
they obviously did not connect, or even attempt to
connect, Malo's childhood to his adult behavior.
They believed he had been born the way he was and
also that he could not be expected to change. Solo
did speculate that Malo's problem was his failure to
be initiated and follow the proper male ritual. But
Solo, along with others, agreed that Malo had
characteristically stolen even before that stage of
the initiation rites. But unlike me, they were
relatively unconcerned to explain his behavior,
accepted him as he was, and tried to make the best

of it. But also, unlike Peter Wilson's clever *Oscar* (1974), they were never able to work out a compromise. Try as they might to include Malo in their activities, to help him with a garden or a wife, to feed him and overlook his behavior, Malo invariably went too far and was himself apparently either unwilling or unable to compromise. Their tolerance was remarkable. It was, as Read wrote: ". . . whether a man is characterized as good or bad, dominant or ineffectual, generous or selfish, he is, at the same time, a member of one's own clan or patrilineage, kin of one's wife or mother, and age-mate, member of the tribe or sub-tribe . . ." (1955:277).

I think I understand in some limited fashion how somewhat like Genet (Sartre 1964), once Malo was defined as "a man who steals" he perhaps felt he was more or less forced to continue in that mode. Even his curiosity about and behavior towards little girls might conceivably be explained by his clansmen's unwillingness to furnish him with a bride and the fact that he was never able to participate in the formal and informal courting ceremonies with his age-mates and the other young men and women. Like the Bena Bena themselves, I have no real explanation for the origin of Malo's deviance. I believe his case illustrates much of what Read claimed for tribal morality. I am not certain, however, whether New Guinea Highlanders are unable to make universal moral judgements in at least some cases, or whether they are merely unwilling.

24   L. L. Langness

                     REFERENCES

EDGERTON, ROBERT B.   1976 *Deviance: A   Cross-
    Cultural Perspective*. Menlo Park, California:
    Cummings.
HEELAS, PAUL and LOCK, ANDREW 1981   *Indigenous
    Psychologies: The Anthropology of the Self*.
    New York: Academic Press.
LANGNESS, L. L.   1963 Notes   on   the   Bena Council,
    Eastern Highlands, *Oceania* 33(3):153-170.
LANGNESS, L. L.   1964   Some   Problems   in   the
    Conceptualization   of   Highlands   Social
    Structures, Special   Publication.   *American
    Anthropologist* 66(4) part 2:162-182.
LANGNESS, L. L.   1965 Hysterical Psychosis in the
    New Guinea Highlands: A Bena Bena Example,
    Psychiatry 28:259-277.
LANGNESS, L. L.   1967 Sexual Antagonism in the New
    Guinea Highlands: A Bena Bena Example, *Oceania*
    37(3):161-177.
LANGNESS, L. L.   1968   Bena   Bena   Political
    Organization,   *Anthropological*   Forum
    2(2):180-198.
LANGNESS, L. L.   1974   Ritual, Power   and   Male
    Dominance in the New Guinea Highlands, *Ethos*
    2(3):182-212.
LANGNESS, L. L.   1976 The Nupasafa Cattle: Rural
    Development in the New Guinea Highlands, *New
    Guinea Research Bulletin* 63:67-90.
LANGNESS, L. L.   1981   Child Abuse and Cultural
    Values: The Case of New Guinea. In *Child Abuse
    and Neglect: Cross-Cultural Perspectives*, ed.
    Jill E. Korbin pp. 13-34. Berkeley: University
    of California Pasadena.
NADEL, S. F.   1953   Social   Control   and   Self-
    Regulation, *Social Forces* 31:265-273.
READ, K. E.   1955 Morality and the Concept of the
    Person   Among   the   Gahuku-Gama, *Oceania*
    25(4):233-282.
READ, K. E.   1959 Leadership and Consensus in a New
    Guinea   Society,   *American   Anthropologist*
    61(3):425-436.

SARTRE, JEAN-PAUL   1964   *Saint   Genet: Actor   and Martyr*. New York: Mentor.

SHWEDER, RICHARD A. AND EDMUND J. BOURNE   1984 Does the   Concept   of Person   Vary   Cross-Culturally? In *Culture Theory: Essays   on   Mind, Self, and Emotion*, eds. Richard A.   Shweder and Robert A. LeVine, pp. 158–199.   Cambridge: Cambridge University Press.

WILSON, PETER J.   1974   *Oscar: An Inquiry into the Nature of Sanity*. New York: Random House.

Semen, Spittle, Blood and Sweat: A New Guinea Theory of Nutrition

Anna Meigs

Kenneth Read proposed in 1955 that the Gahuku-Gama concept of person was primarily physical, that the individual's sense of self was rooted in his bodily nature. He went on to assert that this physical self was not narrowly contained within the confines of the skin but present in substances separated from the body in which they originated.

My research among the Hua, an Eastern Highlands population who speak a dialect of Yagaria and are similar in many features to the Gahuku-Gama, reveals a similar attitude toward the self and the body. This paper, very broadly, is an exploration in the Hua context of the themes of self suggested by Read for the Gahuku-Gama.

The Hua are a culturally and linguistically distinct population of 3100 residents at Lufa Station. They conform to the general social organizational model of the Highlands being patrilineal and virilocal. Traditionally a warring society, young males were initiated around puberty into the secrets of the male cult and a segregated life in the men's house. It was, and to a lesser extent still is, a society in which male fighting prowess and tough bold hardness are in much demand. Females were denigrated to young male initiates as repugnant and dangerous.

The Hua are a people who express much of what they know and feel about their selves and their bodies through the medium of food rules. These hundreds of rules are central to Hua culture and definitive in relation to many important issues (Meigs 1984).

There is no edible which the Hua do not pre- or proscribe, nor is there any category of Hua person who is under no form of eating pre- or proscription. Proper regulation of intake of food is a central concern; as a matter of fact the Hua word for "everything" is *do'ado'na* which means literally "that which can be eaten and that which cannot."

The corpus of Hua food rules may be divided into rules of two types. The first type of rule I call homeopathic.

1. An initiate may not eat foods which are slow growing (for example, the slow growing varieties of yam, banana, red pandanus and sugar cane), lest he himself grow slowly.

2. An initiate may not eat food cooked in ashes or foods which exhibit an ashy dry skin (for example, one species of mushroom, all the snakes), lest his own skin become ashy and dry.

3. A girl at menarche may not eat foods which exhibit more than average juiciness (for example, *pit pit*, pandanus oil, sugar cane, leafy green vegetables), lest she stimulate an excessive flow of blood.

The idea of this first type of rule is that the body mirrors the qualities of the foods which it takes in. If as in rule 1 the initiate eats a food which is slow growing then he himself will grow

slowly. If he eats a food which exhibits an ashy
and dry skin (rule 2), then he himself will develop
such a skin which is, incidentally, considered a
prime index of ill health and sexual impotence. If
the girl at menarche consumes fluids (rule 3), then
her body will become more liquid and her menstrual
flow greater.

Although the homeopathic rules represent the
larger corpus and are particularly significant in
inculcating an attitude of disgust toward the female
body in young male initiates, I will not in general
be discussing them here (for a detailed discussion
see Meigs [1984]).

Instead I wish to focus on the smaller half of
the corpus, the rules of food as *nu*. Before
discussing the concept of *nu*, I want to note briefly
that while the homeopathic rules are directed at
individuals in their capacity as exemplars of sex or
age categories, the food-as-*nu* rules are directed at
individuals as participants in social relationships.
Food-as-*nu* rules have withstood the pressures of
contact far better than the homeopathic rules which
are rooted in the traditional sexual ideology.

Nu, which may be translated as "vital essence,"
ensures growth, vitality, and sexual potency. Its
loss leads to stunting for a child, debilitation,
aging, even death for an adult. *Nu* is or is
manifested in all of the body's substances and
products from feces to fingernail, from semen to
shadow. Moreover, all the products of an
individual's labor contain, or perhaps more
correctly, are his or her vital essence. Thus, a
child is the *nu* of his or her parent (and may
literally be referred to as *dnu* "my *nu*"). So too is
an animal which an individual has raised, garden
products which he or she has cultivated, or any
items which he or she has manufactured. The concept
of vital essence is important elsewhere in the
Highlands (Newman 1964; Kelly 1976).

Like the Gahuku-Gama, the Hua have a notion of
self as relatively non-bounded and non-discrete.
Substances released from or produced by the body or

its labor retain their identity as parts of the self
even when removed in both space and time from the
body. The Hua imagine the self as existing both
within the skin and without it, in the latter case
circulating in the environment and subject to
manipulation by others. Thus, if a bit of an
individual's feces or sugar cane pulp (which
contains his or her saliva) is stepped upon, that
individual him or herself will be *bi aina to-*
"pressed or put down." Further, those bits of self
separated from an individual can be ingested by
others with consequent losses of power to their
originator and possible gains to their recipient.
In fact, it is only by careful regulation of all
losses of *nu* in any of its numerous forms and
constant scrutiny of all gains that an individual
can maintain his or her health.

Switching my focus now from *nu* to food, I want
to sharpen my claim that the Hua see food as *nu*, see
food as a part of the self. Further, I want to
establish that it is by seeing food as *nu*, as a body
substance similar to blood, semen, urine, body odor,
sweat, breath, breast milk and so forth, that the
non-homeopathic pre- and proscriptions of it can be
understood.

There are four ways in which foods are
associated with *nu*. The first is, to retrace my
steps a bit, by homeopathic association. (These
rules could be listed with the vast corpus of other
homeopathic rules mentioned earlier but are instead
entered here because of their association with *nu*).
Consider the following:

4. Initiates may not eat red pandanus oil
    because (they say) it resembles menstrual
    blood.

5. Initiates may not eat any of the
    substances which exhibit the loathed *be
    ptu* smell (for example, the *zokoni*
    mushroom, many species of possum) because
    this is the smell associated with

menstruating women (and to a certain extent with rot).

6.   Initiates may not eat foods which are dark on the interior (three species of taro, all the scavenging animals) because this darkness is alleged to resemble that of the interior of the female's body. (In Hua thinking the inside of the woman's body is dark, moist and putrid and thus, probably by analogy with soil, is fertile.)

In each of the above three rules, foods are proscribed because in some way they resemble body substances and thus, through the principle of homeopathy, possess some of their powers. If an initiate were to eat red pandanus oil, he is told it would have a fraction of the same effect on him as if he were to eat menstrual blood, arguably the most debilitating substance known to Hua males. If he were to inhale the *be ptu* smell of the *zokoni* mushroom, it would have an effect analogous to inhaling the dreaded smell of a menstruating woman. And so on.

The second way in which foods are associated with *nu* is through the principle of *contagion*.

7.   A mature male may not eat leafy green vegetables picked by his real or classificatory wife or his first born child.

8.   A mature male may not eat foods stepped over by his real or classificatory wife, his first born child, or his agemate.

When questioned as to why a mature male may not eat leafy green vegetables picked by certain alters, informants point to their hands and simply and directly state that they are dirty. We do not wash our hands and therefore they are contaminated with

spots of genital waste, sweat, body oil, and spots
of menstrual blood -- such is the Hua assessment of
the logic of rule 7. In the case of rule 8,
informants point out that unlike their European
counterparts, Hua men and women do not wear
underpants and, thus, small traces of their genital
waste may drop on to food when they step over it.
Rules of this kind are clearly operating on a
principle of contagion, one which is familiar to us
and therefore needs no further discussion.

The third way in which foods are associated
with *nu* is through the principle of
consubstantiality.

9.   A mature male may not eat pig raised by,
     wild animal shot by, or the largest and
     best garden produce produced by his own
     self, his real or classificatory wife, his
     first born child, or his agemate.

10. A mature female may not eat pig raised by,
     wild animal shot by, or the largest and
     best garden produce produced by her own
     self, her first born child, and her
     co-wife.

The pig which a person has raised, an animal he has
shot, his or her prize garden produce are thought to
contain his or her *nu*, physical essence, self,
lodged or invested there in act of production. This
concept of consubstantiality is more difficult than
the preceding one of contagion but it is not without
analogues in our own culture. According to the
Marxist congealed labor theory of value, the value
of any product is the amount of labor congealed into
it in the process of its production. We speak of
putting our blood, sweat and tears, even of putting
ourselves, into projects or objects over which we
labor strenuously. Of course, we mean those things
metaphorically and it is tempting to assume that the
Hua do as well but, in fact, they do not. They
believe that some of the physical essence of the

person is present in all the things which he or she produces, but most particularly in the foods which he or she grows, raises, or hunts.

Thus, the Hua conception of food is very different from our own. In the vast majority of cases the foods we eat are produced by people we do not know, shipped over long distances to be sold under plastic or in a can in a supermarket run again by people we do not know. Food for the Hua, on the other hand, is the output and intimate product of a person who is known. This person may be loved in which case the food which he or she gives will nourish but he or she may also be hated and feared in which case his or her food will cause sickness. Where a food is proscribed that proscription is directed not at the food itself but at the producer's *nu* in or on the food.

The fourth way in which foods may be associated with *nu* is that *nu* substances themselves may be eaten as foods.

> 11. A mature male cannot eat his own blood; nor may he eat or drink the flesh or blood of any woman, or the flesh or blood of any person in a generation junior to his own.

> 12. A mature woman may not eat her own blood; nor may she eat the flesh or blood of any person in a generation junior to her own, or the flesh or blood of her co-wives.

We are familiar in our own culture with substances which nourish but which are not foods: for example, blood transfusions and intravenous feedings. The Hua have a similar notion of non-foods which nourish, namely the actual substances of other persons' bodies. Breast milk is obvious but semen is also fed to initiates to make them grow.[1] Blood is let from the veins in the arm and fed not only to initiates but to any person who is sick or ailing. The flesh of the deceased was required eating for the real and classificatory offspring. (Failure to

consume the corpse could cause loss of vitality and
fertility not only to the offspring but also to
their crops and animals.)

Whereas non-food nourishments in our culture
are under medical administration, in the Hua case
they are "administered" according to the same rules
as foods, and in fact may be considered as the
ultimate and original nourishment of which foods are
simply weaker counterparts. For example, if a
person is sick, blood will nourish him or her more
rapidly and profoundly than any food.

To summarize what I have said so far: food
nourishes in the Hua conception by virtue of the *nu*
substances which are in it (consubstantiality), or
on   it   (contagion),   or   which   it   represents
(homeopathy), or which it in fact is (blood, semen,
breast   milk).   Little   else   about   a   food   has   an
effect   on   the   eater.   The   Hua   interest   in   the
nutritive   effect   of   foods   is   displaced   from   the
foods themselves to the *nu* substances with which the
food is associated. When talking with the Hua about
eating and nutrition one starts out talking about
foods but inevitably ends up talking about *nu*.

The   food   rules   discussed   in   this   paper   are
governed by a distinction between trusted *nu* that
grows and nourishes and distrusted *nu* that pollutes
and   sickens.   Generally   speaking   trusted   *nu*   comes
from   consanguineal   and   affinal   kinsmen   while
distrusted *nu* comes from non-kinsmen, but there are
some important exceptions. For the mature male (see
rules 7, 8, 9, 11) these exceptions are the *naru'*
(real   and   classificatory   wife),   *baru'* (first   born
child), and *varu'* (agemate). The body substances of
this small lexically marked set are as polluting and
dangerous to the mature male as those of an alien
outsider,   the   most   polluting   category   of   person.
For   the   mature   female   (see   rules   10   and   12)   the
exceptions   are   the   *baru'* first   born   child   and   the
Komipa   co-wife.   Why   are   these   categories   of
exceptionally   close   kin   viewed   by   the   Hua   as
polluting and dangerous? The answer seems to lie in
the fact that the male ego's relationships with his

wife, first born child, and agemate and the female ego's relationships with her first born child and co-wife are ones of emotional ambivalence. I will deal with the male ego's relationship with wife and agemate first, then the female's with co-wife, followed by a general discussion of the ideology of transfers of body substances, after which I will deal with the more complicated issue of male and female egos' relationships with the first born child.

First, the male ego's relationship with *naru'* real or classificatory wife. The Hua are a small population which for the most part imports brides from outside their linguistic and cultural group. In the past when warfare was more or less endemic this meant importing women from groups with which the Hua may have fought in the past or with whom they might fight in the future. Brides represented the potential enemy within the gates. Hua males to this day speak with fear that their wives will steal a bit of their body substance to give to their brothers who will then work sorcery upon them. It was only after many years of marriage and the birth of at least two children that the prohibition for example on eating leafy green vegetables picked by the wife was relaxed (Meigs 1976). The taboos on foods associated with the substances of the wife reflect, I think, the male ego's suspicions of his wife's loyalty. They are an indicator of the high levels of emotional ambivalence with which these arranged marriages across linguistic and cultural boundaries begin.

The *varu'* or agemate was a person with whom the young male was, according to my informants, locked in a competitive race for success and prestige. Agemates were constantly compared in matters of growth, fighting and sexual prowess, and general manliness. Informants report that suicides occasionally resulted from the stresses of this competitive relationship. Taboos on food associated with the *nu* substances of the agemate reflect the

emotional ambivalence engendered by the competitive
pressures of this relationship.

Switching now to the female ego and her
relationships of ambivalence, it should be noted
that the most common kind of fight to be observed at
Lufa where the Hua live is that between jealous and
hostile co-wives. Again with the co-wives as with
the agemates and the husband with his new bride, the
tensions of the relationship receive expression in
prohibitions on foods associated with the distrusted
party. These prohibitions while motivated (at least
according to my theory) by emotional ambivalence are
understood by the Hua in terms of a theory of body
substance. Before discussing the *baru'* first born
relationship, I will present the theory of
physiological substance in terms of which the Hua
understand and explain their rules.

In Hua thinking when one takes into one's body
a fragment or trace of another person's body
substance, one is taking in a literal part of that
other person. If he or she bears you ill will, then
that part of him or her will do you ill. If, on the
other hand he or she likes you, then that part will
nourish and help you. In the context of friendship
and trust, a food (which is a part of another
person's body because it contains its producer's *nu*)
nourishes; in the context of distrust and enmity the
same food debilitates. This is the central single
principle by which the food rules may be understood.

In Hua thinking there is something approaching
balance between the conception of body substances as
debilitating or polluting and the conception of them
as nourishing and clean. Blood, semen, saliva,
sweat, nasal mucus, body oil, breath, hair, and
fingernail are nourishing if they come from a
trusted person. Blood and semen transfers I have
already discussed. A man's sweat, the oil from his
head, and vomit produced under special conditions
were rubbed on the bodies of real and classificatory
sons to increase their growth and vitality. A man's
hair clippings were traditionally burned on the fire
and sprinkled over food to be eaten by his real or

classificatory sons and served as a tonic to their growth. A deceased man's hair or woman's fingernail might be worn in a packet around the neck of his or her children (the deceased's substance thus being ingested through the skin). These fragments of *nu* substance are said to have the power to increase the growth and fertility of the children and of their plants and animals, and even the power to relieve pain if rubbed on the affected area. One of the recommended cures for a man suffering from *kupa* "pregnancy" (for a discussion of this phenomena, see Meigs [1976]) is that he eat a small fragment of his elder brother's wife's feces. It may also be recommended that a sick or stunted person drink water from the Tua River, which flows through the bottom of the valley and which is said to be full of the body substances of the valley's residents, carried there in feces washed down into the river by rain water. Urine has similar curative uses. The relatives of a sick man may commission a sister married into another community to place a stalk of ginger in an area where it will be urinated on or repeatedly stepped over by the men of the village. The ginger is then returned to the sick man who, on eating it, is said to capture some of the body substance and, thus, power of the members of the affinal community. Of course, if any of the above mentioned substances originates in a distrusted party it is feared as polluting and debilitating. Body substances have for the Hua a value relative to the situation and the producer. In American culture we do not grant body substances the same duality. For us all body substances are absolutely polluting, though in varying degrees with feces being the most polluting and breast milk the least.[2] We are able to acknowledge a non-polluting aspect in body substances only in relation to our own very personal ones and those of our infants and lovers.

In American culture food and body substances are two distinct and opposed categories. Food is something which in the normal contexts of our culture we eat without restriction or reservation

(exceptions are made for ethnically diverse and/or
clearly contaminated foods and thus the negative
corner of the diagram, figure 1). Body substances,
on the other hand, are things we want to get rid of:
flush, wipe or spray away. We tolerate body
substances, as the figure shows, only in very
restricted circumstances and with a very restricted
set of others.

For the Hua, on the other hand, foods are body
substances and body substances are foods, or at
least edible cures. The two squares are one.
Furthermore, both are polluting in some contexts but
nourishing in others.

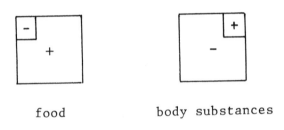

food   body substances

Figure 1. *American conceptions of foods and body
substances*

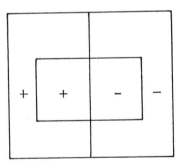

foods and body substances

Figure 2. *Hua conceptions of food and body
substances*

Having demonstrated that the idea of *nu* is central to the Hua understanding of food and nutrition, I want now to show that it also plays a significant role in the understanding of physiological process in general. I will illustrate this claim with a brief study of the Hua conception of sexual differentiation and the related processes of growth and aging.

Males and females are in Hua thinking differentiated primarily in the amount of *nu* they possess. Females enjoy an excess and males a deficiency. Males are *hakeri'a* "hard, dry, slow growing, infertile and hot" and females are *korogo* "soft, wet, fast-growing, fertile, and cool." Most of the many things which males perceive to be wrong with their bodies are due to the fact that their supply of *nu* is limited to begin with and decreases with age. Females, on the other hand, are possessors of mysterious inner fountains. According to males, it is these bounteous supplies which enable females to outstrip males in growth, to age without balding (about which Hua males feel very considerable embarrassment), and most important of all to menstruate, gestate, and lactate (all processes which require a large amount of *nu*) without suffering the same degree of debilitation which males believe they would suffer if they were to make comparable physical contributions.

Males, furthermore, are unable to reach reproductive maturity on their own. One of the primary goals of initiation is to enable males to do what they otherwise could not do: mature. To this end males must first be purified of all female *nu* substances which they have ingested in the process of being nurtured by their mothers and other older females of the community. Nose bleeding, vomiting, sweating, all these are reported by informants to have been practiced in the attempt to wipe the boy clean of female contaminants both internal and external (for a detailed discussion of these modes of purification see [Read 1952; Herdt 1981]). It was only on this foundation of purity that the boy's

growth could be built. That growth was achieved
through feeding the boy pure male *nu* in the form of
blood let from the veins of older males, semen,
sweat and body oils (rubbed on their skins), and
foods produced and prepared exclusively by men (and
thus containing pure male *nu*). Females just grow
needing no assistance or intervention.

Turning now to the rules in regard to the first
born child (see rules 7-10): he or she is almost as
polluting to his or her parent as the menstruating
woman is to the young male initiate. When
questioned about the reason for the taboos on the
first born child, Hua informants will invariably say
that the first born is the one into which the parent
puts the greater amount of his or her *nu*. He or she
is the one on which the mother or father most wasted
him or herself. As such the first born is alleged
to contain more of his or her parents' *nu* than the
subsequent children and, like the first fruit of a
plant, to be larger. And, in what has always seemed
to me a *non sequitur*, the Hua go on to assert that
the *nu* substances of the first born are therefore
polluting to the parent and will cause debilitation,
premature aging, and possibly death.

I attempted for a considerable period of time
to discover the physiological principle involved
here, what it was about the material substances of
first born children, either qualitatively or
quantitatively, which should make them more
polluting to their parents than later born children.
The nearest answer I could construct from the
comments of informants is as follows:

Children are literal parasites on the *nu*
substances of their parents. The fetus, infant and
child grows primarily from donations from his or her
parents. Yet the parent has only a limited supply
of *nu*. What the parent gives to the child is lost
to the parent. The child's gain is literally the
instrument of the parent's loss. Aging is implicit
in being a parent.

Why then cannot a child redress this imbalance
in *nu* flow by return gifts of *nu* substances to his

or her parents? In Hua thinking *nu* in all its forms including of course food, must flow from the senior to the junior generation (see stipulations to this effect in rules 11 and 12). To reverse this direction of flow is, according to numerous persons, like a dog licking its genitals, an act which is not only repugnant but also dangerous. The child's *nu* on entering the parent's body *bi aina to* "presses or puts down" the parent's *nu*. The parent is depleted and debilitated.

The first born being the child in whom the parent invested the greater share of his or her *nu* is the one who can most *bi aina to*. That is the physiological principle as stated by the Hua but I cannot help myself from asking if it does not mask a psychological one.

The first born is the one who initiated the parent's decline and the one who will, in the Hua conception, replace the same sex parent. That there is some anxiety about being replaced is suggested by the following rule:

13. A person may not let his or her first born touch his or her head, shoulder or hair.

When asked why not, informants respond that contact by the first born with the higher parts of his or her parents' bodies will, again, *bi aina to* them, put them down. Further, that the conjoined processes whereby the parents' strength is reduced and the child's enhanced will be speeded up.

Although the Hua are able to justify the taboos in relation to the first born child in terms which are purely physical, it is difficult not to understand them in terms also of emotional ambivalence in relation to the first born child, the one who terminated the parents' period of childhood and freedom and initiated their decline through adulthood into old age. (For a discussion of the near universality of taboos in relation to the first born see Fortes [1974]).

The taboos on the first born represent, or

perhaps I would be more comfortable saying may represent, a folk psychology masquerading as a folk physiology, insights about emotions and relationships presented in a physiological idiom.

I have sought to demonstrate that the central core of the Hua food rules presuppose a theory of food as a kind of body substance and body substance as a kind of food. This identification is not just a peculiar coincidence of Hua thought but a central assumption of their understanding of the varied processes of the body. Oddly though, the more intensely I scrutinized this physiology, the less physiological it appeared. In the end I concluded that what the food rules really tell you about is not what the Hua know about the body but rather what they feel about themselves. Seeing food as body substance and body substance as food provides a perfect vehicle for this kind of expression as it concentrates one's mind on one's dependence on other people because of one's need for food and one's fear of other people because of one's vulnerability to them in the act of eating.

FOOTNOTES

1. Ritual insemination is something about which the Hua are very secretive. Although there were numerous small hints of its existence in the past, only two informants openly "admitted" it had been practiced. See Herdt (1981) for a detailed description of ritual insemination among the not too distant Sambia.

2. Contact with breast milk is so rare in our culture that its pollution may not be obvious. I remember a scene from the movie *Sunday Bloody Sunday* in which a babysitter finds a jar of pale milky looking liquid in the refrigerator, opens it, tastes it and feels totally disgusted and "grossed out" on realizing its identity. I think many of us would react that same way.

REFERENCES

FORTES, MEYER. 1974. The First Born. *Journal of Child Psychology and Psychiatry* 15:81-104.

HERDT, GILBERT. 1981. *Guardians of the Flutes.* New York: McGraw-Hill.

KELLY, R. C. 1976. Witchcraft and Sexual Relations. *Man and Woman in the New Guinea Highlands* (P. Brown and G. Buchbinder, eds.). Washington D.C.: American Anthropological Association.

MEIGS, ANNA. 1976. Male Pregnancy and the Reduction of Sexual Opposition in the New Guinea Highlands. *Ethology* 9:393-407.

MEIGS, ANNA. 1984. *Food, Sex, and Pollution, A New Guinea Religion.* New Brunswick, N.J.: Rutgers University Press.

NEWMAN, PHILIP. 1964. Religious Belief and Ritual in a New Guinea Society. *American Anthropologist* 66:257-271.

READ, K. E. 1952. Nama Cult of the Central Highlands, New Guinea. *Oceania* 23:1-25.

READ, K. E. 1955. Morality and the Concept of the Person Among the Gahuku-Gama. *Oceania* 25:233-282.

"Taboos" and Statements about Taboos: Issues in the Taxonomic Analysis of Behavioral Restrictions among the New Guinea Kafe

Harold G. Levine

In his "Morality and the Concept of the Person Among the Gahuku-Gama," Read (1955) argued that the moral system of the Gahuku-Gama was, in its very essence, contextual and "distributive." By this he meant that general moral precepts were not universalized within this New Guinea Highlands culture and their effects on behavior could not be understood independently of either the individuals involved or the social positions which they occupied. Read's contributions in this article, aside from the interpretive insights afforded by his analysis of Gahuku-Gama morality and concept of personhood, stem from his solutions to then current problems in anthropological analysis. As Read himself was at pains to show, he had first to demonstrate that values and ethical patterns were legitimate objects of comparative analysis and that they were "amenable to logical and systematic explanation" (1955:234). Second, while arguing for the contextual nature of values and morality he had to avoid the "trap" of relativist thinking which would rob him of his comparative exegetic goals. Third, Read had to come to terms with the fact that the Gahuku-Gama "do not explain their value judgments in terms of the concepts which [he was to] employ." He was, in short, confronting covert categories of behavior which nevertheless were believed by him to "underlie a particular, empirically observed, pattern of behaviour" (1955:234). Finally, although he did not systematically explore the problem directly, Read was unavoidably concerned with the very nature of classification as a feature of (or step in) anthropological analysis. What, he in effect asked, can we mean by a cultural category we label as "morality," and what, more specifically, are the "normative criteria" to be used in the comparative analysis of it (1955:247)?

Read's problems in the analysis of Gahuku-Gama morality parallel those involved in analyzing the cultural domain of "food taboos" among the Kafe, another group of the Eastern New Guinea Highlands. "Food taboo," or "taboo" more generally, do not exist as unitary concepts for the Kafe; in fact, they do not have terminological representation in the Kafe language. Further, if we accept for the moment that "taboo" refers generally to "prohibition" or "avoidance," specific prohibitions in Kafe culture are conditioned by, among other variables, the social roles of the actors -- much as Read argued for moral considerations among the Gahuku-Gama. Thus, while the Kafe do not speak of taboos there are clearly areas of prohibition in their everyday lives; and these affect behavior in complex, non-uniform ways (see also Faithorn [1976]).

In this paper I shall argue that shortcomings in our understanding of the nature of taboo stem most fundamentally from the misuse of principles of classification as typically applied in anthropology. I shall first briefly review the uses of classification in anthropological writings, with an emphasis on how different approaches to classification have explicitly been used to model how native classifiers think. I shall then review the status of "taboo" as a taxonomic category and suggest why classification is an important endeavor

in social science research. Finally, I shall
develop a taxonomic scheme which uses the underlying
"relational semantics" of taboo statements as the
salient discriminating variables. The analysis,
which is based upon empirical data collected during
19 months of fieldwork among the New Guinea Kafe[1],
has implications for the modeling of Kafe thought.

I

There are those within anthropology who argue
that classification is the tool of the comparativist
butterfly-collectors, ultimately stultifying to
original speculation and generalization (Leach
1961:2ff.). According to this view any
classification scheme which is used is strictly an
ad hoc procedure to be exploited and then spurned as
new research interests appear (Leach 1962:240).
Entrenched classification schemes are too
value-laden to be of much use. Others in
anthropology, and related disciplines, regard
classification as an essential first step toward
scientific knowledge (Kroeber 1960a, 1960b; Sokal
1974) capable of identifying natural relationships
between real-world phenomena and thus reflecting
something of those natural processes governing the
behavior and taxonomic arrangement of the phenomena
under consideration (Sokal 1974). Rodney Needham is
even more explicit. He argues that classification
is "the prime and fundamental concern of social
anthropology" (1963:viii), crucial to the
understanding of "human thought and social life"
(1963:xxxiv; Needham 1979; Mezzich and Solomon
1980).
  Of course, within anthropology classification
is many things, at once a methodological device, a
topic for study, and an explanatory principle
applicable to both cultural process and product
(Ellen and Reason 1979). As a legitimate focus of
study the introduction of classification into
anthropology probably dates to Durkheim and Mauss'

seminal *Primitive Classification* of 1903 (1963).   In
this work they argued that primitive man was without
the innate capacity to classify.   "It is enough to
examine,"   they   wrote,   "the   very   idea   of
classification to understand that man could not have
found its essential elements in himself. A class is
a   group   of   things;   and   things   do   not   present
themselves to observation grouped in such a way"
(1963:7-8).   Not even simple resemblances between
things could be used to explain how classes were
constructed since there is nothing in the mind
which, at birth, contains the "prototype" for the
classificatory   principles   (1963:8).   Instead,
Durkheim   and   Mauss   maintained   that   primitive
classification   reproduced   the   society's   social
relations: "the   first   logical   categories   were
social categories" (1963:82).   "It was because men
were grouped, and thought of themselves in the form
of groups, that in their ideas they grouped other
things, and in the beginning the two modes of
grouping   were   merged   to   the   point   of   being
indistinct" (1963:82-83).
    In the light of modern research, Durkheim and
Mauss' argument of the absence among primitives or
"modern" children of an innate ability to classify
has been largely discredited, both logically (see
the introduction to the 1963 edition of *Primitive
Classification* [Needham 1963]) and empirically (see,
for   example,   the   cross-cultural   work   of   Rosch
[1973]).   However, Durkheim and Mauss' work has left
an important legacy in the study of classification.
We continue to look for the connection between
classifications and the societies in which they are
developed (Ellen 1979:3).   Even more fundamentally,
we   have   approached   in   a   variety   of   ways   that
"perennial problem in anthropology: the confusion
of the order of nature with that imposed upon it by
man" (Ellen 1979:1).   Beyond this, the Durkheim and
Mauss work has allowed us to see that classification
can be used as a way of learning not only about
thought, but also about the relationship between
thought, words which represent thought (and action),

and aspects of the real world. Finally, Durkheim and Mauss saw an essential continuity between, on the one hand, "primitive classifications" and, on the other, "the first scientific classifications." They argued that the former, however different they may be in detail from the latter, "nevertheless have all their essential characteristics" (1963:81). These include both hierarchical organization and a purpose "to make intelligible the relations which exist between things" (1963:81).

Much has happened in anthropological thinking about classification since Durkheim and Mauss' monograph. Although it is not my purpose, here, to review all of this material, I wish to briefly characterize two of the more recent, and prominent, lines of thought about classification, particularly as these embody a notion of mind and how it works. One is the structuralist tradition, best epitomized by Levi-Strauss, but with significant emendations by Leach, Douglas, Needham, and others. The second is the formalist approach growing out of anthropological linguistics and represented in the work of Goodenough, Conklin, Frake, Berlin, Kay, and many others.

Levi-Strauss' work on totemism (1963) is perhaps exemplary of the structuralist approach and the most directly relevant for the study of Kafe taboos which is to follow. First and foremost Levi-Strauss argues that the concept of totemism cannot be defined monothetically, that is, in terms of necessary and sufficient conditions. He further asks, adapting a line of thought from Lowie, whether such concepts actually do exist or are "merely figments of our logical modes of classification" (Lowie, as quoted in Levi-Strauss [1963:10]). Levi-Strauss then proceeds to look at the "semantic field" occupied by the construct "totemism" as created by the intersection of two underlying features, or "series," *viz.*, nature (further subdivided into "categories" and "particulars") and culture (subdivided into "groups" and "persons"). These features, in turn, are arrived at through a

process which Needham, in another context, has
called an "imaginative apprehension" (Needham
1963:xxxv) and are validated pragmatically, "by
reference to their degree of success in rendering
social facts coherent and intelligible" (Needham
1979:59). What is important for the argument here
is that the principles of articulation which
constitute the classification are not to be found by
examining the thoughts of an informant. Rather,
they come from the mind of the researcher. Even so,
for Levi-Strauss such principles as opposition/cor-
relation, compatibility/incompatibility, exclusion/
inclusion form an "original logic" which is "a
direct expression of the structure of the mind (and
behind the mind, probably, of the brain)" (1963:90).
The elements of this "original logic" would then be
manipulated through a series of psychological
operations akin to Boolean algebra (1963:90-91).

The formalist, or ethnoscientific, tradition
within anthropology has also been involved with
semantic fields, and formalist thinking and
procedure has some similarity with that of
Levi-Straussian structuralism. Both are concerned
with the underlying discriminant features which
define a semantic space and are not necessarily
articulable by an informant. Both employ the
"imaginative apprehension" of such discriminant
features, and the pragmatic testing of the validity
of the classification. However, unlike
Levi-Strauss' concern with symbolic structure, the
primary goal within formalist thinking is the
discovery of semantic universals and general
principles of classification. The data for such
explorations typically include botanical or
zoological term sets. Some effort has also been
made to include covert (i.e., non-named) categories
in formalist analyses as well (e.g. [Berlin,
Breedlove, and Raven 1968; Hays 1976; Hunn 1975b]).

After a rather long period of research one
important conclusion of the formalist line of
inquiry seems to be that, in most cases, folk
classification parallels in important respects the

biosystematics of modern Western science (Berlin, Breedlove, and Raven 1968; Hunn 1975a, 1976). Given these similarities it is not surprising, as Hunn (1976:509) has pointed out, that folk classifications are defined primarily in terms of taxonomic structures with hierarchical organizations featuring set inclusion among the various taxa of the system and a transitive logic that represents the reasoning process by which taxonomic descriptions are generated by informants (Randall 1976).

Such a view of how the mind works has, of course, come under attack. Some time ago Wallace (1965) called for the production of psychologically valid descriptions of native cognitive (semantic) systems (see also [Wallace and Atkins 1960; Romney and D'Andrade 1964]). More recently Randall (1976) quite baldly argued that he could not find any empirical support for the existence of an inherent transitive logic by which individuals generate indirect precedence relations of taxonomic categories. Hunn has suggested a "non-taxonomic cognitive process" (1976:522), arguing that "as models of the *process* of classification they [taxonomic-like structures] are clearly inadequate; the existence of taxa is accepted as a primitive notion of these logical structures, which are then constructed by reference to the relation of set inclusion. The fundamental problem, however, is to account for the *existence* of taxa" (Hunn 1976:520-521). Hunn has also critiqued the logic by which basic folk taxa are defined: "traditional techniques of semantic analysis, which attempt to explain concepts by specifying necessary and sufficient conditions for membership in the concepts [i.e., by using monothetic criteria], have proven inadequate for defining the basic folk taxa, which are semantic primitives" (1976:510).

The nature of classification, whether as studies of cultural categories (and associated practices) such as "totemism" or as studies of folk classificatory systems of plant or animal categories, remains an important concern in anthropology. So, too, are the theories of mind which the studies of classificatory phenomena imply. To date, we have alternative and competing models of how the mind works. In this paper I wish to present data on taboos among the New Guinea Kafe which imply a further plausible model of how the mind may work. Before I do this, however, it is necessary to return to two fundamental and related problems in classification, recognized at once by both Levi-Strauss and in recent formalist writings e.g., Hunn (1976). These are the problems of using monothetic criteria to define categories and use of single taxonomic schemes to mirror reality.

II

Leach's already mentioned disenchantment with classification stems, it seems, from his observation of a lack of fit between the ideal categories of classifications and actual discontinuities found in nature (Ellen 1979). He found that "the species of empirical reality lack objective homogeneity and are blurred at the edges; what is allocated to them is determined by definitions" (Leach as quoted in Ellen [1979:3]). A second problem with classifications, also noted by Leach, is that the real world is characterized by many more natural discontinuities than would be possible for any single classification scheme to fully embody. Leach, and others, seem unprepared to accept the fact that one must economize, selecting only certain features for taxonomic inclusion, and diversify, selecting different sets of features as needs require (Ellen 1979).

These problems in and with classification are now rather familiar ones. The issue, simply stated, is that natural systems, including social and conceptual systems, are not necessarily isomorphic with single, monothetic classification systems (Sokal 1974) since the nature of a real-world system is likely to be polythetic. One cannot, as an example, expect to define a frog by its "green-ness" or any other unitary feature (or set of features) which is both necessary and sufficient for inclusion of the object in the class so defined. To proceed in this way leads to a taxonomic system with internal divisions too rigid to accommodate, to continue the "frog" example, chartreuse animals which, except for their color, partake in every other aspects of "frog-ness." To segregate them on the basis of color alone seems an injustice to the "natural" order of phenomena.

Within anthropology the problem of applying monothetic taxonomic principles to complex natural phenomena is exacerbated by the dual interests of anthropologists in both comparative research and fine-grained, culture-specific empirical studies (Steiner 1956; Goodenough 1956; Kluckhohn 1953). In the former there is the demand for broadly defined, general purpose terms (re: taxa) which can be used for making statements about human society. Terms like "unilineal descent system," "virilocal residence," and "food taboos" fall into this category. In empirical studies, on the other hand, terms must be variously redefined in accordance with peculiarities of a given society and the analytical needs of the ethnographer.

In a recent paper Needham (1974) has reviewed the evidence for regarding such terminological stalwarts in anthropological description as "kinship," "marriage," "descent," "terminologies," and "incest" as monothetic categories. His general conclusion is that while there may be some general, underlying commonality in the reality which each term is thought to index there may not necessarily be "a definite set of characteristic, specific, or essential features" (Needham 1974:70). Classifications employing these and other common anthropological terms are thus spurious at worst or simply misleading at best.

Needham's criticisms of how anthropologists use terms like "kinship," "marriage," and the like are

no less applicable to the word "taboo." This is
due, in part, to the long history of the word and
the particulars of how it first entered Western
usage. The word first appears in a European
language in the late eighteenth century with Captain
Cook's descriptions of practices he observed in
Polynesia (Steiner 1956:22-27); and, as others have
noted (Radcliffe-Brown 1965; Steiner 1956), use of
the word has been colored by its original Polynesian
sense (i.e., certain things withdrawn from everyday
use) and by comparisons with and emendations of
this.

In fact, attempts to define the word "taboo"
and employ it more generally are found throughout
the late nineteenth and the twentieth centuries.
Frazer (1959) defined it simply as "negative magic"
and only one of a number of similar superstitions
(1966). He subdivided taboos into "tabooed acts,"
"tabooed persons," "tabooed things," and "tabooed
words" (1966). Durkheim (1965), although he
preferred the word "interdiction" to "taboo,"
defined the concept as forbidding certain ways of
acting and as declaring certain things incompatible.
Reinach, in *Orpheus* (1930), spoke in terms of
arbitrary interdicts to which were attached
calamitous misfortunes of nature as penalties for
non-compliance. Mead, in her article "Tabu" for the
Encyclopaedia of the Social Sciences (1937) defined
taboo "as a negative sanction, a prohibition whose
infringement results in an automatic penalty without
human or superhuman mediation" and further
restricted its meaning to include only those
"prohibitions against participation in any situation
of such inherent danger that the very act of
participation will recoil upon the violator of the
tabu" (1937:502). Thus, to the general notion of
prohibition, Mead further added the related notions
of "inherent danger" and "automatic penalty."

These and other definitions (for a review see
Kennedy [1967]) form a set of related meanings (a
family resemblance in Wittgenstein's usage [1958])
with notions of "prohibition," "forbidden,"

"dangerous by nature," "automatic penalty" forming the defining characteristics. Unfortunately, however, most researchers tend to ignore the "fuzziness" of the concept, preferring instead to impart to "taboo" a kind of objective, and universal, reality theoretically definable by a limited number of criteria. The problem is that as each new definition is offered it may serve in establishing a general taxon and, often, subordinate taxa with highly determined boundaries. Additionally, each new definition also comes to rely on the tacit assumption that constituent members are comparable in *all* respects. As the following example (and other literature) shows, non-conforming variation can usually be found with little difficulty.

Among the New Guinea Kafe there is a prohibition on trimming the dead leaves of a publicly visible pandanus tree if there is an unavenged death in the village. There is not, however, any inherent danger in the act, at least of a supernatural kind; and there is no automatic punishment for it, supernatural or otherwise. In fact, the function of this prohibition has more to do with inter-village politics and deceptions than with ritual transgressions. It does not therefore readily fall under, say, Mead's definition of taboo stated above, yet it does seem to resemble other prohibitions which might be more obviously categorized as "taboo" under her definition.

While most definitions of "taboo" contain some notion of "prohibition" there *is* some question whether the notion of prohibition is necessarily a key variable in defining taboo. One alternate explanation is that the focus on "prohibition" is a kind of unintended result of the fieldwork process. As Van Gennep (1960:8-9 fn) observed some time ago, one more readily notices instances of acts which one is told he cannot do than those acts which are either allowed or must be done. Both Van Gennep and, later, Radcliffe-Brown (1965) noted that even ritual situations frequently call for acts of both positive and negative volition. It may therefore be more correct to look at "taboos" not as unique entities divorced from other types of behavior, but merely as another perspective on a wide range of cultural acts and items which are permitted and often required. Indeed our traditional conception of taboo seems to assume that there is some universal and irreversible cognitive distinction made by the people we study between things they tell us they cannot do, things they are enjoined from *not* doing, and things which they apparently can do. To my knowledge there is no proof for this assumption; and, given the transmutability of the three logical options, it is not clear what the proof would be.

Further difficulties with a monothetic criterial approach to the definition of taboo arise when one goes beyond the most general type to construct a set of taboo sub-types. In principle any group of apparently "similar" items in the real world can be segregated into single-item classes by the use of increasingly particularistic variables. Since such a procedure defeats any real purpose for a classification, some decisions have to be made about the level and types of contrast desired.

The construction of sub-types in a categorization is a problematic procedure when the "natural" relationship between items are either not known (or specified), or when a wide range of features may serve to define the items (D'Andrade *et al.* 1972). As an example, part of the Kafe "taboo system," broadly defined in terms of certain distinctive "properties," such as material aspect of the culture referred to or occasion of interdiction, may be represented as follows:

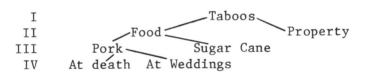

```
  I                           Taboos
 II                  Food                   Property
III          Pork          Sugar Cane
 IV      At death   At Weddings
```

The tree diagram shows four "levels," each level distinguished by an additional variable. However,

using the same variables the tree diagram might just
as "accurately" be written as follows:

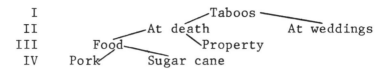

I
II   At death   At weddings
III   Food   Property
IV   Pork   Sugar cane

No priority can be given either of these
classification schemes or any of the ordering
variables since no phylogenetic or logical
relationship can be assumed to exist between any two
items. In one sense this artificiality is
unimportant since most ethnographers presumably
inherently appreciate the fact. Nevertheless the
fact that two equally inclusive schemas of
categorical relationships can be written suggests
that the meaning we and perhaps the people we study
give to a type of taboo may in part be dependent
upon its categorical-taxonomic status.

An example of the effect of categorical status
on meaning will be helpful. In the first diagram on
the previous page food taboos are listed as a
general category which could theoretically be
isolated and studied independently of additional
contextual features. In the second diagram food
taboos exist only as a sub-category of taboos
related to death and may have no meaning outside of
death. To study food taboos, in other words, one
must study death. Further complications occur if
additional features of context are added. Thus,
some Kafe food taboos at death apply only if it is
an adult who has died or if the pork comes from a
pig originally belonging to affinal kin. The
difficulty of specifying increasingly limited
contingencies is again raised and unresolved, and
the question of what we mean when we say we are
studying "food taboos" becomes even more
problematic. The fact that each ethnographer does
assign meaning to the taboos he/she has found is not
helpful if it is based upon an unstated
classificatory scheme thereby making it impossible

to establish a reliable basis of comparison between
accounts. The points to be emphasized here are that
(1) neither "food" nor any other "set" of taboos can
be studied in isolation either from other items at a
comparable logical (or taxonomic) level or from
subordinate and superordinate levels -- in other
words some context must be provided; and (2) the
ethnographer must make explicit the classificatory
scheme from which he/she is operating.

Finally, one additional problem in traditional
approaches to "taboo" as a classificatory category
is that even with a high degree of specificity in
the properties defining classes there will always be
difficulties in sorting certain taboos by category.
The Kafe prohibition against age-mates of a deceased
man eating food in the house where the widow is
secluded is a case in point. Is this a "food"
taboo, a "death" taboo, or something else again?

Given the difficulties in constructing
classificatory schemes and the provisions which must
be made when such a scheme is constructed, one may
reasonably ask whether alternative classification
principles would better serve in the analysis of
socio-cultural data? One answer would seem to lie
in the use of polythetic classification procedures.

In a polythetic classification scheme items are
placed together on the basis of bundles of shared
features. Neither is one feature necessary and
sufficient for class inclusion nor is the presence
or absence of a given feature in an entity
sufficient for including it in or excluding it from
a given class (Sokal and Sneath 1963:14). Whether a
frog is chartreuse or red is irrelevant to its
"frog-ness" except in the sense that its color may
be one of several factors which it shares in common
with other creatures typed as frogs.

While polythetic schemes have found acceptance
in a wide variety of disciplines (Cain 1962; Heywood
and McNeill 1964; Sneath and Sokal 1973), they have
seen relatively little use in anthropology (Needham
1974, 1975; Shweder 1977). The problem has been to
identify the taxonomic variables which could be used

to order cultural data. For reasons outlined above the standard anthropological definitions cannot be used. Other approaches must therefore be employed. One feasible direction is to build upon the substantive possibilities inherent to a data set. Significant contributions have been made along these lines by D'Andrade (D'Andrade *et al.* 1972) and others by using substitution frame eliciting techniques (Black and Metzger 1965; Frake 1964; Metzger and Williams 1963) to generate data on lexical domains such as disease terms and properties related to disease states. The resulting data sets are then subjected to factor analytic, hierarchial clustering, multidimensional scaling, or other multidimensional statistical techniques (Mezzich and Solomon 1980; Shepard 1972) to approximate a conceptual organization of a behavioral-symbolic domain.

A second feasible direction in ordering cultural data follows from Needham's (1974) suggestion to use purely formal criteria which describe the logical, not substantive, possibilities in groups of things or acts. Needham (1974) has demonstrated how this might be done with regard to "descent" and kinship terminologies and less successfully with other domains. In part III I demonstrate how this might be done for "taboo."

With the provisos that polythetic taxonomic systems can be used to mirror a polythetic world (or an uncertainly monothetic one) and that they do not somehow embody explanatory theory in and of themselves (Chaney 1978), there is no reason not to use classification as an important means to scientific inference. Indeed we need a concerted effort to understand the principles of taxonomy in anthropology since not only will taxonomic statements continue to be made and taxa implied in descriptive ethnographic accounts, but also since unknown relationships among cultural data may not otherwise be uncovered. Beyond the job of constructing polythetic classes we also need procedures by which data can be displayed and compared as required by a variety of theoretical interests such that neither the data set nor the basic classificatory scheme need be discarded with each new analytic purpose.

III

In polythetic classification one typically constructs taxa from observations of the features of large numbers of individual entities (whether organisms, words, etc.). Taxa are "built up" from clusterings of these features, a process referred to as "classification from below" (or agglomerative clustering -- Sneath and Sokal [1973:22-23]). "Classification from above" (or divisive clustering), on the other hand, proceeds in the opposite direction by initially grouping all entities into one set and then making successive subdivisions as appropriate. Even when the goal is an agglomerative clustering of entities, classification from above is a necessary first step in order to conceptually and numerically restrict the general universe of entities for study (Sneath and Sokal 1973:23).

Classification from above often depends upon monothetic criteria. The danger is that sole use of such criteria may unnecessarily exclude certain material which does not conform in full to the working definition used to define the taxon. The "solution" to this potential problem is to define the original taxon as broadly as possible and to include atypical or otherwise unsatisfactory material which may *later* have to be excluded (Sneath and Sokal 1973:68-69). This strategy seems particularly crucial when the object of classification is some aspect of the conceptual/semantic system of a foreign culture such as the notion of "taboo." It is misleading to assume that other cultural groups employ an any less complicated system of semantic usages than we do; and that they necessarily operate with

straightforward, monothetic criteria in their
conceptual systems. In cultures where members *do*
use a single word gloss such as "taboo" we must
recognize that even a broadly drawn definition of
it, while both possible and useful, is nevertheless
imprecise and its boundaries probably will not
coincide with its actual, everyday usages
(Wittgenstein 1958:19).

"Taboo" refers to a variety of behaviors,
beliefs, and everyday meanings in the West and most
likely does so in other cultures as well. As an
initial step toward classifying these various
meanings among the New Guinea Kafe I have chosen to
study verbal expressions which imply some kind of
avoidance behavior. These verbal expressions are of
two types. The majority are statements made to me
by Kafe informants describing things which they do
(or, rather, do not do). A few are statements which
I have generated based upon what I observed the Kafe
doing or saying. With the first type the assumption
is the same as with ethno-semantic analysis: the
way people talk about things reflects how they think
about and construe their world (Frake 1962:74). The
assumption behind the second type is similar --
viz., that what people *do* also reflects their
cognitive constructions of the world and that an
outsider can understand this process through
language. In both cases one can study statements
about behavior as a way of understanding that
behavior. My approach is to focus on the
"relational semantics" of statements about behavior
not as a way of uncovering linguistic principles,
but rather as a way of discovering aspects of
cultural meaning and reasoning. These aspects,
taken from a large number of individual cases, are
used to construct, "from below," a polythetic
classification of types of Kafe behavioral
restrictions.

One frequently voiced behavioral restriction by
the Kafe is that a married man cannot sleep with
(and, of course, have intercourse with) a wife who
is menstruating. Men also cannot sleep with a wife

who is sick, pregnant, or nursing. Though there are
obvious differences in these four statements in
terms of the "state" of the wife, the relationship
between semantic elements remains the same. In each
there is an Actor (i.e., a married man), an Act of
restriction (expressed by the phrase "cannot sleep
with"), and some way in which the act is limited or
qualified (i.e., to wives who are sick, pregnant,
nursing, or menstruating). Each specific item --
e.g., wife -- is infused with a culturally specific
lexical meaning and holds this meaning-set
independently of being in this particular statement
related to restrictions. This is not true for the
elements of Actor, Act, and Limitor which take on
semantic importance only because they are
interrelated in this statement. For this reason I
refer to this level of description as "relational
semantics."[2]

Not all Kafe "taboos" take the same form. In
Table 1 I have listed a sample of Kafe taboos,
intended to be illustrative only, according to the
relational semantic elements which they contain. A
survey of these shows that there is a total of five
general semantic variables. The two elements not
yet discussed are as follows:

1. An Occasion which acts as a pre-condition
    before some form of behavior is manifested,
    such as is contained in the phrase "At death
    . . . " of Example 3.

2. An Additional Contingency which qualifies all
    the other elements of the statement such as in
    Example 2 which stipulates that the entire
    statement applies only if a death in the parish
    remains unavenged.

Arrangement of the data in this way has three
distinct advantages over other taxonomic schemes.
First there is no *a priori* assumption of class types
and therefore no prejudice to cultural meanings.
Thus, instead of regarding some act related to food
intake or some prohibited comestible as a "food
taboo," which may not really exist as a cognitively
identifiable entity in the minds of the informants,

Table 1

A Sample of Kafe Taboos and Their Defining Relational Semantic Elements

Example No.	a (Occasion)	b (Actor)	c (Act)	d (Limitor)	e (Additional Contingency)
1		Married men	cannot sleep with	wives who are menstruating	
2		One	cannot clean off	dead pandanus leaves of a tree near a main road	if a death in the parish remains unavenged
3	At death	one	can deny oneself	a particular object meant for him/herself	if especially grieved
4	Before battle	married men	cannot sleep with	their wives	
5	At *tebe kre nentie* ("counseling session" with bride or groom prior to marriage)	partici-pants	cannot sing or joke		if there has been a recent unavenged death in the parish

we can compare statements related to the act of
eating, to foods or specific types of foods which
are the objects of various acts including eating, or
to any other semantic context in which food-related
items appear. Potentially we thereby have access to
the different ways in which food or eating acquires
cultural significance.

A second advantage of the method is that it
specifies as part of the model the total context for
a taboo statement. Precipitating events, various
qualifiers, and added contingencies are all
specified; and these, too, can be conveniently and
systematically compared. Various pairings such as
contingency and act, act and limitor, precipitating
occasion and remaining elements, and so forth, can
be made because it is the interrelationship of these
elements which is already the heart of the model. A
further advantage of focusing on these
interrelationships is that they automatically
specify the context for any given item since the
context *is* the semantic statement under
consideration.

Using the relational semantic elements of
statements about "taboos," it is possible to
construct a set of polythetic taxonomic classes
which may not only be of use in cross-cultural
comparisons but also may reveal cognitive aspects of
"taboo states" not normally appreciated.

A full list of all Kafe taboo statements
related to or noted by me over a 19-month period
fall into five distinct semantic patterns. These
are listed in the following table:

Relational Semantic Elements Pattern No.	a Occasion	b Actor	c Act	d Limitor	e Additional Contingency
1		b	c	d	
2		b	c	d	e
3	a	b	c	d	e
4	a	b	c	d	
5	a	b	c		e

As can be seen, all five possess two items b and c ("Actor" and "Act") in common, but no combination of only b and c exists. Additional items must be used to complete the statement.

The five patterns listed above require some interpretation. Since b ("Actor") and c ("Act") are constant, significance must come from the remaining elements a, d, and e. In pattern 1 the relationship between b and c is qualified in some way by the Limitor (d), and the relationship implied in b c d is *categorical*. In other words, though the Limitor may restrict the class of objects to which the action applies (e.g., men refrain from having intercourse only with wives who are menstruating) or where it applies (e.g., men avoid cutting off the dead leaves of pandanus trees only for those trees located near a main road) the "taboo" obtains for all such instances irrespective of any prior occasions or other contingent conditions. In that sense it is context free. Nearly one-half (22 of 46) of the Kafe behavioral restrictions used for this study are of this type.

In pattern 2 the "basic" relationship of b c d is *contingent* upon some other factor e, and in pattern 4 b c d is *specific* to a given Occasion (a). Both patterns 3 and 5 depend upon some Occasion and an additional contingency and are thus further contextualized. Pattern 5 occurs but once in the 46 cases studied and represents a slight variation on pattern 3. The four types are summarized below:

```
Type I:     b c d = categorical
Type II:    b c d e = contingent
Type III:   a b c d = specific
Type IV:    a b c (d) e = contingent/specific
```

These four types reveal a number of underlying, *presumably* cognitive, features of Kafe attitudes toward restricted behavior. While a relationship between some Actor and some Act is always present in the Kafe system, the data show no instance in which they can be necessary and sufficient conditions in

defining a class or in imparting cultural meaning to
items and acts beyond the lexical meanings which
they possess individually. Cultural (and taxonomic)
meaning can only come with the addition of some
Limitor such that it is the *kind* of thing it is or
its location that is important, with some
Contingency that has no intrinsic relationship to
the lexical meaning of the statement, or with some
prior triggering Occasion which "actuates" the
"taboo state." Clearly a great deal of higher-order
decision-making and information processing are
required here by the Kafe; and the taxonomic scheme
used suggests that the cognitive component in
situations of restricted behavior is not a unitary
phenomenon either cross- or intra-culturally.

IV

    In conclusion, let me summarize the two main
points of my argument. First, when statements about
restricted behavior are broken down into relational
semantic elements, systematic comparison of lexical
items and the behaviors they index becomes possible
without preconceived notions of what, "by
definition," constitutes a "taboo." Second, the
construction of taxonomic categories based on these
relational semantic items and the examination of
these cross-culturally may tell us about thinking
or, at the very least, something about cross-
cultural similarities in how cultural meanings in
certain conceptual-behavioral domains are achieved
and expressed. In both cases categorizations and
taxonomic principles have been used in organizing
multi-faceted empirical data and in generating new
hypotheses and new relationships about that data.
In addition, the broadened use of polythetic
classification principles based upon the formal
properties of phenomena may be one way of avoiding
the kinds of cross-cultural definitional problems we

so commonly face in anthropology, and may be a
useful first step in scientific thinking.

FOOTNOTES

1. Fieldwork was carried out in the villages of
    Homaya and Bafo between June 1971 and January
    1973. I wish to thank Edwin Hutchins and Keith
    Kernan for valuable comments on points raised
    in this paper. Terry Hays, K. Kernan, L. L.
    Langness, Douglass Price-Williams, and Marilyn
    Strathern read and offered valuable comments on
    the manuscript.

2. I am indebted to Keith Kernan for his
    suggestion of the phrase "relational
    semantics." I am also reminded by him that
    relational semantics bears a resemblance to
    case analysis in linguistic semantics. Both
    assume that humans are capable of making
    judgments about the "who's," "what's," and
    "where's" of real-world events and that these
    judgments are represented in grammar either as
    case notions (Fillmore 1968) or as relational
    semantic elements. However, case grammar is
    more concerned with grammatically embedded
    "sortal" categories. I use case ideas for
    heuristic-analytic purposes.

REFERENCES

BERLIN, B., BREEDLOVE, D. E., and RAVEN, P. H. 1968. Covert Categories and Folk Taxonomies. *American Anthropologist* 70:290-299.

BLACK, M. and METZGER, D. 1965. Ethnographic Description and the Study of Law. *American Anthropologist* 67(pt. 2):141-165.

CAIM, A. J. 1962. Zoological Classification. *Aslib Proceedings* 14:226-230.

CHANEY, R. P. 1978. Polythematic Expansion: Remarks on Needham's Polythetic Classification. *Current Anthropology* 19:139-143.

D'ANDRADE, R. G., QUINN, N. R., NERLOVE, S. B., and ROMNEY, A. K. 1972. Categories of Disease in American-English and Mexican-Spanish. *Multidimensional Scaling, Vol. II: Applications.* (A. K. Romney, R. N. Shepard, and S. B. Nerlove, eds.), pp. 9-54. New York: Seminar Press.

DURKHEIM, E. 1965. *The Elementary Forms of the Religious Life.* New York: Free Press.

DURKHEIM E. and MAUSS, M. 1963. *Primitive Classification* (R. Needham, trans. and ed.). Chicago: University of Chicago Press.

ELLEN, R. F. 1979. Introductory Essay. *Classifications in Their Social Context* (R. F. Ellen and D. Reason, eds.), pp. 1-32. London: Academic Press.

ELLEN, R. F. and Reason, D. (eds.). 1979. "Preface" to *Classifications in Their Social Context*, pp. 7-8. London: Academic Press.

FAITHORN, E. 1976. Women as Persons: Aspects of Female Life and Male-Female Relations Among the Kafe. *Man and Woman in the New Guinea Highlands* (P. Brown and G. Buchbinder, eds.), pp. 86-95. Special Publication #8, American Anthropological Association.

FILLMORE, C. J. 1968. The Case for Case. *Universals in Linguistic Theory* (E. Bach and R. T. Harms, eds.), pp. 1-88. New York: Holt, Rinehart, and Winston.

FRAKE, C. O. 1962. The Ethnographic Study of Cognitive Systems. *Anthropology and Human Behavior* (T. Gladwin and W. C. Sturtevant, eds.), pp. 72–85. Washington, D. C.: Anthropological Society of Washington.

FRAKE, C. O. 1964. Notes on Queries in Ethnography. *American Anthropologist* 66 (Pt. 2): 132–145.

FRAZER, J. G. 1959. *The New Golden Bough* (T. H. Gaster, ed.). New York: Criterion Books.

FRAZER, J. G. 1966. *Taboo and the Perils of the Soul*. New York: St. Martin's Press.

GOODENOUGH, W. H. 1956. Residence Rules. *Southwestern Journal of Anthropology* 12:22–37.

HAYS, T. E. 1976. An Empirical Method for the Identification of Covert Categories in Ethnobiology. *American Ethnologist* 3:489–507.

HEYWOOD, V. H., and McNeill, J. (eds.). 1964. *Phenetic and Phylogenetic Classification*. London: The Systematics Association.

HUNN, E. 1975a. A Measure of the Degree of Correspondence of Folk to Scientific Biological Classification. *American Ethnologist* 2:309–327.

HUNN, E. 1975b. The Tenejapa Tzeltal Version of the Animal Kingdom. *Anthropological Quarterly* 48:14–30.

HUNN, E. 1976. Toward a Perceptual Model of Folk Biological Classification. *American Ethnologist* 3: 508–524.

KENNEDY, J. G. 1967. Mushahara: A Nubian Concept of Supernatural Danger and the Theory of Taboo. *American Anthropologist* 69:685–702.

KLUCKHOHN, C. 1953. Universal Categories of Culture. *Anthropology Today* (A. L. Kroeber, ed.), pp. 507–523. Chicago: University of Chicago Press.

KROEBER, A. L. 1960a. Evolution, History, and Culture. *Evolution After Darwin: Vol. II, The Evolution of Man* (S. Tax, ed.), pp. 1–16. Chicago: University of Chicago Press.

KROEBER, A. L. 1960b. Statistics, Indo-European, and Taxonomy. *Language* 36:1–21.

LEACH, E. R. 1961. Rethinking Anthropology. *Rethinking Anthropology* (E. R. Leach, ed.), pp. 1-27. London: Athlone.

LEACH, E. R. 1962. Classification in Social Anthropology. *Aslib Proceedings* 14:239-242.

LEVI-STRAUSS, C. 1963. *Totemism*. Boston: Beacon Press.

MEAD, M. 1937. Tabu. *Encyclopaedia of the Social Sciences* VII:502-505.

METZGER, D., and WILLIAMS, G. E. 1963. A Formal Ethnographic Analysis of Tenejapa Ladino Weddings. *American Anthropologist* 65:1076-1101.

MEZZICH, J. E. and SOLOMON, H. 1980. *Taxonomy and Behavioral Science: Comparative Performance of Grouping Methods*. London: Academic Press.

NEEDHAM, R. (ed. and trans.). 1963. "Introduction" to *Primitive Classification* (E. Durkheim and M. Mauss), pp. 7-48. Chicago: University of Chicago Press.

NEEDHAM, R. 1974. Remarks on the Analysis of Kinship and Marriage. *Remarks and Inventions: Skeptical Essays About Kinship* (R. Needham, ed.), pp. 38-71. London: Tavistock.

NEEDHAM, R. 1975. Polythetic Classification: Convergence and Consequences. *Man* 10:349-369.

NEEDHAM, R. 1979. *Symbolic Classification*. Santa Monica, CA: Goodyear Publishing.

RADCLIFFE-BROWN, A. R. 1965. Taboo. *Reader in Comparative Religion: An Anthropological Approach* (W. A. Lessa and E. Z. Vogt, eds.), pp. 112-123. New York: Harper & Row.

RANDALL, R. A. 1976. How Tall is a Taxonomic Tree? Some Evidence for Dwarfism. *American Ethnologist* 3:543-553.

READ, K. E. 1955. Morality and the Concept of the Person Among the Gahuku-Gama. *Oceania* 25:233-282.

REINACH, S. 1930. *Orpheus*. New York: Liveright.

ROMNEY, A. K. and D'ANDRADE, R. G. 1964. Cognitive Aspects of English Kin Terms. *American Anthropologist* 66 (Part 2, Special Publication):146-170.

ROSCH, E. H. 1973. Natural Categories. *Cognitive Psychology* 4:328–350.

SHEPARD, R. N. 1972. A Taxonomy of Some Principal Types of Data and of Multidimensional Methods for Their Analysis. *Multidimensional Scaling, Vol. I: Theory* (R. N. Shepard, A. K. Romney, and S. B. Nerlove, eds.), pp. 21–47. New York: Seminar Press.

SHWEDER, R. A. 1977. Likeness and Likelihood in Everyday Thought: Magical Thinking in Judgments About Personality. *Current Anthropology* 18:637–658.

SNEATH, P. H. A., and SOKAL, R. R. 1973. *Numerical Taxonomy*. San Francisco: W. H. Freeman.

SOKAL, R. R. 1974. Classification: Purposes, Principles, Progress, Prospects. *Science* 185:1115–1123.

SOKAL, R. R. and SNEATH, P. H. A. 1963. *Principles of Numerical Taxonomy*. San Francisco: W. H. Freeman.

STEINER, F. 1956. *Taboo*. London: Cohen and West.

VAN GENNEP, A. 1960. *The Rites of Passage*. Chicago: University of Chicago Press.

WALLACE, A. F. C. 1965. The Problem of the Psychological Validity of Componential Analyses. *American Anthropologist* 67 (Part 2, Special Publication):229–248.

WALLACE, A. F. C. and ATKINS, J. 1960. The Meaning of Kinship Terms. *American Anthropologist* 62:58–80.

WITTGENSTEIN, L. 1958. *The Blue and Brown Books*. New York: Harper & Row.

Laying Down the Law in Their Own Fashion

Marie Reay

Whenever I return to the New Guinea Highlands, as I try to do every year, it is with some nostalgia for the days that are no more. The Wahgi Valley, which visitors used to call "the Garden of Eden," is still beautiful. Even with steel power pylons marching along the South Wall, the near and far risers of the Kubor Range are layered like the colored cardboard shapes of an old-time stage set. But where people used to walk along hand-made roads bordered with bright flowers, motor vehicles ply busily on the sealed stretches of highway and put up thick screens of dust between Minj and Kudjip. Plumed birds no longer "flash like vivid thoughts" among the trees, as K.E. Read so gracefully put it. Writing in the field an essay to do honor to him, the greatest impediment is being unable to quote directly from his own work any but the most memorable and striking phrase. Indeed I feel that a most appropriate tribute from one pioneer New Guinea Highlands ethnographer to another might be to marshal a series of passages from my own two favorites, *The High Valley* (1965) and *The Human Aviary* (1971), and add little in the way of commentary besides saying "Yes, that is how it was in the enchanted valleys of the early 1950's." He

captured with such astonishing accuracy the
atmosphere of the time and the place that I have
decided to write about an institution that did not
then exist and, even as I write, is ceasing to be --
the unofficial "outside" (*an-dara*) court of the
Village Magistrates. To the author of "Morality and
the Concept of the Person among the Gahuku Gama" I
offer a case-study of law outside the formal courts.
The names are fictitious but the events occurred at
Minj in the Western Highlands during 1982.

Missionaries, in their devil-haunted ravings,
preached that the wearing of beards was sinful
because (they alleged) these aroused carnal desires
in women. One result of this pronouncement was a
sudden proliferation of beards outside the
missionaries' own sect. Similarly, the law of the
kiap may have had consequences not consciously
intended. The Minj people (the Kuma and their
congeners) have lived through three different phases
of law. Most recognize pre-colonial law simply as
custom (*mamb'n'm*), not as law. But all recognize
colonial law, "the law of the [white] *kiaps*," and
distinguish it sharply from the reign of the Village
Magistrates in the years since political
independence. The Village Magistrates are supposed
to observe traditional custom, but many of the cases
that come before them have no traditional precedent.
Some of the Village Magistrates are former *tultuls*
and councillors and so embody in their own persons
elements from more than one system of law. Some are
contemporary fight leaders who see nothing anomalous
in urging their groups to battle while being paid to
implement the law, for their magisterial duties are
strictly within the context of courts. Outside the
court clans take up arms against each other with
paltry provocation to settle old scores and they
continue fighting for many months, obstructed but
not deterred by the barbarous punitive actions of
the Police Mobile Riot Squad and pompous parodies of
peace-making on the part of the Provincial

Government. Every clan has its *raskol* gang which
raids stores, private houses, and public utilities.
Few *raskols* are caught, fewer convicted, and fewer
still serve their jail sentences without escaping.
Defeated electoral candidates erect road blocks;
they send their *raskols* to harass men they think
should have voted for them and to pack-rape the
womenfolk of the defaulters; and they beat up their
own wives and mothers when these have not voted for
them. Unofficial courts held in the village
discriminate against women, who pay whatever
compensation is demanded of them for real and
imagined wrongs to avoid being sent to jail. These
are not, however, the unofficial courts that concern
me here.

As Aldous Huxley said in one of his dialogues
between Aldous and Huxley, "At every instant every
transience is eternally that transience." It is
significant in itself and for itself, but the
significance of a minutia of history changes over
time. The flower-bordered roads and the wooden
bridges with thatched roofs so reminiscent of the
gingerbread cottages of fairy tale, part of the
transient magic of the early 1950's, acquire a new
meaning when a man demands compensation from the
government for the death of his father from the
strain of hauling logs 30 years ago. The unofficial
court, formerly held by councillors, is a tradition
firmly established over 20 or so years. (A. J.
Strathern 1974; M. Strathern 1974; M. Reay 1974).
Now both Village Magistrates and litigants prefer
the unofficial "outside" court to the rule-bound
formal Village Court. But the "outside" court of
the Village Magistrates is apparently a transient
phenomenon, having been banned in January 1983.

In the Village Court, which is designed to cope
with offenses committed in the village and disputes
over traditional concerns, an uneven number of
Village Magistrates has to hear the case. Peace
Officers (popularly known as *Plis* [Police] *Opisa*
because of their possession of handcuffs and powers
of arrest) are in attendance, together with a clerk

to record proceedings. The courts became more
centralized when three of the four clans nearest to
Minj were embroiled in a tribal war. The records of
the Village Courts had been unsatisfactory and the
black *kiaps* who had the task of inspecting the
records hoped that the performance of the clerks
would improve under the new arrangement. One very
large group retained its own Village Court but the
other three combined in a single existing court at
Gabingal, three miles from Minj. This is
inconveniently situated for two of the clans which
are located the same distance from Minj on the
opposite side of the township.

In this area of dispersed settlement the entity
that is equivalent to the village is the
clan-community. Thus the Village Court is not a
"village" court, even though it is situated within
the territory of one of the clans that use it.
Cases are heard by and in the presence of persons
belonging to other clans besides that of the
principals. Whatever is revealed in the Village
Court becomes public knowledge. Magistrates settle
minor matters at home, where they also hold
preliminary hearings of some more serious cases.
They confer with their fellow magistrates as to
whether these should be settled in the formal
Village Court or "outside." Halfway between
Gabingal and the two more distant clans is the
station or township of Minj itself. This is not
gazetted as a Village Court area, so the "outside"
courts held here are not only unofficial but
illegal. But the men prefer to air their
grievances, answer accusations, and settle other
people's differences here in the open air. Any
number of Village Magistrates, odd or even, may
preside over the discussion to its conclusion in the
transfer of compensation or a decision concerning
bridewealth. Often nearly all members of the
clan-community of the principals, except for the
very sick and the very old, are in attendance. Some
men consider it to be their duty to come and listen
to these unofficial courts concerning their

clansmen, for the knowledge of who has said what may
be useful later. The women sit far outside the
charmed circle of the male participants and
spectators, giving some of their attention to the
care of children and the manufacture of net carrying
bags.

The Village Court (in its "inside" and
"outside" forms) is an all-male institution run by
and for men. Women are constant casualties.
Pathologically brutal husbands keep their victims
trapped by getting them dragged before the Village
Magistrates. The women's agnates refuse to take
them back for fear of losing the bride-price that
has been promised or already given. The situation
of the bride-price is crucial for the magistrates.
They do not recognize chronic brutality as
pathological and they simply recommend that a woman
so treated should not return to her agnates but
should go to the Village Magistrate or Peace Officer
of her husband's community and seek a little
compensation. This is cold comfort for a woman
whose husband beats her up every time he comes home
drunk and sometimes holds a gun to her head or a
bushknife to her throat. One such woman's father's
brother instructed her to obey the magistrates and
complain to the lawmen of her husband's clan and not
to himself. He added, laughing, that it would not
matter if her husband killed her since he himself,
as her closest agnate, would receive a good
compensation payment. Men, who are often so careful
to spare one another's feelings, treat women as if
they were not sentient beings at all. When a young
widow went to live with a man of her choice her
father summoned her to the formal Village Court and
had her returned to him so that he could arrange a
different marriage for her later when he received
the promise of a better bride-price. This is a far
cry from the white *kiaps'* law of *laik bilong meri*
("what a woman wants") and their strenuous efforts
to see that girls were able to marry as they
pleased. The contemporary chauvinism of the men of
Minj is their reaction to the new freedoms women

enjoy as a result of the efforts of both Administration and missions to raise their status from that of chattels and jural minors. A woman may complain to the magistrate of her husband's clan and he may even find the matter important enough to hold an unofficial intra-village court; but her case rarely reaches the wider arena of the Village Court or the "outside" court of a panel of magistrates unless the overt intention of the men is to discipline her.

In trying to infer the principles of law Village Magistrates follow when they are not inhibited by the rules of the formal court, I propose to examine in some detail two cases which, being closely related and involving the same persons, were heard by a panel of magistrates in a single series of discussions lasting three days. One, a robbery by breaking and entering a tradestore in Minj township, was only a village matter insofar as the alleged culprits belonged to a single clan-community. The other offense took place in the village but had implications for the authority of law officers generally and for the legitimacy of the law they profess to follow. One of the *raskols* held responsible for the robbery tore off the insignia of office of the Village Magistrate and Peace Officer and broke the magistrate's chain. This was the third such offense in the area; in both the earlier cases the offenders had paid cash compensation to the officials.

Ken's clan has three subclans. In 1953 K was slightly larger than P while B was very small. K is now, 30 years later, much larger than either of the other subclans; B is greatly expanded; and P is the smallest group. The clan's *luluai* was in P subclan but in 1961 that group was in mourning for a prominent leader and a man of K subclan became the clan's first councillor. In 1965 the clan lost its councillor with the amalgamation of two wards and elected a man of P subclan as its ward committee man (*komisi*). In 1967 the same man, Ken, was elected councillor and he held that office for most of the time until the dissolution of the Wahgi Council in 1980. With the establishment of a smaller South Wahgi Council and a state of war between Ken's clan and the other group in the Wahgi Council ward, the southern councillors agreed that Ken's clan should have its own councillor. Ken attends council meetings and receives sitting fees pending the amendment of the council's constitution and an election for councillor. In 1976 he was also appointed Village Magistrate, an office he still holds.

The young men of K subclan await impatiently the promised elections for councillor and Village Magistrate and suspect Ken of getting them delayed so that he can continue to hold office. They point out that their subclan is larger than Ken's; that P group has monopolized the positions of power and monetary reward; and that the aged magistrate practices the *wantok* system, favoring men of his own subclan and sub-subclan. He has certainly done this on several occasions, requiring men in other segments to compensate his close agnates without inquiring closely into the truth of the allegations. He has been able to implement his decisions through force of personality and threats of jail for defaulters. A most glaring confusion of his kin and magisterial roles occurred when he provoked his own wife to strike him in the presence of some other magistrates and had her sent to jail. Women who injure their co-wives also go to jail, but Ken goes to extraordinary lengths to see that his clansmen stay free and atone for their wrongs simply by paying compensation. He has often acted as if he believed the threats of *raskols* that if they died or fell ill in jail the person who sent them there would have to pay massive compensation to their relatives. He is so much their clansman that he cannot, as magistrate, decree that no such compensation can be exacted. Thus his own involvement in prescribed roles interferes with his performance as magistrate.

        In July 1982 a rumor circulated that there was
to be an election of Village Magistrates. Ken
himself was silent about this. Soon the rumor
crystallized into the knowledge, gleamed from men of
other clans, that the magistrates were to be
reviewed at Gabingal and if any were found to be
unsatisfactory their clansmen could elect new
magistrates. On the appointed day several young men
of K and B subclans went to Gabingal. They
protested loudly that Ken was an unsatisfactory
magistrate and demanded an election. Ken tried
futilely to silence them, for they were shaming
their bigman in the presence of men from other clans
and an excited crowd was hemming them in. Ken tried
to ward them off by spreading his hand over Gordon's
face to push him away. Gordon alleged later that
this had made his face bleed. Ken did the same to
Terry King, who retaliated by striking him. After
some confusion the D.O.I.C. ("A.D.C.") agreed
reluctantly that the clan could hold an election for
Village Magistrate.
        The young men of B and K subclans understood
that it was accidental that Ken held simultaneously
the two offices of councillor (officially with no
voting powers) and magistrate and that these would
eventually accrue to two different men. Terry King
(who was a K man) himself wished to be councillor,
so the young men of K decided that a man of B should
hold the office of magistrate. Several young men of
B also wished to be councillor, but only Gordon had
a fervent desire to become Village Magistrate. A
surprising number of young men expressed support for
him. I found this surprising because from the time
Gordon had left school he had been an active member
of the *raskol* gang and, further, he was easily
angered and quick to display violence. It seemed to
me that the responsibilities of being a magistrate
were unlikely to reform him and that the *namba*
(insignia of office) would give him the power he
needed to become a bullying tyrant. But suitability
for the post in terms of character, intellect, and
personality was irrelevant to the young men's

choice. There were several men of K subclan who
seemed to me to be suitable in these terms. (One
was a reformed bully and former drunkard who had
harbored, as a youth, the impossible dream of
becoming a judge.) But the young men did not
consider them. Their resentment at Ken practicing
the *wantok* system was not a protest against the
wantok system as such: they wanted their own *wantok*
system to prevail. Impartiality could prejudice
their own interests. B and K were united in this
ambition and since the councillor was to be a K man
the Village Magistrate had to come from B. But no
one in B wanted the job badly enough to challenge
Gordon: some were afraid to do so and some did not
relish spending two arduous days each week in the
formal court.

The election, with supporters lined up behind
their candidates, was a shambles. Recounts were
necessary when lines of supporters who had already
been counted moved over to join the uncounted
supporters of other candidates. Many young men
tried to vote for two or more candidates
simultaneously. Some young men, seeing men and
women of K among Ken's supporters, castigated them
for lining up in the wrong subclan. Several
additional young men of both K and B contested the
election and split Gordon's expected vote, for the
men and women of P were solidly for Ken. A young K
raskol, Carl, stood for election as a joke. The
young men who had been plotting Ken's downfall were
angry at his win and Gordon was infuriated at his
own defeat. The election was held in the limited
space of Ken's hamlet, where his little village
courthouse was situated. The previous year Gordon
had presented Ken with some good quality chairs
(stolen from houses in Minj) for the courthouse.
Now he dragged them outside and smashed them. He
swore at Ken and stormed about threatening to set
fire to the little courthouse. He assaulted both
his parents, who had voted for Ken, knocking them to
the ground. No one interfered with Gordon's
expression of rage: all looked on with guarded

interest. Four months later he was still ambitious
to supplant Ken as Village Magistrate but had not
given up his *raskol* activities.

Most of the young men who wished to become
councillor saw the office as a sinecure -- a source
of regular remuneration and a springboard to a
political career. Also they considered it was
unjust that the three available offices (Village
Magistrate, Peace Officer, and councillor) should be
concentrated in the one subclan. Terry King had an
additional reason for wanting to become councillor.
He had noticed that all the *raskols* were
concentrated in K and B subclans whereas P had no
raskols because men with *namba* kept their
subclansmen in order. If there were an
office-bearer in each of the other two groups the
clan would be free of *raskols*. (In fact P did have
a few *raskols*, but not enough to carry out
independent large-scale operations.) He saw his
intended role of councillor as keeping law and order
within the clan-community. In deliberations of the
council itself he intended to support those
councillors who wanted to put a stop to tribal
warfare. He blamed the increase in *raskolism* for
the renewal of warfare.

One night in November 1982 *raskols* broke into a
tradestore in Minj and stole a quantity of goods.
The theft was doubly daring because the store
belonged to Peter Ali, commander of the Police
Mobile Riot Squad. His mother and two young girls
were sleeping in the dwelling behind the store. The
old woman heard the *raskols* and went outside, where
she could dimly discern four figures. One appeared
to be wearing a football jersey bearing the number
"12." A *raskol* threatened that he and his
companions would rape and perhaps kill her and the
girls if she did not go back inside the dwelling.
She thought she recognized the voice of a certain
young man of Ken's clan. The next morning she went
in search of the *raskols*. She took with her two
men, one of them a prominent Seventh Day Adventist.
They followed the route the *raskols* would certainly

have taken if they belonged to Ken's clan and soon found fresh footprints which led straight into the heart of that group's territory. They also found a trail of biscuit wrappings and soft drink bottle tops.

The police arrived to search the *raskols'* houses and tradestores. Henry, the clan's only young bigman, also of K subclan, showed them which buildings to search. They confiscated manufactured beds and mattresses; other items of furniture of recognizably government issue; electronic equipment including an expensive radio cassette recorder stolen from the D.O.I.C.'s house; a sporting shield belonging to a local school; and numerous alien objects. These were the spoils from earlier robberies that the *raskols* had kept for themselves after making lavish gifts to their clansfolk. The police also confiscated many cartons of food and soft drink. They did not find the *raskols'* firearms, which were hidden elsewhere, and most of the goods stolen from Peter Ali were missing. But they did discover a Seventh Day Adventist poster which Peter and his mother identified as coming from the store.

It was already common knowledge that the *raskols* who had rifled Peter Ali's store were Gordon (the B youth with ambitions to become Village Magistrate), George (of P subclan), and as prime movers in the operation, two young men of K subclan, Bob and Carl. Bob was a hardened criminal who had committed numerous robberies and was still at large after escaping from custody. He was the only one of the four with "a name" (not as a renowned leader, but in the police and court records). The special position of Bob made it imperative for his clansmen to treat the robbery as a matter for the unofficial court. If it went to a formally constituted court he would certainly go to jail, no matter what the outcome.

Bob and Carl were not present at the police search. They had not gone into hiding but were away helping the clan's most qualified mechanic to build

a house. The *raskols* had acquired an unregistered
motor vehicle and had manually pushed it home. The
mechanic was to restore it to running order as soon
as he had finished building his house. The police
had departed with their ungainly load of loot before
Bob and Carl arrived at the assembly place.

Carl was intractable. He abused the law men,
Ken and Kevin, for calling in the police and letting
them search his house without his knowledge. The
Village Magistrate and the Peace Officer protested
that the police had come at Peter Ali's behest, not
theirs. Nevertheless, Carl insisted, they should
have informed him that the police were coming and
given him a chance to be present. The two officials
tried to quiet him, but he continued to revile them
at close quarters as if daring them to strike him.
At last he reached out and pulled Ken's chain of
office from him, breaking it. Then he tore Kevin's
badge off his shirt.

The two village officials were astonished and
embarrassed, but soon they were calculating with
satisfaction that Carl would have to pay them K300*
each as compensation and a fine of the same amount.
Meanwhile Peter Ali was forcefully demanding that
the *raskols* Carl, Bob, Gordon, and George must
reimburse him K1,000, the amount of a government
loan he had received to purchase the stock they had
stolen, together with a few pigs, two or three of
which must be fully grown. He threatened that if
they did not pay he would send the Police Mobile
Riot Squad to capture as many of the clan's pigs as
he wanted. Ken and Kevin reckoned that an
unofficial court of the assembled Village
Magistrates would award them five pigs each in
addition to the cash compensation. All these
expectations were unrealistic. The last coffee
flush had brought very low prices; that was six

*K (Kina) is the official currency of Papau New
Guinea; roughly equivalent in value to the
Australian dollar.

months before and there was little legitimate money about. If the four *raskols* had jointly tendered nearly K2,000 (as well as all those pigs), this would obviously be stolen money and more charges might be brought against them. After the unofficial hearings began, Ken and Kevin reduced their demands for compensation to K100 each with no pigs; and Peter Ali extended the time for payment from a few days to two weeks. At the end of the unofficial court Kevin accepted the K10 (*sic*) offered. The *raskols'* spokesman, Terry King -- not himself a *raskol* but bitterly opposed to Ken, eager to supplant him as councillor, and determined to have him replaced as Village Magistrate -- offered Ken, as a deliberate insult, K10 also. Ken tried to conceal his emotions. He made a careful speech explaining that the *raskols* did not understand the seriousness of the offense. It was not simply an offense against himself personally: it was an offense against the government. K20 would be fitting. The *raskols'* spokesman took another fold of K10 promptly from his pocket and handed over the K20.

Then it was time for the *raskols* to give compensation to Peter Ali for the robbery. The young bigman, Henry, had arrived late dressed conspicuously in work overalls and brand-new gumboots and gone into private consultation with each of the presiding magistrates while the court proceeded. He persuaded Peter Ali to accept K200, which he himself would lend the *raskols*, and the eight pigs of varying sizes they had brought to Minj. Terry King called the value of each pig. The values were grossly inflated. The pigs were led and presented not by the *raskols* themselves but by fathers and brothers and subclan brothers as a gesture of solidarity with them.

Under the "law of the *kiaps*" the family and close agnates of a man arrested for stealing might sorrow for him but they recognized that he was wrong or foolish to commit the offense because he knew the law. Now, however, there is a feeling that habitual

criminals (*raskols*) are not really law-breakers
because there are no strong laws to break. A common
argument runs as follows. The white *kiaps* who
brought the law have long gone and taken their law
with them. The black *kiaps* are weak and do not
concern themselves with law and order. The
councillors draw their pay and if they talk about
anything important in their meetings no one ever
hears of it. They do nothing to introduce strong
laws that could curb the *raskols*. The *raskols*
themselves are disadvantaged: they are hopelessly
unemployed school leavers who are ill-fitted for
subsistence farming and cash cropping, have no
prospects of any kind of job, and are forced by
circumstances to steal for a living. It is quite a
lavish living for a villager to have double beds,
innerspring mattresses, plenty of sheets and
blankets and convenient items of furniture; ample
supplies of store food and soft drink; and money to
buy clothes and beer and contribute to each other's
bride-price.

The evidence against the four *raskols* was
flimsy; but the magistrates found no occasion to
assess or review it.
1. Peter Ali's mother thought she recognized the
voice of Carl's brother (also a *raskol*) and, since
the brothers' voices were similar, she believed it
must have been Carl she had heard.
2. She said she noticed a football jersey with the
number "12." The only person in Ken's clan who had
such a garment with the appropriate number on it was
a public servant who did not follow the common
custom of letting his subclansman wear his clothes.
3. The fresh footprints, biscuit wrappings, and
soft drink bottle tops were superficially
incriminating. But there were precedents for
raskols sneaking through other groups' territories
and leaving such a trail to mislead the police.
4. The house search had uncovered the spoils of
several earlier robberies, but the only item Peter
Ali and his mother could definitely identify as
coming from his store was the S.D.A. poster.

5.   There were no S.D.A. converts in Ken's clan.
But young men who were regular visitors at the
raskols' houses were certain that the poster had
been there long before the robbery. It was one of a
set of posters the *raskols* had acquired some months
earlier in robbing a store owned by another S.D.A.
convert. The others, recognizably of the same set,
decorated the house of Kevin the Peace Officer.
6.   Some unspecified person had informed Peter Ali
that Gordon, George, Bob, and Carl were the
culprits.
7.   On the last day of the unofficial court Maurice
of B subclan related that he had been present when
the four *raskols* had been planning to rob a number
of establishments, beginning with Peter Ali's. They
had invited him to be their *komisi* (literally
council ward committee man but here their organizer
and leader), but he had declined. (Carl admitted
that the conversation had taken place but insisted
that it was simply a "game" using the English word,
and not a "plan," again an English term.) Maurice
related this not as evidence against the *raskols* but
during an attempt to clear himself publicly of their
suspicion that he might have been the person who
betrayed them to Peter Ali.

The unofficial court lasted from about 10 a.m.
to 4:30 p.m. each day. In the mornings and the
evenings Carl tried to find out who had reported him
and his companions. The informer, he said, would
provide the compensation he had to give to Peter
Ali. All the men he named as suspects went to a
great deal of trouble to convince him, either in
personal conversation or in the court, that they had
not informed on the *raskols*.

The *raskols* accepted the fact that they would
be required to pay compensation, but they continued
to protest their innocence of the robbery. Carl's
father, Kim, was eager to defend his son and he
demanded to know the identity of the "witness" or
informer. He recognized that the case against the
boys was weak and he wanted to know how the person
who had made the report had discovered the identity

of the *raskols*. The magistrates insisted that the
report to Peter Ali was confidential. Kim stressed
that the report was vital evidence and the boys were
entitled to know what evidence the court had against
them. Was it an eye-witness account or was it
hearsay? If the case were heard in the Local Court
the witness would be required to give evidence. Two
of the magistrates contradicted Kim in an
authoritative way, telling him that if the case went
to the Local Court the magistrate would know the
identity of the witness but keep it secret. In any
case, they said, if the Local Court were to hear the
case the *raskols* would certainly go to jail. Would
they not prefer to give compensation? Kim made no
further reference to the Local Court but continued
to demand that Peter Ali must reveal the identity of
the witness. Eventually Peter Ali assured Kim that
he would do so once the *raskols* had paid
compensation. (According to one of the *raskols* and
two of their associates, he did not honor this
promise.) The mystery of who had reported the
raskols to Peter Ali so dominated the last day of
the court that Ken, Kevin, and Henry all made
lengthy denials that they had done so.

Despite the flimsiness of the evidence (which
rested on little more than the unrevealed say-so of
an unidentified informer), the magistrates were
presuming all along that Gordon, George, Bob, and
Carl were guilty of breaking, entering, and stealing
from Peter Ali's store. Plainly they saw their role
as that of talking out the case and seeing that the
known offenders paid compensation. The presumption
of guilt and the inevitability of compensation
emerge clearly in the following extracts from the
speeches of Village Magistrates during the hearing.
1. "You have committed a serious offense (tearing
off the insignia of office of a Village Magistrate
and a Peace Officer) so think well. Would you
prefer to give compensation here in the open air or
go into the office and see the *kiap*? You are also
accused of theft, so you have committed two
offenses. What do you want to do?"

2. "We know about courts. When a man has stolen, no matter what he says we are in the habit of getting pay from him and giving it to people. If we accuse him of stealing and he denies it he must still give a little pay."

3. "When we sit in the Village Court we ask the accused whether he has stolen before and his parents have given compensation or not. If he says he is not a thief we let him go if no one has seen him steal. But if we decide to let him go and everyone says he is indeed a thief we say to him 'Everyone has identified you as a thief, so why do you deny it and lie to the court?' Certainly we did not see him commit the theft, but we require him to give a little pay: we cannot let him go scot-free. He has to pay a fine or give compensation to the person from whom he stole. If he does not have the means to do this we send him to jail."

The night of the robbery was dark and Peter Ali's mother, who saw the *raskols* at close quarters, could only make out the number "12" on an inky background. It would have been impossible for any witness to the robbery to identify the four men. On their way home they had to pass Maurice's house. But if he had seen them he would certainly have spoken to them and, since they were trying to recruit him for their gang, they would have given him a bag of rice or a carton of tinned meat as an inducement. But Maurice appeared to have no motive for reporting the *raskols*: he was benefitting from their robberies and he was flattered by their invitation to be their leader. The young bigman, Henry, also had an opportunity to report the *raskols*. When he told the police *which* houses to search he could have conceivably been telling them *whose* houses to search. But by this time nearly everyone in Ken's clan-community knew that Gordon, George, Bob, and Carl were either responsible for the robbery or at least being blamed for it and it seems more likely that the police already shared this knowledge. Several men in the clan described Peter Ali as their friend on the strength of having

occasionally drunk with him, but Henry's alleged
friendship with the officer was more plausible
because they shared several interests. Henry had to
pass through Minj on his way to work and he could
easily have called at Peter Ali's house, which was
on the main road. But Henry was paternalistically
protective of the young men of his subclan and would
certainly not have betrayed Carl and Bob with a high
risk of sending Bob to jail.   In saying that he
would lend the *raskols* the compensation money, he
could well have been covering up knowledge that they
could easily afford it.

Another member of Ken's clan who had an
opportunity to inform the police and Peter Ali of
the identity of the *raskols* was Ken himself.   He
went to see the police and came back and informed
his clansmen that Peter Ali had said these four were
responsible.   Ken could have told Peter Ali simply
that all his clansmen knew that these four were
responsible and then made certain that they did know
by saying that Peter Ali himself had told him.   If
the four were innocent, as subsequent events
suggested, the report of the mysterious "witness"
was a fabrication.

Peter Ali had relatives in one of the groups at
Minj and he prided himself on his good relations
with the local people. Many say that during the
1979-81 war he helped his relatives and Ken's clan,
using a police vehicle to ram the shields of their
enemies and to ferry new shields to his relatives.
As well as being angry at having his store plundered
and being affronted at the *raskols* robbing a store
belonging to a police officer, he was startled and
deeply disappointed that the men in Ken's clan who
called him their friend had not protected his
investment from the clan's *raskols*. Throughout the
unofficial hearing his manner and speech were
emotional.   He was plainly disappointed with the
amount of compensation he received, and he only
accepted it because Henry persuaded him to do so.
He must have been sorely tempted to reveal the
identity of the informer to one of his drinking

companions in the knowledge that this would stir up
trouble in Ken's clan. The fact that he did not do
so suggests strongly that the informer was a bigman
whose co-operation he required in the performance of
his work. There were only two such men, Ken and
Henry.

If the informer did fabricate his report he
must have had a very strong motive for doing so.
Kevin had clashed with Carl and had his badge of
office torn off, but he was not a man to harbor
grudges. The compensation he received was paltry,
but once he had accepted it he resumed his former
good relations with the *raskols*. Ken, however, had
still been waiting futilely for Carl, Gordon, and
Terry King to compensate him for the extremely
humiliating (*nandidl og-ma nggorom*) experience at
Gabingal — judging that in the circumstances he
himself did not owe compensation to them — when
Gordon shamed him further by explicitly trying to
unseat him as Village Magistrate. The chain of
office of Village Magistrate constituted official
recognition that Ken was a bigman with an assured
place among the most important traditional leaders
of the area. The breaking of the chain was a
serious threat to Ken's position and his future.
All these recent confrontations sprang from a
resentment dating back to 1967. At that time the
men of K and B had supported Ken in the council
election against candidates from another clan in the
same ward. They expected him to stand down in favor
of a K or B man at the next election; but Ken told
them tactlessly and arrogantly that he had no
intention of standing down and expected to remain a
councillor for life. The expectation became
increasingly a determination to hang on to the
offices of councillor and Village Magistrate as the
rebellious opposition of the young men of the other
subclans became more articulate and more aggressive.
He could no longer ignore the threat to his
position, whereas earlier he had been assuming
unrealistically that his two sons would succeed him
in the two offices.

Thus Ken had a strong motive to lay the blame
for the robbery on Gordon of B subclan and on the
young men of K. But if only K and B subclans were
implicated it would be obvious to all that the
informer belonged to P subclan. He would need to
name one *raskol* of his own subclan. The *raskol* did
not, of course, belong to Ken's own sub-subclan.
George was the son of a quiet and gentle-mannered
man who would certainly not be inquiring into the
identity of the informer.

Peter Ali and the Village Magistrates accepted
the information concerning the identity of the
raskols as authoritative, as they would certainly
have done if the informer himself were a magistrate.
Throughout the hearing they assumed that Carl, Bob,
Gordon, and George were guilty of the robbery.
When, a month later, another store (belonging this
time to a company) was robbed the police assumed
that Ken's clan was again responsible. They raided
the clan's houses, smashing doors to get inside.
They broke all the shields, bows, and arrows that
they found there; they confiscated all axes and
bushknives; and they destroyed other property,
including cooking and eating utensils. But they did
not find the stolen goods. They had sacked the K
and B houses and were about to attack those of P
when a P man named Keith arrived and intercepted
them. He told them that the *raskols* of Ken's clan
were not responsible for this robbery. Walter, a P
raskol, had a house nearby which he was not using
and Walter's brother-in-law had been sleeping there.
At five o'clock in the morning Keith had seen this
man setting off for home carrying two heavy net
bags. The police went immediately to the man's clan
territory and burst into the houses. They found
there the proceeds of the last night's robbery.
They also found goods that Peter Ali identified
positively as coming from his store.

Peter Ali suggested that the clan of the
culprits should give compensation to Ken's clan
instead of to the company whose store they had just
robbed. This was a neat and simple solution: the

guilty *raskols* would not have to pay double compensation (to him and to the company) and he himself would not have to return Henry's K200, which he had already spent on restocking, and the *raskols'* pigs, some of which he had already sold for a fraction of the values called at the end of the unofficial court. The only loser would be the company, not a person, and its goods would have been insured. Ken endorsed Peter Ali's suggestion. But the men of K subclan had other ideas. They resented having their possessions destroyed in the police search while those of P subclan had escaped. They blamed Walter for harboring the outside *raskol* and letting blame fall upon themselves. Since Walter was a P man they demanded that P subclan should pay them compensation for their losses in the police search and the blame attached to them unjustly for the two robberies. They impounded Walter's pigs as hostages. Meanwhile Kevin and many other supporters of the clan's *raskols* decided that the police search had gone unreasonably beyond the requirements of such an operation and they confronted Peter Ali demanding compensation from the police. Peter Ali scuttled off to the provincial headquarters to consult his superior officer.

On the following day the Minj men heard that some Hagen men had murdered a man of Minj who held a senior position in the province. There had been similar deaths in recent years. This event reawakened the periodically articulated ambition to secede from the Western Highlands and set up an independent Jiwaka province (the name being an acronym using the first two letters of Jimi, Wahgi, and East Kambia). If the Government refused to grant this wish their provincial representatives would resign and Jiwaka would become "a free country." (This English term, absorbed intact into the vernacular, signified an area without provincial government.) Mid-Wahgi men would dynamite the bridges on and near the Hagen border and blockade any Hagen vehicles that approached. But unfinished happenings tumbled over each other to claim men's

attention. Some *raskols* bailed up a truck carrying
beer to Mt. Hagen and in the ensuing raid a
policeman shot a man dead. This act aroused the
hostility all men felt towards the police. Not
towards the "Law Police," among whom they had
"friends" who would help them, but towards the
Police Mobile Riot Squad and the special detachment
sent from Port Moresby to curb tribal warfare and
raskolism. Peter Ali was their trusted *wantok*, but
the others were aliens who were not susceptible to
influence and showed no mercy towards the local
people. Many young men spoke with bravado of
shooting a policeman in retaliation for the man's
death, and a former policeman of the dead man's clan
was strongly (though incorrectly) rumored to have
done so. None of these issues had been settled by
the end of the year. In the distraction provided by
the secession move the K men had returned Walter's
pigs, leaving the whole matter of compensation to be
concluded later. One of the K *raskols* threatened
that if a P man won the council election (which was
as far in the future as ever) he would build a house
on the access road and block P cars from going in
and out.

    Carl's father, Kim, was the only participant in
the unofficial court who invoked principles of law
that had ruled in the courts of the white *kiaps*. He
recognized the distinction between eye-witness
accounts and hearsay; and he insisted that vital
evidence should not be withheld from the defense.
But the invocation was futile. The magistrates had
learned from a source they believed unquestioningly
that the boys had committed the robbery, so the
protestations of innocence did not shake their
presumption of guilt. Carl gave an account of his
movements spontaneously in his own defense, not at
their request. The magistrates knew from the same
source that the boys were habitual criminals and
they stated openly that a reputation for stealing
was proof of guilt.

    There was no question of Carl's innocence in
respect of the lawmen's insignia of office, for many

eye-witnesses had observed his actions and he
himself made no denial. One of the magistrates
referred to the offense as a serious one, but they
did not treat it with great seriousness: they
seemed to regard it as the sort of thing that could
easily happen when there were young *raskols* in the
village. Two individuals, Ken and Kevin, had been
stripped of their customary decorations. One of the
magistrates referred to these as *egin*, decorations,
and another referred to them as *bilas*, the Tok Pisin
equivalent. A little compensation was fitting, but
the magistrates made no attempt to determine the
amount that would be appropriate. A "big"
councillor (*kaunsil og-ma*), not himself a Village
Magistrate, dropped by to listen to part of the
first day's proceedings and, hearing of Ken and
Kevin's initial demands, queried whether the
magistrates were empowered to exact as much as K300
in compensation. The clerk of the Village Court had
taken home the books containing this information and
had gone away leaving his house locked, so the
magistrates adjourned the unofficial court for a
day. Ken and Kevin modified their demands as soon
as the information was available. But the *raskols'*
spokesman (Terry King) and negotiator (Henry)
determined the amounts actually given, which were
the lowest the complainants could be induced to
accept. So far as the magistrates were concerned,
the acceptance of compensation ended the matter.
They ignored the obvious displeasure of two of the
complainants, Peter Ali and Ken, as they would not
have done if they had been seriously concerned to
see the matter settled. When the Riot Squad raided
the houses of Ken's clan after the further robbery,
Peter Ali's drinking companions told me that he had
assured them that these policemen had acted on their
own initiative. But it seems unlikely that a
so-called "disciplined" force would carry out such a
raid without being ordered to do so.

Bob was named throughout as a member of the
gang of four. The magistrates, however, did not
require him to be present at the court out of

consideration for the fact that he was an escapee
who was wanted by the police. This was a most
telling demonstration that although they were
designated "magistrates" and everyone referred to
the gathering over which they presided as a "court"
(*kos* or *kot*), it was not in fact a court *of law*
unless we stretch the concept of law to include a
variety of common law that is different from,
antithetical to, and aims to subvert the law of the
country. Helping habitual criminals to evade
capture secures the goodwill of the criminals' clan
and strengthens the prestige of the magistrates, for
they are above and more powerful than the law. The
proceedings of the unoffical court are not recorded,
so discussion can flow freely and ignore or set
aside points of law. When Carl was accounting for
his movements he mentioned casually that he had
helped himself to a knife he had seen a woman (from
another group) drop. No one commented on this
behavior, but some other young men said later that
it was not stealing: the woman had already dropped
the knife without discovering its loss so it no
longer belonged to her.

This kind of subversive common law is not
unique to the Village Magistrates and the people who
come before them. The police did not want Bob very
urgently. It was well over a year since he had
escaped from custody the first time and, although he
kept away from the government station, they could
easily have found him at home if they had come in a
vehicle that did not look like a police car. One
night, emboldened by beer, he went to the hotel
where a policeman recognized and arrested him. He
was placed in a cell but escaped. No record of the
arrest survives, but the earlier charges against him
were listed for November 1982. He did not appear in
court and the Law List for March 1983 again carried
his name. His escapes from custody would not have
been possible without the collusion of some member
or members of the police force. *Raskols* cultivate
friends (*pren/wantok*) among the police and ply them
with beer, food, and more substantial gifts.

According to my informants, some of the police require money in exchange for particular services. This requirement places them, as individuals, in a position of power over the donors -- a power as individuals which few can attain as members of the force. The help they give illegally in return is often not the simple fulfilment of obligation but the imposition of continuing indebtedness.

In January 1983 the newly appointed Village Court Inspector decreed that magistrates must hear their cases exclusively in the formal Village Court where they were supposed to hear them. He would not tolerate their hearing cases and determining compensation "outside." They protested that there were too many cases for a court that sat only two days a week and if they had to preside in the formal court on other days they should be paid more. They had not been requesting extra pay for the "outside" court work that had engaged them on other days. Evidently the satisfaction they derived from presiding "outside" was at least equivalent to the pay they were receiving as magistrates, since they interpreted this as payment for the less congenial duty of holding formal court. The Inspector can easily enforce the ban on holding unofficial courts in Minj township, since this highly visible site is not in a gazetted Village Court area. He would be unable to prevent the magistrates from holding unofficial courts at Gabingal itself or in other places outside the town and out of sight. But the very visibility of the unofficial court at Minj has been its strength and the source of their satisfaction with it. The sight of them presiding -- as officials, if unofficially and illegally -- has made them known and given them prestige.

The white *kiaps*, who did not recognize the councillors' courts, dismissed them as "conciliation," though the councillors themselves considered them to be courts of law and the people who passed through them treated them as authorized legal institutions. Prior to the arrival of the Village Court Inspector, black *kiaps* were referring

to the magistrates' unofficial courts as "courts"
and tended to assume that the magistrates were
following the same law as they administered in the
formal Village Court. Ostensibly they were
following traditional custom except when this
conflicted with the law of the country, the lineal
descendant of the law of the white *kiap*. But
breaking and entering a store in the township is
only remotely analogous to stealing a pig from a man
in a neighboring clan, and to treat the matter of
Ken and Kevin's insignia of office as an insult to a
bigman and his offsider is to neglect the questions
of the authority of village officials and the
legitimacy of the law.

In bending the law to the shape of political
expediency and settling cases in accordance with
principles that are at odds with the law of the
nation, the recent unofficial courts of Minj have
been closer to "conciliation" than the former
councillors' courts. If conciliation had been the
magistrates' primary aim, however, they would not
have ignored the complainants' obvious
dissatisfaction with the compensation they received.
The principle of conciliation has emerged most
clearly in a decision in a recent land case, not
heard by the Village Magistrates as such but by one
of their number in his capacity as Land Mediator or
Adjudicator. Some men had squatted on an enemy
clan's land in an attempt to incite them to attack.
When ordered off they had displayed their shields,
but the owners, who had no wish to be penalized for
starting a fight, reported the matter instead. The
Land Mediator awarded half the disputed land to each
group, leaving the squatters triumphant and the
owners indignant. But the mediator told a spokesman
for the owners privately that he knew the squatters
had no valid claim to any of the land: he had
divided it simply to placate them and prevent the
eruption of tribal warfare. His aim was not to
establish legal entitlement to the land but to
prevent conflict.

Whereas the Local Court, like the court of the white *kiaps*, concentrates on the offense (Was it committed? Did the accused commit it?) and the person accused (Is he guilty or innocent of the offense?), contemporary conciliation concentrates on placating the aggrieved. Peter Ali was the central character of the magistrates' illegal court. For Ken's clan the presence of Bob in the *raskol* gang was a powerful deterrent to having the case heard by the Local Court or the District Court; but Peter Ali had another powerful reason. Those courts would punish the *raskols* but would not award him compensation.

The language of Minj has no direct equivalent of the concept of punishing or penalizing someone for a crime. Various circumlocutions, based on the idea of capturing or "holding fast" (*ambel nggi*) the culprit, usually refer to particular offenses. The expression that comes closest to the English "I punish" is *kan ngonts*. Literally "rope I-give," this actually signifies "I tie him up." But *ambel nggi*, *kan ngo* -- hold him fast and tie him up -- is scarcely an adequate rendering of "to punish." Further, although to give someone rope has always meant to tie him up, nowadays it also means to put handcuffs on him or put him in jail. The punishment is associated with the law of the white *kiaps* and the Local Court. (Villagers draw no distinction between the Local Court and the District Court, which uses the same building.) And yet in traditional law there were offenses that were, as we would say, "punishable" by more barbarous methods than imprisonment. But shooting an arrow through the thigh of a reluctant bride or driving a stake through the foot of an adulterous woman was not simply punishment: it was an effective, though cruel, means of anchoring her to the ground and preventing her from escaping or finding other lovers. This was the overt reason for the act, which conforms closely with the idea of capturing her, holding her fast, and tying her up. The arrow for the reluctant bride was not a hunting arrow but

a weapon used in inter-clan warfare, appropriate for
use against someone from a different group. Both
arrows and spears figured in the "punishment" of
witches, for they had disassociated themselves from
the clan and worked to its detriment. The overt
concern of the spearsmen and archers who drove the
witches to a high bank and then dispatched them was
not to execute them for their crime, but to make
certain that the witchcraft creatures they harbored
in their bodies would be carried away with them in
the rushing river and be incapable of finding new
hosts within the clan. The "punishment" of the
witches was for the good of the clan, the group that
formed the moral community. But again, it was
conceived of not as a punishment in our sense but as
a preventive measure. Barbarous indeed was the
practice of cutting off an ear or thrusting a stick
through the eyeball of a chronic thief or male
adulterer. The same term, *kunump*, covers theft and
adultery, the latter being conceived of as a special
kind of theft, and the two offenses received much
the same treatment in traditional law. A person
caught thieving food had to pay compensation to the
owner, just as a man had to pay compensation to the
husband whose rights he had stolen to a woman's
sexuality. But a man who continually breached other
men's rights in their womenfolk or who continually
stole food from other people's gardens had to be
halted. He was branded by mutilation so that
wherever he went his appearance signalled a warning
"Here is a thief: watch your food and watch your
wives." The mutilation was not seen as a punishment
for his crimes. Rather, it was foward-looking like
the prevention of the bride's escape or the woman's
wandering and the safeguarding against those
witchcraft creatures finding new hosts within the
clan-community.
      Of course there was indeed punishment, in our
sense of the term, within traditional law. All of
these offenders must have known what to expect as
consequences, unfortunate for themselves, of their
actions. Kuma are not Kalauna, among whom "there

are no 'crimes' . . . and therefore no 'criminals'"
(Young 1971:114). Punishment, however, was not a
preoccupation of Kuma traditional law, which was
concerned with satisfaction for the aggrieved and
the future prospects of the group. For the good of
the community it recognized an offense not
acknowledged in formal modern courts of law, that of
being a habitual thief or adulterer. The offense
that concerned the Village Magistrates in their
illegal court was the theft of goods from Peter
Ali's store. They did not accuse Carl and his
companions of being habitual thieves, for they
recognized no such offense. And yet implicit in the
hearing was everybody's certain knowledge that these
youths were *raskols* who had already committed
numerous robberies and lived by stealing. It did
not really matter to the magistrates whether the
boys were guilty of this particular robbery since
they were certainly guilty of others.

All but a few of the clan names at Minj end in
-*ka* (sometimes modified to -*ga*), signifying "birds"
and "good," the ultimate good being traditionally
the clan. Thus Kondika is Konts's flock and Ngeniga
phratry is Nginabil's flock. But groups do not
necessarily bear the names of mythological ancestral
figures. Some commemorate the physical
peculiarities of unnamed individuals among their
founding ancestors. There is a clan descended from
a man with rotten teeth and another from a man with
badly cracked soles to his feet: almost any such
feature would do to mark off one particular flock or
colony of men. Traditionally these were indeed
Read's "iridescent congregations of people," groups
of men proud in the knowledge that their plumage was
more spectacular than that of any bird that flew.
But few men remain who visualize their group,
without prompting, as a flock of birds. Instead of
feathers they wear big woollen caps with pompoms on
them, designed surely for toddlers, or cloth caps
advertizing consumer goods or political parties, or
striped knitted or netted tea cosies. One man wears
a party boater perched like a jam tart on the crown

of his head. Women, however, still have to keep
their heads free for carrying babies, fencing posts,
and loaded net bags. Missionaries who take the
Cyclopean strictures of Paul seriously require them
to cover their heads in church, but a piece of torn
laplap or Christmas decoration can serve this
purpose. The hens of the beautiful creatures men
revered and emulated were themselves drab and
undecorated.

In pre-colonial days flocks of men took off
from time to time like birds in flight and alighted
elsewhere out of reach of their enemies. Some
stayed away from their old territory for years and
some were never able to return. Less territorial
than the birds, they harbored no resolve to defend
their homes, which they could rebuild elsewhere.
The group itself was the entity they had to preserve
and increase for their own continuance. They had
rules for living together but no general concept of
law that contained the rules. There was no overall
framework that combined the definition and treatment
of offenses inviting punitive sanctions and the
definition and treatment of offenses people could
expiate by giving a little compensation. *Mamb'n'm*,
which translates loosely as "custom," is really
closer to "fashion" than to "law." An explanation
of how a rule of behavior came into being is "the
bigmen conferred, reached a firm consensus, and
informed the rest of the people" (*Yi og-ma mag'r'
peng en-di kendjip*, literally "Men big
being-gathered-together head one they-threw-away").
This referred generally to a cultural innovation (a
new style of dancing or a new element of ritual) or
a major group activity (when to hold the pig
festival; whether to retire to the hills). The
bigmen (orators of subclans, headmen of
sub-subclans, and any other prominent men) laid down
the law on these matters but they did not lay down
moral commandments, for the moral precepts that had
formerly served the clan were already well known. A
spectator did not have to be a bigman to remind
disputants "It is not good for brothers to quarrel."

Yu mamb'n'm, "the word of custom," was any kind of instruction and it issued from parents as well as from bigmen.

Witches have not been executed, nor thieves and adulterers branded, for over 30 years. The custom of driving stakes and arrows through the limbs of wilful and wanton women took longer to eradicate, but there are many people who who have never seen it happen. When the white *kiaps* introduced the concept of law they saw the punitive sanctions of the Minj people as offenses themselves. It was homicide to execute a witch, and even to mention witchcraft was spreading false report. Cutting off somebody's ear or poking his eye out, or disciplining a recalcitrant or lustful female was inflicting grievous bodily harm. The erstwhile offenders were now the victims who received the protection of the law. Habitual thieving, the progenitor of *raskolism,* was no longer an offense. Each act of stealing or adultery was a separate offense in a law that concerned itself with individuals and had no regard for the welfare of the group. The magistrates in the illegal "outside" court did not find it necessary to examine the *raskol* gang individually and establish degrees of culpability. They held the gang to be collectively responsible for the theft and required Carl and his companions to collectively pay the compensation. Similarly, an inter-clan homicide or serious physical injury becomes the concern of the clan to provide satisfactory compensation.

When the *kiaps* abolished the punitive sanctions for offenses they did not recognize, the way was still open for the Minj people to use less barbarous and violent methods for the same purpose. For nearly two decades witches grew less fearful, knowing that they would simply be banished if discovered, and ultimately people became less interested in prosecuting them. From the late 1960's onward the serious investigation of witchcraft has given way to surmise in gossip that particular persons must be witches. Prohibited from

causing grievous bodily harm, men beat up unwilling
brides and adulterous wives, most men soon learning
not to draw blood which a woman could allow to dry
and show to the *kiap* at the earliest opportunity as
evidence of common assault. Under the law of the
magistrates a man who would have gone to jail for
wife-beating in the early 1950's has now to pay
compensation to her male agnates. Traditionally
this applied only when the woman's injuries were
radically disabling, as, for example, broken limbs.

In pre-colonial times a habitual thief might
sometimes receive more gentle treatment than
mutilation: the man from whom he had stolen the
most could require him to work for him, in
conditions comparable to serfdom, for a period of
some months or as long as he needed him. This was
usually a bigman, since he had more wives and
therefore gardens than most and more valuables in
the way of pigs and shells and plumes for others to
steal. It may be surprising that the punishment has
not survived the crime and spread to other offenses.
Village Magistrates are authorized, and it is well
known that they are authorized, to pronounce
community work as an alternative penalty to fines
and imprisonment. But they do not pronounce it, for
although their authority carries weight within the
courts, it does not enable them to see that a
sentence of laboring work in the village is carried
out.

A component of traditional law the Village
Magistrates are proud to retain is the custom of
giving compensation (*kumap*), though they administer
it differently from the pre-colonial and colonial
dispute settlers. In the case of Peter Ali versus
the *raskols* the magistrates let the litigants decide
the amounts and they did not inquire whether these
were just and satisfactory to all parties. (I have
discussed the concept of *kab'g'* in the Epstein
volume already cited.) Coming from different clans
they do not take account of the consequences for and
welfare of the group. The law of the white *kiaps* is
confined now to the formal courts. The formality is

forbidding and the atmosphere punitive. Magistrates
and Peace Officers rarely bring a formal charge
without first holding an unofficial court or
preliminary inquiry. Thus they charge the miscreant
on the basis of their certain knowledge that he is
guilty and he goes to court knowing that he will be
penalized. The formal court is a ritual prelude to
the penalty. When I tried to discuss with some
modern warriors the unconstitutional Section 11 of
the Group Fighting Act they were mystified by the
notion of considering a person innocent until proven
guilty. They themselves, they said, considered an
accused person to be guilty unless he could produce
witnesses to establish that he was not. They were
referring here to the official courts, but the
Village Magistrates followed this principle quite
explicitly in their illegal unofficial *kos*. Ken did
not hold a preliminary village inquiry to establish
the guilt or innocence of the *raskols*, but he went
to court in the certain knowledge that they would be
found or presumed to be guilty.

Pre-colonial law at Minj, like that of the
Gahuku Gama, was embedded in community morality.
The law of the white *kiaps* was generally accepted
and respected as part of an exciting new regime.
Here it was not the gun and the jackboot that
effectively suppressed tribal warfare. Several
great men (i.e., bigmen who were very big indeed)
gathered together and decided that there were
political advantages for their own groups as well as
material benefits for the people of the area as a
whole if they refrained from fighting as the *kiaps*
demanded. They gave instructions that this new
fashion must continue until the *kiaps* left. The
departure of the white *kiaps* lifted the taboo on
fighting. The black *kiaps* are administrators rather
than field officers and have no authority away from
the government station. Men who are politically
ambitious look for support from prominent men of
other groups. So long as no one else in their own
groups is a rival candidate they have a ready-made
power base, irrespective of their policies and

personal qualities. Everyone recognizes the
material advantages that can accrue to the group to
which a member of the national parliament or
provincial government belongs. The politician does
not have to prove himself a bigman by leading and
guiding his group in everyday activities and in its
relations with other groups.

A man may be the recognized headman of his
sub-subclan and act as its spokesman on some
occasions, but he no longer directs its members'
work activities. Few subclan orators continue to
coordinate the activities and regulate the marriages
of their groups. Ken, who is orator of P subclan,
is a strong leader of his own sub-subclan but he has
little to do with the other sub-subclans of P, whose
members respect him and are happy to have a Village
Magistrate in their own subclan. Henry, the young
bigman, deposed the traditional orator of K in 1970
and effectively abolished the role, setting himself
up as a modern leader with ideas he brought in from
outside the area. He has since changed the image he
wants to present to that of the traditional bigman,
specifically that of a man who is materially well
off and generous to a fault. He does not adjudicate
disputes or lay down the law. What leaders there
are in the village are partial or part-time leaders,
not the generalized leaders of pre-colonial times
and the heyday of the local government council. Men
of renown (*kang'm ep minya mim*, literally "name up
on-top he-is," i.e., "his name is on high"), such as
those who presided at Minj to see that the *raskols*
paid due compensation to Peter Ali, wear bigman
masks which mark them off from the ordinary run of
men.

K.E. Read wore no such mask when he came to the
New Guinea Highlands, but he soon made his mark as a
bigman of Highlands ethnography. He was the first
to notice the pervading sexual antagonism. He was
the first to note a change in settlement pattern as
demarcating different cultural areas. No one seems
eager to follow up this observation even yet.
Perhaps our commitment to our narrow ethnographic

areas prevents us from sketching in the fine details within Read's broad brush strokes. We know now that there is a striking cultural discontinuity between Mid-Wahgi and adjacent Hagen (Strathern 1969), two areas of dispersed settlement; and we know of cultural continuities in the east of Chimbu Province across the disjunction of settlement patterns. But we have so far shirked the task of discovering what are the precise cultural correlates of dispersed and nucleated residence. K.E. Read was the first to be so modest in reviewing his findings that he chose to write of his personal relations with his informants and the feel of fieldwork. He has shown a more intimate understanding of New Guinea Highlanders than he admits to in his work. And he has been unique in conveying his insights in a literary medium. Here I am giving a special meaning to the word "literary." Margaret Mead, a writer of a very different kind, possessed a talent for making the dry, scholastic messages of anthropology intelligible to the publishers' ideal catchment, the so-called "general reader." Mick, however, has produced works for anthropologists to ponder which are inspired literature of the kind any lover of fine writing is delighted to read.

108   Marie Reay

REFERENCES

EPSTEIN, A. L., ed. 1974. *Contention and Dispute: Aspects of Law and Social Control in Melanesia.* Canberra: Australian National University Press.

READ, K. E. 1955. Morality and the Concept of the Person Among the Gahuku-Gama, *Oceania* 25(4):233-282.

READ, K. E. 1965. *The High Valley.* New York: Charles Scribner & Sons.

READ, K. E. 1971. *The Human Aviary.* New York: Charles Scribner & Sons.

REAY, M. 1974. Changing Conventions of Dispute Settlement in the Minj Area. *Contention and Dispute: Aspects of Law and Social Control in Melanesia*, ed. A. L. Epstein, pp. 198-239. Canberra: Australian National University Press.

STRATHERN, A. J. 1969. Finance and Production: Two Strategies in New Guinea Highlands Exchange Systems, *Oceania*, 40(1).

STRATHERN, A. J. 1974. When Dispute Procedures Fail. *Contention and Dispute: Aspects of Law and Social Control in Melanesia*, ed. A. L. Epstein, pp. 240-270. Canberra: Australian National University Press.

STRATHERN, M. 1974. Managing Information: The Problems of a Dispute Settler. *Contention and Dispute: Aspects of Law and Social Control in Melanesia*, ed. A. L. Epstein, pp. 271-316. Canberra: Australian National University Press.

YOUNG, M. 1971. *Fighting With Food: Leadership, Values, and Social Control in a Massim Society.* London: Cambridge University Press.

Church Law, Court Law: Competing Forums in a Highlands Village

George D. Westermark

The anthropological writings of K.E. Read on the Highlands of Papua New Guinea set the agenda for the work that was to follow in later years from that area. His early articles included such varied topics as land tenure (1952a), a regional comparison (1954), and ritual (1952c). In his essay "Morality and the Concept of the Person Among the Gahuku-Gama" (1955), he went far in describing the social context of individual responsibility, and with his study of missionaries, "Missionary Activities and Social Change in the Central Highlands of Papua and New Guinea" (1952b), he made one of the first examinations of the impact of conversion and education in the Highlands. Inspired by the latter two examples of Read's work, this chapter studies how new sets of obligations created through church membership influence the use of contemporary legal institutions.

The law-ways of the Agarabi of the Kainantu District, Eastern Highlands Province were like those of Read's Gahuku-Gama, as well as those of other traditional New Guinea societies (Epstein 1974; Koch 1974; Lawrence 1969; Podolefsky 1978; Strathern 1972). Social relationships between Agarabi in conflict influenced their responses strongly; closer

relationships led to easier settlements, and more
distant relationships led toward fighting. As Read
notes:

> To the Gahuku-Gama . . . man is primarily
> a social individual, a member of this or
> that particular social group, someone who
> occupies a particular position in a system
> of social rights and obligations . . . His
> responsibilities are not conceived as
> being constitutionally determined, nor
> have they any explicit extra-social
> reference; they are dependent on the
> presence or absence of particular social
> bonds. Thus, it is not to human beings as
> such that men are morally bound, but to
> human beings as members of a particular
> collectivity (1955:233).

Agarabi life was dramatically transformed by
their first contact with Europeans in 1927. Since
that time they, like other Highlanders, have
continued to increase their understanding of the
world beyond their mountain homes as they have come
to participate in a more extensive social system, one
which includes peoples and places unknown to their
forbears. The changes associated with this expanded
world have created new collectivities and new social
bonds.

An increased range of alternatives is also
available to the Agarabi in the legal field. While
economic linkages with the world economy increased
during the past three decades, political
decentralization has opened new opportunities in
self-government. Disputes can be handled officially
by a number of agencies from the welfare office to
the village court, and for members of organized
churches, the informal handling of disputes is
possible through church officials. The latter
possibility is the focus of this chapter. I will
explore how Agarabi Seventh Day Adventists respond to
grievances by combining the use of the national
village court system with church officials and
rituals. By examining a number of disputes between

Adventists, I hope to add to our knowledge of how changing social relationships are affecting Highland dispute management.[1]

BACKGROUND

With the Gadsup, Kamano, and Tairora, the Agarabi are one of four ethnolinguistic units found in the Kainantu District. Numbering approximately 13,500, the Agarabi are distributed in some thirty villages, whose populations range from 250 to 800. All but one or two villages are connected by vehicular roads to the Highlands Highway, Papua New Guinea's major artery, which links the more western Highland provinces to the coast. Bisecting Agarabi territory, the Highway passes through Kainantu town, the district's bureaucratic and trading center. Kainantu town is located in Agarabi territory, and no Agarabi village is more than nine miles from it.

Contemporary Agarabi villages were demarcated during the colonial period. They roughly reflect settlements that existed in the pre-colonial period, though in some cases villages were created where none had been before. Traditional settlements were small, nucleated hamlets, palisaded for protection. Several neighboring hamlets united by ties of kinship, marriage, exchange, or cooperation in war formed the most extensive political unit, which I call the *phratry*. Settlements usually joined a number of clan segments, with the men of each segment co-residing in one or two houses. Frequent wars led to the dissolution and recombination of settlements, and the redefinition of political alliances (Westermark 1981a).

The Agarabi settlement of today is far less nucleated than before the arrival of the Australians. The pacification that began in 1933 made it possible for many Agarabi local groups that had fled to escape conflict to return to their previous settlements. Although Australian patrol officers encouraged the formation of large villages to facilitate government supervision, the decreased threat of attack led gradually to the less nucleated pattern.

Agarabi economic activities are still largely concentrated in subsistence agriculture. In the 1960's and 1970's, however, the inroads of Western capitalism were increasingly felt, as land was devoted to cash crops and cattle production.

The Australian administration introduced coffee to the Agarabi at the close of World War II. The first Agarabi who experimented with coffee began to earn cash in the early 1950's, thus stimulating an interest in the crop in other villagers. By 1955, nearly every Agarabi village had some coffee gardens, and a coffee census in 1956 revealed that more than 36,000 trees had been planted (K.P.R. 1955/56). Production increased among the Agarabi and Gadsup from ten tons in 1957, to eighty tons in 1960, to 400 tons in 1970 (Young 1973: 36). In addition to actual production, many Agarabi who own trucks act as coffee buyers, purchasing coffee in the more remote villages of the district for resale at a better price to coffee factories in Kainantu town, Goroka, the provincial capital, or as far away as Lae, the coastal terminus of the Highlands Highway.

Agarabi began the first cattle project in the Kainantu District in 1961 (Young 1973:37). Agarabi projects have since expanded in number and grown in size, as they have elsewhere in the district. Although cattle are not sold to companies in town, some of the Agarabi animals are sold to non-cattle owning villagers. The profits are used both for traditional purposes such as exchanges associated with birth, marriage, and death, and for business projects such as the purchase of trucks. Since Adventists refrain from eating pork, cattle have been of particular interest to them.

The Agarabi were one of the earliest Highland peoples brought under the control of the Australian administration. In 1933, the first census was taken and the first *luluai* (Pidgin "village headman") appointed in Agarabi villages (Aitchison 1964; Radford 1972, 1977). With the introduction of this official position, new possibilities for dispute management opened for the Agarabi. The administrative definition of the *luluai's* role did not include judicial powers; however, unofficially most *luluai* heard cases, levied fines, and administered corporal punishments.

Recent years have seen other political innovations. The Agarabi were the first Kainantu District ethnolinguistic group to participate in an Australian-sponsored local government council organized in 1960. Councilors replaced the *luluai* at this time, and adopted their unofficial role in handling disputes. Since 1973 they have participated with the other peoples of the district in an experiment in sub-council government unique in Papua New Guinea. The current district-wide council concerns itself with general services such as schools, roads, and health aid-posts. The district is divided into mini-councils, or *Eria Komuniti* (Pidgin "Area Community"), concerned with problems pertaining to its member villages. Villages voluntarily join the mini-council of their choice; villagers elect their own officials; and each council collects its own taxes. Because the district-wide Kainantu Council operates on the profits from its business interests, each mini-council is able to use its tax money for whatever projects or investments it chooses (Westermark 1978a).

The most significant legal development for the law-ways of the Agarabi in the 1970's was the introduction of village courts in 1975. As with the mini-councils, court officials are elected at the village level and incorporate several villages within their geographic jurisdiction. Unlike the councils, however, the village courts are part of the national judicial hierarchy. Thus, for the first time, village leaders have official judicial powers. Part of the magistrates' salaries come from the national government; magistrates can sentence offenders to imprisonment in government jails; and cases heard by the courts can be appealed to higher courts. Despite these differences, together the councils and village courts form the basis for a true participatory village government (Westermark 1978b).

The creation in 1976 of a land mediation system was another recent development that has expanded official village level legal machinery. Land mediators are appointed in parts of the country where land disputes are prevalent. One mediator and five ad-hoc mediators were appointed for the Kainantu District, based on recommendations made by the district council. The mediators are the primary official method for handling land disputes, although difficult cases can be taken to a local land court. Land disputes cannot be heard by the village courts (Westermark 1981b).

AGARABI SEVENTH DAY ADVENTISTS

Christian missionaries were among the first Europeans met by the Agarabi. In 1927, two Lutherans, Leonhard Flierl and Karl Kaueracke, passed through Agarabi territory, visiting several villages (Radford 1972:91). The first Highland Lutheran mission station, however, was established in Gadsup territory, south of the Agarabi. Seventh Day Adventist missionaries established a station in 1935 at the Upper Ramu Patrol Post, the eventual site of Kainantu town. Hence, early Adventist missionary activities concentrated on the Agarabi; indeed, they were the earliest converts to Adventism in the Highlands.

The beliefs and organizations that distinguish church members are fundamental to an understanding of disputing behavior among them.[2] Agarabi Adventists perceive themselves as followers of the true Christian faith. A number of their beliefs set them apart from and place them in opposition to other churches. In the traditional pig-loving Highlands, the Adventist abhorrence of pork, in accord with Old Testament dietary proscriptions, is one of those beliefs. Adventists also believe in baptism by immersion -- "Just like Jesus" -- another practice

that sets them apart. An emphasis on healthful
living also singles out the Adventists. They
consider the body to be the temple of the Holy Ghost,
and they ban the comsumption of things that they
believe to be harmful to it, e.g., beer, coffee,
betel nut, liquor, and tobacco. Cleanliness is
stressed as an important means of maintaining the
"temple."

Perhaps the most significant tenet of Adventist
belief for Agarabi church members is their adherence
to Sabbath worship. They believe this tenet creates
an unavoidable conflict between them and other
Christian groups. Agarabi Adventist sermons seldom
fail to point out that Jesus said that he came to
fulfill the laws of the Old Testament, not to break
them; since the Fourth Commandment indicates the
importance of Sabbath worship, Jesus did not intend
that Christians should alter their holy day. In
fact, when asked why they converted to Adventism,
many Agarabi say they did so because of Saturday
worship.

The importance of the Sabbath worship was
impressed upon me at a showing of slides of Biblical
sites by a Highland Adventist from Goroka. He and a
number of other Highland businessmen had accompanied
an Australian Adventist missionary to Israel in 1977.
In his presentation, he drew attention to one slide
that showed an urban scene on the Sabbath, with shops
and businesses closed in accordance with Jewish
practice. The implication of the slide was clear to
those present: in the land of Jesus, Israelis, like
Adventists in Papua New Guinea, worship on Saturday.
A question that many in the audience posed was, why
had the other Christian churches attempted to mislead
them into believing that Sunday was the Christian
holy day?

Sabbath worship also figures prominently in
Agarabi Adventist visions of the Second Advent of
Jesus. Their scenario for the events of the Last
Days includes the following: other Christian
churches, led by the Roman Catholics, will conspire
with the world's governments to enact a law in favor

of Sunday worship; Adventists, holding true to the
Fourth Commandment, will be discriminated against in
various ways for their faith; because they have
failed to influence the Adventists, the churches and
governments will move to destroy them; finally, with
the Adventists facing destruction, Jesus will return
to save God's chosen people.

Adventist beliefs regarding dietary
prohibitions, baptism, and Sabbath worship are
followed more strictly because of adherents' belief
that the Last Days are near. That many church
members do regard the imminence of the Second Coming
as a real possibility was demonstrated to me shortly
before the conclusion of my field research. A number
of church elders came to me to request that I watch
for signs of the Last Days after my return to the
United States. Because all things happen first in
America, they reasoned, I could warn them of these
signs, enabling them to prepare for the End.

The identity of Agarabi Adventist church members
is reinforced by their well-developed organization
and its activities. Each church has a number of
offices to be filled from its membership: deacon,
deaconess, and church elder. These individuals
perform such duties as supervising seating in church,
collecting offerings, and assisting with the service.
Groups like the Women's Welfare Society, the Laymen's
Society, and the Youth Choir provide social and
recreational activities outside the religious
ceremonies.

Strictly religious pursuits can demand much of a
church member's energies, however. Worship is
performed for brief periods (45-60 minutes) twice
daily, in the morning and again in the evening. On
Saturday, when services usually extend from nine
until noon, Adventists often meet again in
mid-afternoon.

Periodically during the year, Coastal pastors
organize revivals and camp meetings. Revivals last
for several days, with the pastor beginning the
evening worship in mid-afternoon. Usually a revival
is devoted to some particular topic, e.g., marriage,

child-rearing, or the Second Advent. It provides a time when the pastor can explain the Adventist approach to these topics in greater depth. Camp meetings are larger gatherings, the members of the district's churches gathering at the Kainantu town Adventist headquarters. These meetings sometimes mark the visit of a church official or the initiation of a new program.

It should be made clear, however, that though the beliefs and organization of the church demarcate a singular Adventist identity, Agarabi church members do not live in isolation from non-Christians or the members of other churches. Approximately 1000 active members (i.e., those listed on the church rolls) and many nominal members live among non-Adventists, either within their own hamlets or in neighboring villages. Although the Adventists are energetic evangelizers and church membership has been growing strongly in recent years, daily activities bring church members into contact with many who do not share their beliefs.

ADVENTIST DISPUTE PROCESSING

Research in the ethnography of law in different cultures has frequently demonstrated the significant impact social relationships have on the methods disputants select for handling their disputes. This has been shown to be as true of peasant societies as it was of the pre-colonial societies of New Guinea. Recent studies have related the use of ritual reconciliation in dispute management to social relationships (e.g., [Dillion 1976, Koch *et al.* 1977]). Based on a comparative study, Koch *et al.* suggest that such ritual methods for handling disputes will be found where people in close-knit groups or networks cannot afford to test their social relationship in the fires of public debate. They propose that:

> Disputants will use avoidance as an initial response to a grievance and

subsequently repair their relationship
through the performance of a
reconciliation ritual if a dissolution of
their relationship gravely jeopardizes
their common interests and if other
procedures are either unavailable to them
or incapable of effecting a mutually
satisfactory settlement (1977:269-270).
Given the Adventists' religious affiliation,
their sense of doctrinal opposition toward other
Christian sects, and their social involvement in
church organizations, one might suppose that forms of
ritual reconciliation would be used by Adventists in
handling their disputes. Such a supposition would
not be totally incorrect.
Adventists do employ several church-related
activities in their dispute management. However,
Adventists use village courts as often as
non-Adventists, even though the courts tend to
emphasize their adjudication rather than their
mediation component (Westermark 1978b). In the
Agarabi village with which I am most familiar, a
community noted as a stronghold of Adventism, 53% of
the village court cases in a one year period involved
church members, and in 36% they acted as
complainants.
This active Adventist involvement in the village
judicial system is somewhat puzzling given the
negative attitude taken by Agarabi church elders
toward the court. There is no opposition to the
courts from the official church hierarchy, but local
church elders believe that use of the court does not
instill the proper feeling in church members. One
elder explained the problem thus:

It is better for church members to finish
their troubles with other church members
without going to court. When they go to
the village court, Satan enters their
hearts and they think only of winning
their case, not of their life after death.
Another elder gave a more vivid account:

The Bible says that the court is like
shooting a man with an arrow; it is like
killing him. It is not good.

As noted above, the elders' perception of court
proceedings is accurate. Magistrates do not perceive
reconciliation to be their primary objective; they
expect that litigants in the court will be clearly
opposed. They feel that the litigants should be
enemies at that moment, and they order those who may
easily resolve their disputes once the anger of the
moment has worn off to attempt mediation outside the
court.

The attraction of the courts for Adventists may
be explained, in part, by the fact that Adventist
beliefs receive a sympathetic hearing in the courts
from the many officials who are church members.
Magistrates sometimes infuse greater religiosity into
the proceedings by beginning the day with prayer:

Alright, before we hear the peoples'
disputes, we must pray. Jesus Father, on
this morning we ask you. True, we are
leaders on this earth, but we do not have
much power, we do not have much strength.
You, you have more power, more strength.
Whatever our thoughts, you must give us
understanding. When we want to make a
decision, you must sit with us and give us
understanding. We ask you in the name of
Jesus Savior. Amen.

By equating Adventist rules with the laws of the
government, they also sometimes give precedence to
Adventist beliefs, as was demonstrated in the
following case.

Case 1. The plaintiffs, parents-in-law of the
defendant, were pressing the latter for a
brideprice payment. The young defendant argued
that, as a member of the Adventist church, he
was forbidden to make such a payment. In the
parent's favor was the fact that the *Eria
Komuniti* of the litigants, like others
throughout the District, had set standards for

brideprice payments. It was claimed that these
standards would end the exorbitant demands being
placed upon some grooms, but magistrates also
argued that these payments were the *kastom lo*
(Pidgin "customary law") of the Agarabi. In
this case, however, the magistrates supported
the defendant's argument, adding that "the law
of the mission is the law of the government."
During their remarks following the decision,
they admonished the defendant (a wage-earner),
saying that he must help his parents-in-law with
money when they were initiating business or
ceremonial projects.

The attitudes of Agarabi Adventists toward the
court thus present us with a complex blend of
attraction and opposition. In the cases discussed
below I hope to show that, although Adventists do
avail themselves of the court's services, the church
elder's criticism of the court modifies the manner in
which litigants handle their disputes into two ways:
some Adventists do not pursue their cases as avidly
as they might otherwise (Case 2), and others take
advantage of several alternative methods for handling
their disputes open to them through the church (Cases
3-4).

Case 2. After receiving back the large sum of
money he loaned his fellow church member, the
complainant felt that he should receive some
additional "profit money" (i.e., interest). He
went to the village court, but he made it clear
that he did not want to bring the borrower in
for a hearing. All he wanted was a letter
instructing him to make the additional payment.
The court clerk wrote the letter which was
delivered by the complainant, and the borrower
said he would consider the matter. After
several months passed with no action, I asked
the frustrated lender what course of action he
would now pursue. He responded that he would
just wait, and if he never received anything
more, "he (i.e., the borrower) will be judged by
God."

The Church elders do not merely advise other
Adventists to refrain from using the village court,
but also act as mediators. They urge their fellow
Adventists to bring their cases to them, and when
they hear of disputes, they go to visit the disputing
parties. The elders encourage the disputants to
forget their grievance, and offer to pray with them
in an effort to ease their anger. To persuade the
disputants to accept their efforts, the elders argue
that one can never know the time of the Second
Advent. Those with outstanding disputes may be
excluded from heaven. Furthermore, they insist that
those who have obstinately pursued disputes will have
negative marks on their record on Judgement Day.

The next two cases illustrate the type of
dispute in which an elder might intervene; his
involvement at different stages of the dispute; and
the factors that might lead to the success or failure
of his mediation.

Case 3. The young wife of a man who had
recently returned for a vacation from his work
in the Papua New Guinea Islands went off in the
afternoon with some other young women, and did
not return until late that night. The husband,
who had been searching for his wife during the
evening, heard reports that she had been to the
cinema in town. When the wife returned, the
husband met her in front of her parents' home,
yelling at her for going away all day and for
attending the cinema. As his anger increased,
he picked up a stick and began to hit his wife.
The wife's father went to his daughter's defense
and punched the husband, knocking him to the
ground. The husband did not retaliate, but he
and his father, who had arrived in time to see
the wife's father punch his son, initiated a
shouting match with the wife's father,
criticizing the wife's behavior while the wife's
father objected to seeing his daughter beaten in
front of him. At this point, a church elder
came with two male church members and tried to
calm the disputants. They responded positively

to the elders' exhortations to end their
yelling, but the wife's father asserted that the
next day he would take his son-in-law to the
Local Court in town. The church elder and the
two church members continued to urge them all to
end their dispute through prayer, and not to let
the night go by without reconciling. After
about an hour's discussion, the church elder was
able to convince all the participants to pray
together and promise not to revive the dispute.
When I spoke with the main participants, they were
all agreed that the dispute was resolved. In the
months that followed this altercation, there was no
further trouble.[3]

Case 4. A man had taken a second wife, and as
is common in such marriages, the first wife was
not happy about the situation. During the year
that followed the marriage and that preceded the
case in question, there had been a number of
fights and court cases growing out of the
animosity between the co-wives. As a result,
the first wife had left the house that she
shared with her husband and returned to live
with her parents. One afternoon, the husband
brought home meat that he intended to give to
his first wife, but as he was met initially by
his second wife, she convinced him to give her
the meat to cook for his mother and siblings.
The husband then went off with his father in
their truck on business. Unfortunately, the
first wife had seen her husband in town after he
had bought the meat, and she knew that it was
meant for her and her children. When she
learned that the co-wife had intercepted the
meat, she, along with her mother and a sister,
headed for her husband's parents' house. The
ensuing argument quickly became a fight, with
the first wife, her mother, and a sister on one
side, and the second wife, the husband's mother,
and another daughter-in-law of the husband's
mother on the other side.

The first wife's father, a village court magistrate, arrived at his house shortly after the women of his family had set off after their rivals, and he arrived at the scene of the fight after it had begun. Attempting to separate the women, he was struck by his daughter's mother-in-law, and he, in turn, gave her a shove that sent her tumbling across the floor of the house. With that the fight ended, and the first wife's father took his family back to their house. The husband and his father arrived home later that evening, and were angered by what had occurred. The husband's father, perhaps motivated by the fact that his daughter-in-law's father was a village court magistrate, decided to take his case to the local court in town, rather than to the village court.

The next morning a church elder, hearing of the dispute, tried to convince the husband's father to give up his intention to go to the local court, and, instead, to handle the dispute through prayer. The husband's father was adamant, however, and he took the case to court, where the first wife, her parents, and her sister were all fined and placed on a year's probation.

After the court hearing, the two families remained angry and refused to speak, and though the church elder continued to seek to effect a reconciliation, it was almost a year before he was able to get the two mothers and the first wife to pray together. After that, relations improved, with the first wife frequently visiting her mother-in-law, and the other members of the two families speaking with each other.

In each of these two cases, the church elder tried to intervene soon after the trouble began, and attempted to keep the parties from taking their case to court. His effort in the first case was more successful, it appears, because the dispute did not have the long-term animosities that had built up

around the second dispute. Both disputes had
involved violence, but the second dispute was
preceded by a number of other fights and court cases.
That the church elder was able to establish a
reconciliation in the second case, however temporary
it might prove to be, was a tribute to his
perseverance. At least by the time I left Kainantu,
approximately six months after the reconciliation, no
further disputes had arisen between these parties.

Another method for dispute management available
to Adventists is embodied in their communion service.
The ritual consists of a preliminary washing of feet
by church members, the men in one group and the women
in another, followed by the consumption of bread and
wine, symbolic of the body and blood of Jesus. Prior
to the communion ritual, Adventists try to settle
their disputes, since they believe that one should
not celebrate the "Lord's Supper" with a conflict
unresolved or a sin unrepented. Apparently, in the
years prior to my arrival in Kainantu, public
confession of sins and disputes was made before
village gatherings of Adventists.

Shortly before I arrived, however, the system
was changed to one in which disputes would be settled
privately with one's fellow disputant, with or
without the mediation of the elder, and a sin would
be repented in prayer with the elder. Several older
men did not believe that the new system would work,
because it would not leave the same impression. They
said that standing up in front of others and
confessing was like standing before an enemy with a
drawn bow: your mouth went dry, your perspiration
flowed, and your legs shook. Without this type of
mandatory public recitation they doubted that people
would truly confess their shortcomings. Other
Agarabi Adventists believe, however, that to take the
bread and wine of communion without first resolving
one's conflicts would be to risk illness, and this
belief may motivate them to use private repentance.[4]

The washing of feet prior to the communion has
special significance for dispute management, since
the act, which parallels Jesus' washing of the feet

of his disciples before the Last Supper, serves to affirm ritually the conclusion of a dispute. Adventist informants cited this as a good way to handle a dispute, because then both parties would know that the dispute would not be reopened.

It is difficult, however, to determine how often this aspect of the Lord's Supper is associated with disputes. Having learned of this aspect of the ritual, I asked the male participants after one Communion whether they had chosen a partner because of a dispute with that person, and found that only one pair had selected each other on that basis (See Case 5). It may be that some who were participating in the ceremony were unwilling to reveal a conflict that had remained private, but it does not appear that this method is frequently used. I did not record any instance of a dispute responded to in this way in the memory case record collected from Adventists.

Case 5. A son built his house near that of his father, in an area where his uncle had formerly resided. The father had adopted the son elsewhere in the Eastern Highlands Province as a child, and the son's wife also was from another ethnolinguistic group.

The uncle claimed that he planted a small garden of coffee trees near where his house had stood, and though he had not cared for it or harvested it in years, he decided in 1978 to use the garden. It was the son's contention that the trees the uncle planted died before maturing. The son said that the trees in question had sprung from the seed of unpicked coffee from his father's nearby trees, which he had cared for after building his house. When the uncle would not heed the son's warnings to leave this coffee alone, he threatened his uncle with his knife. The uncle responded by reminding him that he was adopted and that neither he nor his wife were from their village. This was an insult to the son's position in the village, and the confrontation nearly resulted

in a fight. Each man remained angry with the
other, and several weeks passed without a change
in the status of the dispute. A church elder
attempted to mediate the dispute with no
success. The approach of the Lord's Supper
encouraged both men to ease their antagonism.
The uncle approached the son first, but he did
not apologize for his remarks; rather, he simply
said that the coffee was not worth fighting
over. At the Communion, they selected each
other to wash feet and end their dispute.

A final way in which disputes can be managed
through the Adventist church is by an oath taken on
the Bible. I observed only one instance of this
oath-taking, and as far as I am aware, it was the
first time that it had been applied in Kainantu.
Although an oath is used in the government courts
before a witness testifies (but not in the village
court), and Agarabi see the two oaths as related, the
Adventist oath is thought to be much more powerful
and serious. In the case I observed, one of the
participants described the relationship between the
two oaths in the following way:

This way of holding the Bible is the law of
the Seven-Days and the law of the
government too. If there is an
insignificant dispute or a serious dispute,
when you go to the Office (District Office
or Court) with a dispute you hold the Bible
first . . . Inside the Seven-Day mission,
it is one *kot* of ours (i.e., a way of
handling disputes). If someone holds the
Bible and lies, then some misfortune will
befall him or his family. The basis of the
government law comes from the Seven-Day
mission. God gave the Bible to Seven-Days
first and then the government took it and
used it. God gave the bayonet to the
government to clear the road and make a way
for the Bible to follow. The government
uses the bayonet to cut men who make
trouble, but it is God who has given power

to the government. They gave the government this power so that the mission could later bring the Bible to the villages. The government cleared the bush and they punished the trouble makers. As for those who made trouble, the government cut off their ears, cooked them, and fed them back to the trouble makers. After that, all the the trouble makers were quiet and listened to the mission. We deacons or church elders sometimes fight with other people and our faith is not strong. But pastors or men who have strong faith, men who speak with God, have the strength of God, and when trouble comes they can gather and pray and perform the Bible oath. If (the defendant's name) caused the trouble and lies while holding the Bible, God will see it. He will say, "You sinful man, you have lied in my sight," and then God will do something to that man. Sometimes he will kill him, but sometimes he will only make him sick or have an accident. The Bible is strong law and you must tell the truth.

The mixture of methods for dispute management exemplified in Case 6 makes it particularly interesting, with village and national legal agents, and indigenous and Christian religious practices, introduced in handling the case.

Case 6. A large house, recently built by members of one lineage, and shared by four families, was burned to the ground. Besides the house, many household items such as plates, cups, pots, and blankets were destroyed. It also was claimed the K800 (U.S. $1000) hidden in the house was burned. The defendant was the wife of one of the lineage men. Her husband and accusers said that she had burned the house because her husband had brought her co-wife to live with him in the new house while the accused lived in a house nearby. The husband had become

an Adventist, and supposedly given up his second
wife in accordance with Adventist doctrine. But
he had fallen away from the church, and when his
family finished the new house, he brought back
his other wife from her parent's home where she
had been staying.

There were two types of evidence against
the defendant, although she denied that she was
responsible for the fire. Her husband's
brother's wife saw her go into the house shortly
before the fire began. Though she did not claim
that she had seen the defendant start the fire,
the complainants argued that there was no reason
for the defendant to be in the new house,
especially since her co-wife was now living
there. Second, the elder brother of the
defendant's husband consulted a diviner who,
through his dreams, identified the accused as
the culprit.

Armed with this evidence, the elder brother
went to the police with his case. The police
counseled him to go back and handle this trouble
in the village, since the defendant was his
sister-in-law. Several Adventists then
suggested to the elder brother that he consult
the Coastal evangelist about the possibility of
performing the Bible oath. He did so, and the
evangelist agreed to come hear about the
dispute.

There were approximately fifty to sixty
people present for the Monday morning hearing,
including the defendant, her parents, the elder
brother, a village court magistrate, and the
Coastal evangelist. Conspicuously absent was
the defendant's husband. The hearing began with
a statement by the father of the defendant, a
leading Adventist and the village councilor
(quoted above), and the elder brother, also an
Adventist, detailing the evidence that he had
against the defendant. Her father then
criticized the elder brother for trying to solve
the dispute three ways -- the police, the

diviner, and the mission -- instead of just using one. He added that he had experience with diviners, and that he no longer believed in their truthfulness. Further, he said that one could not take such evidence into court, since the government only believed what a witness actually had seen, and he asked the village court magistrate whether or not this was true. When the magistrate agreed that it was, the elder brother said that the father was trying to frustrate his attempts to settle the dispute, and that he would immediately take the case back to the police. To impress the gathering with his seriousness, he began to ready his truck for the trip into town. Many present called out for him to wait, to give the defendant time to speak, and to try the oath before going to the police. After a considerable exchange of words, the elder brother agreed to let the evangelist administer the oath.

The evangelist began by explaining what could happen if the defendant took the oath: if the defendant lied while holding the Bible, she would die; but, if she was falsely accused, her accuser would die. The evangelist said that he he had seen many people die on his home island after an oath was taken on the Bible. For example, his father's brother had had an adulterous relationship with a woman, but he refused to admit it. A pastor had him take the oath, and within two weeks he was dead. He warned that once the power of the oath is set in motion, there is no way to avoid its consequences.

Following the evangelist's speech, several people, the father, the elder brother, and a brother of the wife, urged the wife to come forward and take the oath. The village court magistrate, who described himself as the father of both co-wives (actually an elder member of their clan), took a more conciliatory tone. He told the wife that he knew why she was angry:

her co-wife was living in the house that the
defendant had helped to build; the co-wife rode
in the truck that the defendant helped to pay
for; and her husband had given her co-wife money
to play cards. All this money had come from the
sale of coffee that was a result of the
defendant's efforts, not those of her co-wife;
everyone knew the co-wife was lazy. Wasn't it
because of these things, the magistrate asked
her, that she was angry? And hadn't she gone in
to burn something of her co-wife's, but had
accidentally set the entire house on fire? With
that the defendant broke down and admitted that
what the magistrate suggested was true.

The magistrate said he understood her
anger, and that it was good she had admitted
causing the fire, since now the family could end
their trouble. He criticized her husband for
giving her co-wife the defendant's money, as it
was their *kastom lo* (Pidgin "customary law")
that a husband should not give the things of one
wife to another wife. The defendant was right
to be angry. Now that the defendant had
admitted setting the fire, the elder brother's
wife said, they could take the case back to the
police; but the magistrate asked her why they
had ignored the village court in this case, and
he encouraged them to go there next.

Some people began to leave the gathering at
this point, while others sat and discussed the
case. The general feeling seemed to be that the
husband was at fault: if he had behaved
properly the trouble would never have occurred.
Eventually the case was taken to the village
court, where the husband and the defendant were
ordered to rebuild the house and pay K200 (U.S. $250)
to those who had lost household goods or cash in the
fire. By this stage in the dispute a diviner, the
police, the village court, and an Adventist oath had
each been brought into play. The oath was never
enacted, though I believe that its threat was
crucial, along with the persuasiveness of the

magistrate, in breaking down the resistance of the
defendant. Neither village court order had been
satisfied when I left Kainantu two months after the
decision; nevertheless, the flexible combination of
legal and religious resources applied in this case
had reestablished relations between the wife and her
in-laws while generally easing tensions within the
village.

CONCLUSION

The changes which the Agarabi have experienced
in the last fifty years have drastically altered the
way they organize their society. New relationships
have emerged that go beyond the ties of kin and
community; sources of authority have entered their
lives that have established different bases upon
which to manage their interactions; ideas have been
introduced to them that foretell a previously
unimagined end for all human strivings. Yet gardens
are planted much as they were before, and the homes
of grandfather's descendents can still be found in
the same vicinity. As has been the pattern in many
newly independent nations with a relatively recent
growth in pluralistic organization, they display an
intricate blending and manipulation of the new and
the old. There has been change, but there has been
continuity as well.

The examination of Adventist dispute management
in this chapter presents one form of the cultural
integration common to Agarabi experience. It is
clear that the distinctive identity demarcated for
Adventists through their beliefs and organization
limits only partially their use of the secular
methods for handling disputes. Judicial hearings are
utilized even though church officials disparage them;
yet dispute outcomes are shaped also by the Adventist
desire for group harmony and religious merit. While
the private nature of some ritual mechanisms for
handling disputes makes it difficult to ascertain the
extent of their use by active church members, I

believe the application of these mechanisms is relatively slight when compared to the use of the village courts.

What of the broader implications of the Agarabi Adventist situation? An examination of the cases cited in this paper lends support to the suggestion by Koch *et al.*(1977) that ritual methods for handling disputes will be found where public hearings threaten significant social relationships. Adventist affililation leads disputants to favor processing their grievances through such ritual techniques as communion services, oaths and prayers. Furthermore, the cases discussed indicate that the existence of an additional social relationship (e.g., neighbor, daughter, father-in-law) is associated with the use of ritual. In this respect Agarabi Adventist conceptions of individual responsibility continue to parallel Read's description of the Gahuku-Gama (see first page of this chapter).

On the other hand, the alternatives available to Adventists through official forums are appealing, and as the argument of Koch *et al.* (1977) also would imply, the resort to ritual techniques is diminished. Adventist social bonds are set within a broader field of relationships today. Local and religious associations are affected by the bonds created through economic and political activities at the regional and national levels. Consequently, there is no simple formula Adventists adhere to for handling their disputes. Perhaps if the village courts took less heed of Adventists' beliefs, or if the preponderance of signs for the Second Coming indicated that the End loomed just over the horizon, dispute management through the church would prove more attractive.

FOOTNOTES

1. An earlier version of this chapter was presented
    to the Symposium "The Anthropology of
    Melanesia," at the 1980 Northwest
    Anthropological Association meeting, Ellensburg,
    Washington. I wish to gratefully acknowledge
    the support for my research from the following
    sources: National Institute of Mental Health
    (IF31MH076); National Science Foundation (BNS
    77-14886); Bollingen Foundation; Department of
    Anthropology, University of Washington.

2. The beliefs I describe are those held, to
    varying degrees, by knowledgeable Agarabi
    Adventists. It is not my concern here to
    determine whether or not they are identical with
    those held by the Papua New Guinea pastors or
    the Australian missionaries who work with them.

3. I did not observe this dispute. The account
    given here is based on the reports of the
    participants, who were interviewed the day
    following this incident.

4. Several Adventists independently discussed with
    me the possibility of becoming ill in this way.
    Although the Coastal evangelist made a general
    announcement before one Communion I attended,
    telling those present that they need not fear
    sickness, it did not convince everyone.

REFERENCES

AITCHISON, T. G. 1964. *As I Remember It: Early History of Kainantu.* Goroka District Newsletter No. 32.

DILLON, R. D. 1976. Ritual Resolution in Meta' Legal Process. *Ethnology* 15(3): 287-299.

EPSTEIN, A. L., ed. 1974. *Contention and Dispute: Aspects of Law and Social Control in Melanesia.* Canberra: Australian National University Press.

KAINANTU PATROL REPORT (K.P.R.) #2 & #10, 1955/56.

KOCH, K. F. 1974. *War and Peace in Jalemo: The Management of Conflict in Highland New Guinea.* Cambridge: Harvard University Press.

KOCH, K. F., *et al.* 1977. Ritual Reconciliation and the Obviation of Grievances: A Comparative Study in the Ethnography of Law. *Ethnology* 16(3):269-283.

LAWRENCE, P. 1969. The State versus Stateless Societies in Papua New Guinea. *Fashion of Law* (B. J. Brown, ed.) Sydney: Butterworths.

PODOLEFSKY, A. 1978. *Pattern, Process, and Decision-Making in New Guinea Highland Dispute Handling.* Doctoral Dissertation, State University of New York at Stony Brook.

RADFORD, R. 1972. Missionaries, Miners and Administrators in the Eastern Highlands. *Journal of the Papua and the New Guinea Society* 6:85-105.

RADFORD, R. 1977. Burning the Spears: A "Peace Movement" in the Eastern Highlands of New Guinea. *Journal of Pacific History* 12(1):40-54.

READ, KENNETH. 1952a. Land in the Central Highlands. *South Pacific* 6:440-449, 465.

READ, KENNETH. 1952b. Missionary Activities and Social Change in the Central Highlands of Papua and New Guinea. *South Pacific* 5(11):229-283.

READ, KENNETH. 1952c. Nama Cult of the Central Highlands. *Oceania* 22(1):2-25.

READ, KENNETH. 1954. Cultures of the Central Highlands, New Guinea. *Southwestern Journal of Anthropology* 10(1):1-43.

READ, KENNETH. 1955. Morality and the Concept of the Person Among the Gahuku-Gama. *Oceania* 25:233-282.

STRATHERN, M. 1972. Official and Unofficial Courts. Legal Assumptions and Expectations in a Highlands Community. *New Guinea Research Bulletin, No. 47.* Canberra: Australian National University.

WESTERMARK, G. D. 1978a. *Eria Komuniti* in Kainantu: Observations after Five Years. *Decentralization: The Papua New Guinean Experiment,* (R. Premdas and S. Pokawin, eds.). Port Moresby: University of Papua New Guinea.

WESTERMARK, G. D. 1978b. Village Courts in Question: The Nature of Court Procedure. *Melanesian Law Journal* 6:79-96.

WESTERMARK, G. D. 1981a. *Legal Pluralism and Village Courts in Agarabi.* Doctoral Dissertation, University of Washington, Seattle.

WESTERMARK, G. D. 1981b. "Old Talk Dies Slowly": Land Mediation in Agarabi. Paper for Symposium "Mediation and Society," American Anthropological Association Meeting, Los Angeles.

YOUNG, E. 1973. *The People of the Upper Ramu: A Socio-Demographic Survey of Agarabi-Gadsup.* Occasional Paper No. 8, Department of Geography, University of Papua New Guinea.

Em Strongpela Meri: A Female Leader in the Eastern Highlands of Papua New Guinea

K. J. Pataki-Schweizer

INTRODUCTION

The relation between culture and identity holds great fascination for anthropology, and the role of gender in this relation piques further, as in K.E. Read's lucid expositions for the Central Highlands of Papua New Guinea. More recently, formal interest in gender in role, status, and symbolism and in authority and decision-making has become marked in the social and biological sciences. Scrutiny has also been directed at the function of gender and sex roles in cultural and political ideology, and it is apparent that the study of female persons in cultural life and social processes has not received due recognition. It is also evident that skewing in the collection and analysis of data has occurred, of particular import for our understanding of human behavior in pancultural perspective (Milton 1979; Slocum 1975). This paper offers some observations about an unusual woman, Hirihaka'au of Tontaina, from a society of the Eastern Highlands, the Tairora, in relation to these issues.

Tontaina is one of the local groupings or "bounded complexes" (Pataki-Schweizer 1980:31-37) in this part of the Highlands, organized around both

residence and kinship. In 1963, Tairora included 45
such complexes with an average population of 223 in
some 660 square kilometers of varied topography and
ecology.   Its 10,800 people, comprising several
dialects, practice subsistence horticulture and pig
husbandry with some hunting and gathering. Tontaina
included 81 people in 1963 and an estimated 140 in
1978, with 5.3 square kilometers of territory. To
its immediate west was the complex of Norai'eranda
from which Tontaina traditionally originated, and to
its immediate south Tondona (also called Ontora), a
Tairora complex with ties to the Auyana language
group further south. Both Tondona and Norai'eranda
were considered enemies (Tok Pisin: *birva*) by
Tontaina, and are referred to again.[1]

HIRIHAKA'AU, OF TONTAINA

Hirihaka'au, born in Tontaina, was in her late
forties or perhaps fifty years of age in 1972. Her
father was Kam'ora of Tontaina, who was known as a
prominent fighter in that area, *numbatu Matato*
refering to Matato, a legendary Tairoran warrior
(Watson 1970). Her mother was Naina, also of
Tontaina, who was Kam'ora's second wife; both
parents were deceased in 1972. The number and
sequence of Hirihaka'au and her siblings are marked
by some uncertainty in her recall, which may reflect
disproportionate age differences, early mortality,
and her position as the second-last child. Of seven
siblings, only Hirihaka'au and her younger sister
were alive in 1972 (Fig. 1).

The extraordinary feature of Hirihaka'au with
respect to the Highlands is that she had been the
luluai or paramount leader of the Tontaina complex
for at least 10 years. She was appointed to this
position in the mid-1950's by an Australian patrol
officer or *kiap* who had first selected her as *tultul*
or village translator (she was fluent and articulate
in Pisin), and subsequently was promoted by him to
the position of *luluai*.[2] Preparation for
independence was in progress in 1972, and areas of
the country had shifted from the *luluai-tultul*
system to local councils. In this newer system,
communities (bounded complexes) elected or chose a
committee of several representatives (*komiti*,
singular and plural) with a chairperson (*cheman*).
These committees were combined into larger Local
Government Councils (*kaunsil*) usually conterminous
with a language group, e.g. the Tairora, Kamano and
Gadsup Councils. It appears that Hirihaka'au had
coped well with this political change, since she was
cheman of the committee in that area; her colleagues
were a man from Norai'eranda and two men from
Tontaina.

Hirihaka'au's demeanor drew the visitor's
attention even before one learned about her unusual
situation and capacities. She was particularly

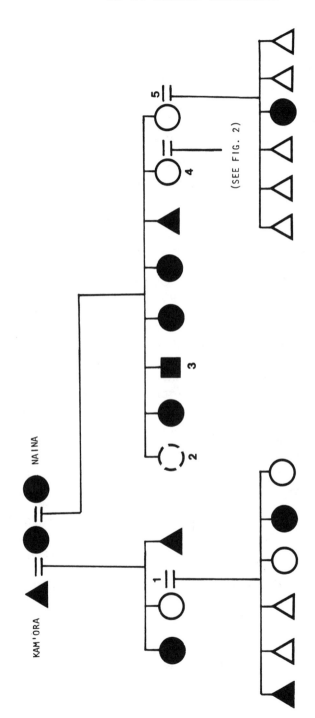

FIGURE 1

HIRIHAKA'AU GENEOLOGY, 1972

KAM'ORA

NAINA

(SEE FIG. 2)

CHRONOLOGY: LEFT-RIGHT/EARLIER-LATER

● : DECEASED

1- HUSBAND FROM TONTAINA

2- BIRTH UNCERTAIN

3- SEX UNCERTAIN

4- HIRIHAKA'AU

attentive and forcefully articulate beyond the hardly-restrained pattern of her people. She maintained eye contact, unusual among women in this area of the Highlands at that time and earlier, and showed few if any of the particular expressive behaviors of shame and embarassment for females in this society. Her eyes were striking: in a milieu of irises ranging from deep brown to near-black, Hirihaka'au's were greenish-brown and contrasted dramatically with her skin color, something one grew to feel she knew and used to effect. Her appearance in 1972 was relatively traditional at a time when acculturation and the climate at an altitude of 1800 meters encouraged loose pullover blouses, cotton sarongs and sweaters. She wore the traditional married woman's skirt (layers of plant-fibre strips encircling the body, covering the hips to knees) and a well-worn short-sleeved man's shirt, and she regularly used a traditional bamboo pipe in which she smoked *brus*, locally-grown tobacco, a practice more usually the purview of males. She was married to Neneara of Tontaina with whom she had seven children. Her sister was also married to a man of Tontaina; both had been married only once.

An overriding quality of Hirihaka'au recognized by her kinfolk and of clear relevance to her position as *luluai* is that she was "strong," *strongpela meri tru*, "*kaymbuka*" in her language. She was described, and she agreed with the description, as being like her father; he was in turn compared with Matato, a legendary Tairoran warrior and despot who had lived out his cultural scenario as few men have the opportunity to do, before being in effect assassinated by his own people. Her sister was described as being "also strong"; together they were "one kind," although how the deceased siblings had ranked in this spectrum of power was less clear. Their husbands appeared relegated to some reverse of traditional roles: though male, "they worked in the gardens." During conversations with Hirihaka'au and her relatives, her husband usually remained far to the rear of his

spouse with a somewhat deferential demeanor, sitting
with several men of similar age. He was
considerably older than his wife, perhaps in his
sixties, more than the five to ten-year difference
one might expect of this generation.

It is also of interest that in the Tairora
language group, hardly a cohesive cultural entity in
precontact times with at least four distinct
dialects, there had been two other women in similar
positions of leadership, both *tultuls*. One was from
the Barinabuta complex several kilometers to the
east, and was reported (1972) to be deceased. The
other was said to be living in Tondona, a
traditional enemy of Tontaina.[3] The same *kiap* had
made the appointments for Tontaina and Tondona, and
it is probable that he appointed all three women;
some informants reported this. Whether these three
selections reflect the whimsy of a European
administrator in the field remains an open question.
However, the prevailing norms of the Administration
and the Tairora, plus the rigors of political
survival in a culture where leadership is desired,
competitive, and essentially achieved within each
generation tend to negate the possibility. That
Hirihaka'au survived and to all appearances thrived
for a period of at least twenty years indicates
other salient reasons, including a particular
conjunction of culture, family and personality.[4]

She had travelled widely for a New Guinean in
the pre-independence period before and during her
position as *luluai*: by her own account she had
visited Goroka and Mount Hagen in the Central
Highlands, Lae on the northeast coast and also Port
Moresby, the administrative capital on the southern
coast. She said that she did this because she
wanted to see these places and liked to travel, and
because she was not afraid of new or different
situations ("*mi no savi poret*"). She still visited
Kainantu, the administrative center some 25
kilometers to the north, and was involved in the
sale of locally-grown coffee (sun-dried coffee beans
or "parchment") at Kainantu and to buyers who

visited the area in trucks. This cash business was becoming a significant economic factor in local life and economics, and had just begun when I visited the area in 1962-1963.

A particular *noblesse oblige* in Hirihaka'au become evident as time and conversations proceeded. Apparently feeling that we had sufficiently covered our topics, she maintained her humorous (or bemused) demeanor yet withdrew in terms of more direct exchanges. One sensed that she was thinking of other times and situations lived in a life which spanned more change than most humans would experience, and which she had coordinated if not directed for her immediate group (Kiki 1968; Somare 1975). I remained for a while longer and while we conversed, her daily activities often took her elsewhere. One had the distinct feeling of being an attendant at a court, if egalitarian in style, with little choice other than to relax and appreciate it.

I revisited the area again in mid-1978, hoping to renew acquaintance with this unusual person. Residence is very mobile in the Highlands, and the village was no longer where it had been in 1972. Quite by mistake due to decay of the vehicle track, I arrived at the complex of Tondona and was led to a woman of authoritative bearing: this was A'rio, one of the two female *tultuls* mentioned earlier, now in her late fifties or early sixties and no longer in active political life.[5] Tondona had been involved in an altercation with Tontaina the previous week, and feelings were high. It was inadvisable to visit Tontaina directly from Tondona, and my borrowed motorcycle had to be returned to Kainantu. An afternoon's discussion with A'rio and Tondona confirmed the essential story of Hirihaka'au given here, and also that there had been a female *tultul* at Barinabuta, Tubi'mo, deceased for several years.

And of Hirihaka'au: she had died that March (1978) and was buried at the western periphery of the Tontaina area bordering Norai'eranda. Her husband had died earlier and she had remarried a man from Norai'eranda (one notes that a Council member in 1972 was from there). While A'rio commanded respect, her people's attitude towards her had more of the honorific quality befitting a retired dignitary recognized as such, rather than the state approaching awe that Hirihaka'au could evoke. A'rio, as with Hirihaka'au, had lived fully as a woman by Tairoran standards: married, several children, gardens, and grandmother. She agreed that Hirihaka'au was certainly Tairoran by their norms of behavior ("*em i pasin tru bilong Tairora*"); indeed a woman among women, conceivably in terms of behavior (role) a "man among men"; in any case, an unusual female in their perception and an unusual human by mine.

DISCUSSION

Why Hirihaka'au was able to attain and maintain her position, given the constraints against a woman as leader and the fluid nature of local politics in her cultural setting, can be used as a focus or vivid metaphor for the question of gender bias and its implications in ethnographic reporting mentioned earlier. Serious recent attention has been given to the function of gender in anthropological research, distinct from the broader politico-historical context of the past twenty years. Several substantial efforts have contributed to the anthropological study of women in sociocultural and socioevolutionary perspective (Tiffany 1979; Kessler 1976; Friedl 1975; Reiter 1975; Sanday 1973), and such efforts extend beyond ethnography or social rectifiction into newer paradigms with epistemological import for the sciences (cf. Strathern 1981).[6]

Male-female relations *per se* in Papua New Guinea have also been a continuing focus of interest, and the structural, functional and conceptual separations between the sexes, with varying degrees of male dominance and starkness, are acknowledged characteristics of the Highlands (Brown

and Buchbinder 1976:1-2). These are amply confirmed
in the ethnographic literature concerning gender
ideology and female behavior (Sillitoe 1979;
Godelier 1976; Strathern 1972; Langness 1967;
Meggitt 1964) and earlier attention (Bateson 1958
[1937]; Blackwood 1936; Thurnwald 1934; Seligman
1915). The nature of male-female relations within
Melanesia, whatever it might be in broader
comparison, includes a particularly intimate
relationship between gender contrast (e.g.
Josephides 1983:296-297) and its cultural
elaboration. From the ethnographic evidence, it
appears that the pattern of that relation involves
learned demeanors in cultural domains (of which the
now-classic contrast of Highland "prudes versus
lechers" is an example [Meggit 1964:221]); symbolic
dimensions in which gender is ritually emphasized
(as in initiation [Read 1965:113-140]), transposed
(Hogbin 1970), or transmuted (Kelly 1976)[7]; and the
leavening of circumstance and idiosyncracy, which
operated to unprecedented effect in Hirihaka'au's
situation.

It was evident that Hirihaka'au fulfilled both
male and female roles for Tontaina and that area of
Tairora, and that this duality was sanctioned by her
people. This also required that individuating
facets of her personality be to some degree subsumed
by her innovative use of the category of "roles,"
which in the interactive context preeminently
involves the use of appropriate learned behavior,
e.g. a public demeanor or persona.[8] Hirihaka'au
fully confirmed her culture's expectations of a
"female" (meri) which included marriage and
children. She was also accepted as having those
characteristics held necessary for a leader, which
were linked to Tontainan/Tairoran conceptions of
"male" (man) or "maleness" and embedded in their
behavioral expectations for the masculine role.[9] It
is necessary to make a contrast between these last
two since it is unlikely that they are simply
isomorphs of each other, and it appears that in the
interface between them as, respectively, cultural

model and acted behavior, Hirihaka'au and her two colleagues were able to situate themselves initially.

There is, overall, a very wide range of cultural criteria operating in the assessment of gender in the Highlands and of exceptions like Hirihaka'au. In any case, obtaining such information requires more than research design and hypotheses. Cross-sex interaction involves potentially high affect loading, and psychodynamic factors exist in this[10] area of fieldwork which have yet to be elaborated. There are also "structural" constraints which affect the transfer of information, noting Megitt's observation that "dyadic social relationships . . . hold inherent contradictions" with specific regard here to cross-sex exchanges in fieldwork, if not triadic male/female/investigator relations (1976:72; Caplow 1968). There are thus pervasive psychosocial issues in the ethnographic investigation of gender, as noted by Langness about the categories of "male and female" in the Highlands (1976:101-105).

With respect to our "*lady luluai*" as some European administrators put it, there was a particularly strong quality of *praxis*, sheer actuality or existential happening palpable in her situation and derivable for her two colleagues. First, she was at a juncture of historical time and cultural milieus in which an unorthodox act was initiated; whether by individual or mutual whimsy, frustration, aggression or insight, she was appointed. Second, she did have the idiosyncratic "potential" for leadership necessary which almost no[11] women and relatively few men had in that society. Third, her culture, while it might be labeled deeply if not utterly chauvinist, still provided structural options and behavioral opportunities for transformation or transcendence of its strictures for sex roles: it could in this sense be creative. Fourth, a rather special set of historical circumstances and familial factors had primed her situation, i.e. European contact and pacification

and a father of prowess. Fifth, Hirihaka'au like
any perceptive and healthy human, had adjusted to
changing life situations and coped effectively at
the local political level, e.g. promotion to *luluai*
and selection for the Local Government Council.
With regard to the latter, not all *luluais* were
elected to the position of councillor and the
transition was on occasion used to remove
individuals who had lost support, as in the Auyana
language group further south.

It is interesting to speculate on the future
for Hirihaka'au's progeny given their tradition, the
particular example of personalized authority from
which they derive, and the sanction for this style
in Tairora. With independence in 1975 and the rapid
"decentralization" of government authority to the
nineteen provinces now comprising Papua New Guinea,
one might expect her descendants (*lain*) to continue
in her pattern. Hirihaka'au had two daughters, a
son who was working in Port Moresby, three grandsons
and three granddaughters alive in 1972, who could
provide a sizeable pool for potential Totaina if not
Tairora leaders (Fig. 2, information from
Hirihaka'au). The quest for authority and political
power is a major part of Highland life, repeating
itself in every complex, and the emergence of a
profitable coffee economy in the Highland provinces
now links individuals and complexes in new spheres
of local, regional and national activity. The
future for Hirihaka'au's descendants will in any
case involve them in expanded political settings,
greater cultural mixing, pervasive acculturation,
and new options (e.g. provincial loans for local
business development) affecting self-concepts as it
did, albeit uniquely, for their mother and
grandmother a generation earlier.

IMPLICATIONS

Detailed ethnographic attention has been
directed at male initiation, ritual, status and the

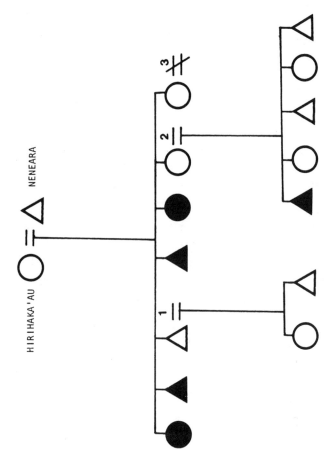

FIGURE 2

NUCLEAR FAMILY, HIRIHAKA'AU AND NENEARA, 1972

1- WIFE FROM NOMBIA, HUSBAND IN PORT MORESBY

2- HUSBAND FROM TONTAINA

3- DIVORCED

CHRONOLOGY: LEFT-RIGHT/EARLIER-LATER

▲ : DECEASED

"producing of man" in the Highlands (Herdt 1982; Read 1965:124-140). It is not the purpose of this paper to assess Hirihaka'au in relation to such descriptions or those few statements available for females (notably Strathern 1972; Hays & Hays 1982; Newman & Boyd 1982:277-282; Poole 1981; Weiner 1976; Glasse & Meggitt 1969; Read 1965:191-194), and the limited information about Hirihaka'au does not permit this. It does however appear that this unusual individual and her Highland situation justified some attention, given the themes motivating this volume. Concerning the last, Read has elaborated on the situational nature of morality and by implication, its ethical context in relation to self-hood for the Gahuku-Gama, some 100 kilometers to the west. His general description of their demeanor also applies to the Tairora, and is quoted at some length:

> Both men and women are volatile, prone to quarrelling and quick to take offence at a suspected slight or injury. They are jealous of their reputations, and an undercurrent of tension, even latent animosity, accompanies many interpersonal relationships. Dominance and submission, rivalry and coercion are constantly recurring themes, and although the people are not lacking in the gentler virtues, there is an unmistakeable aggressive tone to life. The majority of social rewards go to the physically strong and assertive, to the proud and the flamboyant . . . As a result, we find that people are markedly aware of themselves as individuals. They possess a strong feeling for or an awareness of . . . the idiosyncratic 'me,' and the majority of social situations reveal a high degree of ego involvement (1955:254).

Granting such a psychodynamic setting, it is not my intention to analyze Hirihaka'au in terms of morality and selfhood, i.e. "the concept of the

person as an ethical category" so well critiqued for
the Gahuku-Gama by Read (1955:247). Yet such a
category relates to what is culturally permissible
and personally possible, and his observations are
applicable here. He asserts (and I agree) that
"certain values are recognized in all cultures" and
"it is the essence of personal consciousness that
the individual is immeasurably more than we are able
to   infer   from   .   .   .   social   status"
(1955:241,249-250). With respect to authority and
its use, "certain duties are felt to be independent
of status" and while "people may and in fact do move
out of position and thereby in a somewhat
paradoxical sense, lose or forfeit their identity,"
these factors do also permit new social identities
for the person able to generate them at the right
place and time, as Hirihaka'au did (1955:259,276).
Furthermore, different or even unorthodox behaviors
tend to be seen as "curious possibilities, neither
intrinsically   right   or   wrong,"   e.g.   the
non-judgemental perception of homosexual practices
by Highlanders who do not traditionally practice
them (1955:261,261f.; Herdt 1981) or, I suggest,
anomalous   yet   socially   positive   actions   by
individuals such as Hirihaka'au.

     Similarly, one was struck by the excitement and
emotion of ritual activities and at the same time
their utter casualness if not improvisatory nature,
at   least   as   I   observed   them   in   the   Eastern
Highlands.   As   with   the   Gahuku-Gama,   it   was
"extremely   difficult"   if   not   "almost   .   .   .
impossible . . . to observe anything one could
describe as a distinctly religious fervor, awe or
reverence at . . . ceremonies I have witnessed . . .
a casualness which contradicts their importance as a
symbol . . . " There is no necessary reason why
this casualness (which is my point and not the
religious or ritual element) should not extend to
roles and role-behavior, a psychosocial flexibility
evocative of the "looseness" of social organization
and kinship so intensely discussed for the New
Guinea Highlands. Indeed, it may well be that it is

the felt violation of *internalized* tenets which
elicits strong reaction rather than the normative
breach itself, abetted also by the "strongly
developed sense of self" and the "full recognition
of the idiosyncracies of others" in the Highlands
(1955:272,274).

Thus the "distributive morality" of these
people, of such anathema to fundamentalist missions
and their similars, does provide a flexible datum
for those individuals who could perceive and use it.
Underlying this datum is "the fact that each agent
recognizes that his moral obligations to others are
differentially apportioned," plus the additional
buffer that "the manner in which people behave . . .
outside the tribal system of relationships . . . is
virtually a matter of indifference" (1955:256,257).
Significant behavioral options and elasticities for
both sexes would appear to follow from this,
implicit and tolerated regardless of the constraints
or rigidities in their sanctions. Read concludes
that "they do not distinguish as clearly as we are
accustomed to between the individual and the status
which he occupies" and thus "tend . . . to see men
largely in terms of their position in a system of
social rights and obligations" (1955:276). I
believe this determinate position can be turned upon
itself and would suggest that since they do *not* make
the strong distinction, those very facets and
characteristics of the individual are instrumental
potentials to be exploited towards newly-structured
social identities; that is, they represent a
flexibility which was recognized and in effect
sanctioned. While this would occur as part of some
social scenario, i.e. through a cultural veil and
perhaps darkly at times, this is not the final
measure of what was possible for the individual who
could coordinate rules and persons in their place
and time.

With respect to Hirihaka'au, it was clear that
she was diverging from but not violating Tairoran
ethical norms, for she received personal support
from her relatives and sanction from her community

in her positions and activities. One would posit
that what Hirihaka'au did was seen by both her and
her people as "ethically" permissible and "morally"
acceptable, although it is unclear if these terms
are directly applicable; at this point the
actor/observer, emic/etic enigma also rears its
head. Insofar as traditional Highland societies
could act directly and harshly when a member stepped
far out of line as in cases of incest, repeated
adultery, theft of pigs, the birth of twins in some
areas or the example of Matato's death given above,
we may state that more abstruse criteria of right
and wrong were a part of their cultural fabric. In
the example of Tontaina, a woman was not only
sanctioned but approved by her people both before
and after her death. She was an effective leader
and a productive mother, her actions had a strongly
pragmatic flavor, and these could be fitted by
Tontaina into less specific notions, felt or
articulated, of what was held to be correct
according to their way of life. Moreover, the
unprecedented historical nexus, a specific catalyst,
buffered her activities and buttressed her
unorthodox position. Clan fighting and skirmishes
continued intermittently after her appointment, yet
she appears to have resolved them to the
satisfaction of both her people and the
administration.

It is not that Hirihaka'au "broke the rules" as
Matato did; it is, in fact, clear that she followed
the rules, except that she did this in both male and
female capacities. This unusual sort of
sociocultural androgyny was acceptable to her people
(and indeed, the Australian administration), and
indicates the flexibility inherent in cultural
systems regardless of stated rules or what they
appear to be. Probably a two-fold model is
indicated for individuals such as Hirihaka'au, who
could follow the established moral code and yet
perceive within it an adaptive if not permissive
quality. As such, a culture may appear blatantly,

seductively or brutally monolithic, yet remains a
heuristic device of considerable option.

This adaptive quality, however liminal, would
be present whatever the traditional constraints upon
gender and sexual roles, and Hirihaka'au used it
fully. It too is part of what one might consider a
more inclusive behavioral complex bridging societal
continuity and individuation: biological capacity
(gender) is culturally articulated with individual
consciousness to produce an acceptable and stable
sexual identity. In the socio-evolutionary context
of Tontaina in the 1950's through the 1970's, the
meaning of being "female" was just beginning to
evolve from an intense monocultural adumbration of
reproduction for social continuity. This was
nevertheless amenable to change by a female despite
the pressures of a persisting traditional,
small-scale, subsistence orthodoxy: in Strathern's
trenchant phrase, "the dominance is not
unchallenged" (1972:306). It will be interesting to
see the pattern of encroachment, to put it one way,
which should follow given the nature of Highland
acculturation, its traditional cultural stratum, and
seeding such as Hirihaka'au. It is of considerable
import that Hirihaka'au had in effect transcended
millenial teleological assumptions about her gender
and biological functions, perhaps a forerunner of
today's activism by women.[12] Such improbable
traditional examples are significant in their
successful sociocultural variance even for a
Tontainan universe of one, a significance which
increases when expanded to a Tairoran universe of
three.

CONCLUSION

The intimate relation between social
continuity, human contiguity, heterosexual
reproduction and the cultural nexus appears, within
the ecological context of the Central Highlands, to
have required particular elements. These include a

vivid   contradistinction   of   gender,   physical
exlusions and separations between the sexes, and
dramatic   ritual   reinforcement   and   symbolic
reiteration for males. This condition is, of
course, not unique to the Highlands. Yet it
definitely includes expression of a Highland "male"
style which, paradoxically, requires both sexes in
its contradistinction. This style may thus be seen
as a strong aesthetic of these cultures as they deal
in   their   own   way   with   the   exigencies   and
profundities "simultaneously asserted for the fields
of sex, social organization and death" (Bateson
1972:152). To this writer, the rather extraordinary
example of Hirihaka'au, a definite achievement by a
definite individual, indicates the psyche-protecting
defensive nature of sexual roles and sexual identity
in the traditional setting, as they mediate the
polarities of biology, social life and individuation
toward immediate ends and needs. Yet option for
major change is reflected in the sometimes-notable
variations and exceptions in presentation of self,
self-perception, and cross-sex transactions. These
are aspects of identity which go well beyond
immediate ethnographic interests or curiosity. The
domain of gender in traditional societies thus
remains a very pervasive and very personal focus for
both the observed and the observer with respect to
our understanding of the human condition.

FOOTNOTES

1. The ethnography of Tairora is given elsewhere (Watson 1983; Pataki-Schweizer 1980:54-75).

2. During fieldwork in the Australian Trust Territory of New Guinea in 1962-1963, I recorded information about the local *luluai-tultul* administrative system, the former the senior authority and the latter the *Tok Pisin lingua-franca* translator and assistant for their community. Both were government-appointed positions, usually one each for a complex. In the preeminently male composition of the system, I was struck by the anomalous inclusion of three women in a total of over 100 positions for the Tairora and in fact, for a study area including 100 complexes, four languages and 36,000 people. Marriage in this area was often exogamous between friendly complexes, especially for traditional leaders, and this practice continued with the *luluai-tultul* system. Thus it was interesting that all biological parents and grandparents for each of the three women (recall is usually limited to two generations) were also from the same complex. I intended to follow this further and did so during a visit in 1972.

3. T. E. Hays, speaking of fieldwork among the Ndumba (Habiina) Tairora to the far south of Tontaina in a different dialect group, reports that the Ndumba use the phrase, *nronra tua nraase* (1979). This glosses via Pisin as "big bilum woman," one whose net-bag is capable of "carrying others" which appears to be semantic recognition of special female capability. It is also worth noting that Tondona is not a "pure" Tairora complex since it has considerable admixture from the Auyana language group. Thus the ethnographic context for the Tondona *tultul* is not identical to Hirihaka'au

and extends the possible conditions for such leadership.

4.   I obtained Hirihaka'au's agreement to record her history in 1972 with which her people concurred, and with Tondona in 1978. Hirihaka'au, in discussing her two colleagues, mentioned the Tondona *tultul* as "my friend" ("*pren bilong mi*"), a noteworthy denotation given the traditional enmity between these two complexes.

5.   Her appearance was marked by the loss of her nose due to yaws. This disease of the pre-contact period was halted by penicillin; the disfigurement preceded her appointment as *tultul*.

6.   They may also help to undo a persistent and almost teleological duality, polarity or dichotomy holding male and female as separate *conceptual* entities and confirmed by sexual roles in daily behavior, as one reads the contemporary public situation.

7.   Gender can also be negated, e.g. the belief by groups in the Eastern Highlands such as the Pundibasa Gadsup in a spirit-entity generically termed *masalai* in Pisin, usually found in forests and sometimes protective of group territory. This entity is the size of a "tall" human and has pale white skin, very long straight black hair, glowing eyes, and extremely long earlobes. It is sexless and can take either male or female form to seduce for malevolent purposes.

8.   This may have contributed to my perception of her "withdrawal" mentioned above, once the propieties and more formal exchanges had been completed.

9.   The Highland male stylization of authority and
      strength through dramatic and histrionic
      demeanors is exacerbated, if not made all the
      more stressful, by the particular intensity and
      vagaries of local politics in the Highlands.
      These roles are very dynamic and include much
      option for the gifted individual, even though
      they appear essentially as given or a fixed
      theme to most members of the society. In
      reality roles are probably endlessly modified
      at the social microlevel, and at times
      transcended as with Hirihaka'au (Read 1980:167;
      Wikan 1977; Kaplan and Bean 1976).

10.   It is of interest that a number of earlier
      anthropologists, e.g. Boas, underwent
      psychoanalysis and saw it as germane to field
      research (Devereaux 1967).

11.   I am grateful to Lorraine D. Sexton for
      providing the following Highland vignette
      (Bergmann 1955), (emphasis added):
      In the beginning of this year there appeared a
      queer new movement. I called it the women's
      movement. It was going on already when we
      arrived here. First we noticed the women, not
      only the girls, dressed up, singing and dancing
      when we travelled from one place to another.
      Soon we heard that the men were bitterly
      complaining about the behavior of their
      womenfolk. They did not work in the garden,
      they did not prepare the meals properly, etc.
      The men kept quiet, they said, we have still
      our axes . . . All that I could find out about
      how this movement started concerned a
      misunderstanding about the English Queen. As
      she is a woman, the women here thought to play
      a big role in the native life now too. *They
      wanted to be appointed luluais* . . . etc,, etc.
      When I heard about it, I suggested to the
      teachers to quiet the men down and told them

this movement would die out soon. And so it did. I have not heard anymore about it now for several months.

Such events and activities are noteworthy and their genesis intriguing, given "the rarity with which women as such ever come together to solidary groups, or even combine on the basis of their sex in the expression of opposing interests" (Strathern 1972:313).

12. Assessment of the symbolic aspects of being female does not provide direct explication of the present situation (1983) in Tairora or practical assistance for female individuals in transition there, as acculturation preceeds apace. A host of questions about the function and meaning of gender remain, e.g. concerning reproductive exploitation, parenthood, learning opportunities, expressive behavior and style, interpersonal communication, social organization and political participation.

REFERENCES

BATESON, G. 1972. Style, Grace and Information in Primitive Art. *Steps to an Ecology of Mind*, pp. 128-152. New York: Ballantine.
BATESON, G. 1958 (1937). Second Edition. *Naven*. Stanford: Stanford University Press.
BERGMANN, W. 1955. *Annual Report for Ega Lutheran Station, 1955*.
BLACKWOOD, B. 1936. Life on the Upper Watut, New Guinea. *Geographic Journal* 94:11-28.
BROWN, P. and B. BUCHBINDER, eds. 1976. *Man and Woman in the New Guinea Highland*. *Special Publication Number 8*. Washington, D.C.: American Anthropological Association.
CAPLOW, T. 1968. *Two Against One: Coalitions in Triads*. Englewood Cliffs, N.J.: Prentice-Hall.
DEVEREAUX, G. 1967. *From Anxiety to Method in the Behavioral Sciences*. The Hague, Paris: Mouton.
FRIEDL, E. 1975. *Women and Men*. New York: Holt, Rinehart and Winston.
GLASSE, R. M. and M. J. MEGGITT, eds. 1969. *Pigs, Pearlshells and Women*. New York: Prentice-Hall.
GODELIER, M. 1976. Le Sexe Comme Fondement Ultime de L'Ordre Social et Cosmique Chez Les Baruya de Nouvelle-Guinee: Mythe et Realite. *Sexualite et Politique* (A. Verdiglione, ed.), pp. 254-306. Paris: Payot.
HAYS, T. E. and P. J. HAYS. 1982. Opposition and Complimentarity of the Sexes in Ndumba Initiation. *Rituals of Manhood* (G. H. Herdt, ed.), pp. 201-238. Berkeley: University of California Press.
HAYS, T. E. 1979. Personal Communication.
HERDT, G. H., ed. 1982. *Rituals of Manhood*. Berkeley: University of California Press.
HERDT, G. H. 1981. *Guardians of the Flutes*. New York: McGraw-Hill.
HOGBIN, I. 1970. *The Island of Menstruating Men*. Scranton, London, Toronto: Chandler.

160   K. J. Pataki-Schweizer

JOSEPHIDES, L. 1983. Equal But Different? The Ontology of Gender among Kewa. *Oceania* 53:291-307.

KAPLAN, G. A. and J. P. BEAN. 1976. *Beyond Sex-role Stereotypes: Readings towards a Psychology of Androgyny*. Boston: Little, Brown.

KELLY, R. C. 1976. Witchcraft and Sexual Relations: An Exploration of the Social and Semantic Implications of the Structure of Belief. *Man and Woman in the New Guinea Highlands: Special Publication Number 8* (Brown and Buchbinder, eds.), pp. 36-53. Washington, D.C.: American Anthropological Association.

KESSLER, E. W. 1976. *Women: an Anthropological View*. New York: Holt, Rinehart and Winston.

KIKI, A. M. 1968. *Ten Thousand Years in a Lifetime, a New Guinea Autobiography*. Melbourne: Cheshire.

LANGNESS, L. L. 1976. Discussion. *Man and Woman in the New Guinea Highlands: Special Publication Number 8* (Brown and Buchbinder, eds.), pp. 96-106. Washington, D. C.: American Anthropological Association.

LANGNESS, L. L. 1967. Sexual Antagonism in the New Guinea Highlands: a Bena Bena Example. *Oceania* 37:161-177.

MEGGITT, M. J. 1976. A Duplicity of Demons. *Man and Woman in the New Guinea Highlands: Special Publication Number 8* (Brown and Buchbinder, eds.), pp. 63-85. Washington, D.C.: American Anthropological Association.

MEGGITT, M. J. 1964. Male-Female Relationships in the Highlands of Australian New Guinea. *American Anthropologist* 66.4.2:204-224. (Reprinted in *New Guinea: The Central Highlands* [J. B. Watson, ed.]).

MILTON, K. 1979. Male Bias in Anthropology. *Man* 14:40-54.

NEWMAN, P. L. AND D. J. BOYD. 1982. The Making of Men: Ritual and Meaning in Awa Male Initiation. *In* Herdt, ed. (1982), pp. 239-285.

PATAKI-SCHWEIZER, K. J. 1980. A New Guinea Landscape: Community, Space and Time in the Eastern Highlands. *Anthropological Studies in the Eastern Highlands of New Guinea, Volume IV.* Seattle and London: University of Washington Press.

POOLE, F. J. P. 1981. Transforming "Natural" Woman: Female Ritual Leaders and Gender Ideology among Bimin-Kuskusmin. *Sexual Meanings* (S. B. Ortner and H. Whitehead, ed.). New York: Cambridge University Press.

READ, K. E. 1980. *Other Voices: The Style of a Male Homosexual Tavern.* Novato: Chandler and Sharp.

READ, K. E. 1965. *The High Valley.* New York: Charles Scribner's Sons.

READ, K. E. 1955. Morality and the Concept of the Person Among the Gahuku-Gama, Eastern Highlands, New Guinea. *Oceania* 25:233-282.

REITER, R. R., ed. 1975. *Towards an Anthropology of Women.* New York: Monthly Review Press.

SANDAY, P. R. 1973. Toward a Theory of the Status of Woman. *American Anthropologist* 75:1682-1700.

SELIGMAN, C. G. 1915. Torres Straits and New Guinea. *Women of All Nations* (T. A. Joyce, ed.), pp. 151-160. New York: Funk and Wagnall.

SILLTOE, P. 1979. Man Eating Woman: Fears of Sexual Pollutions in the Papau New Guinea Highlands. *Journal of the Polynesian Society* 88:77-97.

SLOCUM, S. 1975. Woman and Gatherer: Male Bias in Anthropology. *Towards an Anthropology of Women* (R. R. Reiter, ed.). New York: Monthly Review Press.

SOMARE, M. 1975. *Sana: An Autobiography.* Port Moresby: Niugini Press.

STRATHERN, M. 1981. Culture in a Netbag: the Manufacture of a Subdiscipline in Anthropology. *Man* 16:665-688.

STRATHERN, M. 1972. *Women in Between - Female Roles in a Male World: Mount Hagen, New Guinea.* London and New York: Seminar Press.

162   K. J. Pataki-Schweizer

THURNWALD, H. 1934. Woman's Status in Buin
    Society. *Oceania* 5:142-170.
TIFFANY S. W. 1979. *Women and Society: An
    Anthropological Reader*. Montreal: Eden Press.
WATSON, J. B. 1983. *Tairora Culture:
    Contingency and Pragmatism. Vol. V.,
    Anthropological Studies in the Eastern Highlands
    in New Guinea*. Seattle and London: University of
    Washington Press.
WATSON, J. B. 1970. Tairora: the Politics of
    Despotism in a Small Society. *Anthropological
    Forum* 2:53-104.
WEINER, A. B. 1976. *Women of Value, Men of Renown*.
    Texas: University Press.
WIKAN, U. 1977. Man Becomes a Woman:
    Transsexualism in Oman as a Key to Gender Roles.
    Man 12:304-319.

Daribi and Barok Images of Public Man:
A Comparison

Roy Wagner

In one of the earliest, yet most conclusive, anthropological definitions of the moral to be essayed, Emile Durkheim (1966:398) claimed all things that make for solidarity, and that force men to take account of others and regulate their conduct, as the province of morality. Kenneth Read's study of the moral person among the Gahuku Gama served, among other things, to reiterate this sense of the specifically moral for an anthropology that could be accused of having lost the moral in its pursuit of the social -- having redefined the collective focus of cultural life as a mechanical effect rather than a meaningful orientation.

A most sensitive and finely drawn image of the moral in a Highlands culture pervades also the intimate portraits of Makis, Asemo, Tarova, and the other personalities that vivify Professor Read's *The High Valley*, a work that gives away less to the impersonal mechanics of integrative "function" than perhaps any other in the anthropological literature. I cannot hope, in doing honor to his rediscovery of the moral, to second Read's achievement -- formalized concepts and observed regularities make a poor second to the immediacy of human impulse, presence, and gesture. Yet I would like to show,

through the means of a comparison, how a species of
the moral person is "found," differently, in two
very different Melanesian cultures. My intention in
doing so is not that of demonstrating, yet again,
that Melanesian cultures are very different from one
another, nor is it to show, as Robert Murphy
paraphrased David Schneider, that "if things were
not the same, they would be different." I would
like, instead, to give a lateral extension to the
idea of the moral person by delineating its
articulation with social form and motivating
contingency.

To this end I would like to qualify the notion
somewhat by turning it into what the sociologist
Richard Sennett has termed "public man." In his
book, *The Fall of Public Man*, Sennett (1977)
provides a wealth of examples from 17th and 18th
century Europe for his argument that the Western
sense of public presentation has changed radically
since that time. Public man involves what would
appear to modern eyes as a highly mannered,
depersonalized and probably "artificial"
presentation of the self before others, as if all
the world were, indeed, a stage. And although the
masquing and mannequin costuming of, say, Louis
XIV's court is not at all the same thing as the
bilas of a Highlands public performer, Sennett's
√ "public man" is in some ways a more apt costume for
the Melanesian moral person than our modern concept
of "the individual."

This is particularly the case when the moral
person is *enacted*, when it becomes a subject of a
public performance or presentation, for then it
engages the consideration of what is known in
Tokpisin as *sem*. "Shame," the etymologically
obvious gloss, is perhaps a less accurate rendering
than Geertz's characterization of the Balinese
"*lek*."

> *Lek* is at once the awareness of the
> ever-present possibility of such an
> interpersonal disaster and, like
> stage-fright, a motivating force toward

avoiding it. It is the fear of *faux pas*
-- rendered only that much more probable
by an elaborated politeness -- that keeps
social intercourse on its deliberately
narrow rails. It is *lek*, more than
anything else, that protects Balinese
concepts of personhood from the
individuating force of face-to-face
encounters (1973:402-403).

Public man is the moral person in the limelight of
sem; to have a sense of it, to "have *sem*," is to
have the morality, and the demeanor, to avoid its
enactment.

Public man is the moral person as demonstration
or exemplification -- what matters is how it is
found, or disclosed. To disclose, or exemplify, an
inappropriate act or intention, to enact "shame,"
or, what is more important, to invoke the potential
of doing so, is to recover a sense of the moral.
And the disclosure, or recovery, of the moral is not
merely an abstraction hovering over the scene of
village life, evidence of "the social" wherever an
ethnographer wishes to make a point; it is not
"solidarity" or "the collective" per se. It is
rather a kind of habitual forum, a "behavior," and
the manner in which it is staged, how and where and
when, bears importantly upon the resultant image of
public man.

The moral may well be a "given" premise, as
Durkheim suggests, of social existence, as is the
collective. But public man is something altogether
more specific -- a dramatic form or elicitation of
the moral. My suggestion here is that it can be a
useful counterpart to the notion of "shame" in
approaching the expression of morality in Melanesia.
The comparison I have to offer is perhaps a contrast
of extremes within the range of such expression. It
involves, on one hand, a highland, non-Austronesian
speaking people, who are normatively patrilineal
(Daribi), and on the other a coastal, Austronesian
speaking, matrilineal society (Barok).[1] Over and
above these "classificatory" details, there is a

striking difference in formality, and in the overt
emphasis on formality, on public occasions between
the two peoples. Daribi have nothing like the
self-conscious formality of Barok feasting, which is
re-enacted on every possible occasion, yet they
could scarcely be accused of being less "moral."[2]
This is part of the data, and not a construction
that I have imposed upon them. The temptation, for
some, would be to seek an explanation for it on
historical or social structural (i.e., that
matrilineal peoples must give an added emphasis to
features stressing male authority and continuity)
grounds. There may indeed be some scope for both
kinds of interpretation (though the formality of
Barok feasting is unusual even among their
matrilineal neighbors), but I shall stress, instead,
a contrast in cultural *ethos*, in the general range
of social ideas and expectations within which public
man is situated, and "found."

THE DARIBI -- "A SOUL IS NOT DISCIPLINED"[3]

The Daribi inhabit two volcanic plateaus, as
well as some adjacent limestone ridge country, at an
altitude of about 3,500 feet above sea level, on the
southern fringes of the highlands in Papua New
Guinea. They live by swidden horticulture, growing
a staple of sweet potato with other crops in forest
clearings, and live in units organized around a norm
of patriliny, and defined through payments made to
the maternal kin. Clans average about 80 persons,
and are grouped into communities of about 250
people. The Daribi were pacified in about 1960.
When I first began to interview Daribi on the
subject of human motivation and their concept of the
soul, I had no suspicion that these ideas had to do
with anything but a kind of native categorization or
description of the world. It was only later that I
realized that these (human) aspects of "world view"
have profound ethical implications. The seat of
spontaneity and discernment, the Daribi *bidinoma'*

("human soul") has a vital but somewhat shaky attachment to the body. Normally it occupies the auricles and ventricles of the heart, whose steady thumping about evidences a healthy ongoing animation. During dreaming, shock, or intense fright the *noma'* is said to leave the body through the coronal suture (*borabe*) or, the nostrils, and it leaves permanently at death to become an *izibidi*, or ghost. Ordinarily it produces normal breath (*mobo*) and speech (*po*), but at moments of extreme anger it rises into the nose and produces angry breath (*sebe*). Illness is often traced to a condition of a "sleeping soul" (*noma' ubo*) or "swollen soul" (*moni noma'*), whereas other forms of physical or mental disorder, or aberrent behavior are associated with the "holding" (possession) of the soul by a ghost or other entity.

A child is said to receive its *noma'* when the coronal suture hardens and it gets teeth -- which is also the time that it gets a fairly definite name (though names are not directly identified with the soul). Before this time, the child must be treated gently, to avoid frightening off the nascent soul, and it is not generally held responsible for bowel control and other verbally communicated behavioral norms, because, lacking a soul, it must also lack the capacity for discernment. Thus a small child or toddler is never punished or held responsible for its actions until the presence of soul is in evidence. Extreme anger is likewise something of an extenuating ethical circumstance; someone giving vent to near-hysterical anger, who speaks "nose talk" (*guni po*) and breathes *sebe* because the soul has gone into the nose, will often, like the *popokl* sufferer at Mount Hagen (Strathern 1972:253ff) be the object of pity and special consideration. Whatever outrageous or unsocial acts might be performed by someone in this state will likely be discounted, and the performer, after he has been calmed and consoled by the inevitable knot of concerned bystanders, will be able to recount them with a cool and detached objectivity. (I have noted

much the same objectivity, retrospective and
otherwise, in Daribi subject to temporary insanity.)
Possession or "holding" of the soul is only the most
extreme of the conditions under which a person's
actions are disqualified as "not his own," for here,
as in the case of anger, the motivational structure
references unknown or impinging factors.

These special cases bracket or outline a
general conception of public action respecting and
accomodating the vulnerability of the soul. Even
casual, day to day encounters and interactions take
account of this premise, incorporating it quite
unconsciously within the rhythm and style of normal
life.

The Daribi word *hare* carries the same
connotations of moral impropriety and moral
discernment as the Tokpisin *sem*; *hare mene* (to have)
"no shame" is the condition of someone who is
shamed. Daribi define shame in terms of kin
protocols, as "that which is felt in the presence of
the wife's father," a relationship enjoining severe
forebearance. The relationship with the wife's
mother, which would be even more evocative of *hare,*
is not mentioned because, forbidding any contact
whatsoever, it is a relationship through the fact of
not relating (Wagner 1977a). Kin relationships, at
all events, constitute the most consistently formal
set of protocols in Daribi life.

Otherwise, the "public" side of public man
involves gatherings of a more or less formal nature
in the *be'mesaro,* the cleared area in front of a
longhouse, for feasts, ceremonials, and exchanges,
and the informal, convivial day-to-day life of the
men's quarters. Daribi traditionally occupy
longhouses, divided into male and female sections;
in the single-story *kerobe',* sections are separated
by a bark partition, with the men's quarters facing
the *be'mesaro,* "in front." In the two-story
sigibe', the men's quarters are located above the
women's. But in either case the women's quarters
are subdivided into individual rooms, each with its
firebox slung beneath the floor, whereas the men

occupy sleeping places adjoining fireboxes along a single, barracks-like corridor. Male socialization is thus relatively "public," as opposed to female privacy, and the ongoing life of the men's quarters, which are seldom deserted, takes on the semblance of a continuous, low-key conversation. The likeness to a conversation is more than a convenient image here, for the major action is verbal -- anecdote, banter, word-play, commentary, and oral narrative carried on casually by men at their ease, sitting or lying and smoking, resting, or perhaps nibbling at a snack. The regnancy of "talk," or verbal art and imagination, is somewhat like what one might expect in an Irish pub, except that here, in this living space, the freedom of anyone to "opt out," to withdraw into his own thoughts or affairs, to doze off, is never questioned. It is the most convivial human institution I have ever encountered.

A cardinal rule, never stated and never challenged, of this and every other occasion is that a person's intentionality and, below a certain threshold, a person's actions, are never questioned, mentioned, commented upon, or constrained. A man is free to break off conversation and interaction, do what he wishes to do, and rejoin again whenever he wishes. Once I watched a man get up from his seat by the fire, walk out into the *be'mesaro*, slash down all his host's young papaya trees in retribution for a grievance, and then re-enter the men's quarters, all without comment or, seemingly, notice on anyone's part, including the host. A public performance indeed, but what of *hare*? The Daribi shaming strategy simply asserts: "go ahead, go right ahead and do it (and we'll all see exactly what kind of person you are)."

Even the more strictly "formal" contexts of Daribi public action might best be defined in terms of speaking, though here it is the speech, the monologue with raised voice, rather than the conversation, that serves to identify "public man." At many, though by no means all, feasts, exchanges, or ceremonials -- especially those where there might

be some doubt or uncertainty as to the event or its
rationale or motives -- one or more important men
(*genuaibidi*) may make a formal speech at the focal
point of the proceedings (just before the cooked
food is distributed, or just prior to an exchange).
Traditionally, an important man may also harangue
the people of a settlement first thing in the
morning, calling their attention to some pressing or
timely collective task, or to some problem or danger
confronting them. He will either stand or pace in
the *be'mesaro* while speaking, or simply stand in the
doorway and call outward. Alternatively a man with
a special grievance might address the community in
the same way, often working himself up to a pitch of
indignation.

A Daribi man becomes "public man" simply by
raising his voice in the presence of others.
Usually this is tacitly acknowledged in the style of
the speech itself, which becomes emotional or
declamatory, and may assume the peculiar Daribi
"balanced rhetoric" of weighed alternation of
positive and negative statements.[4] But in the act
of making his actions "public" in this way, a man
also renders himself acutely vulnerable. He is laid
open to the "stage fright" of *hare*, but he is also
exposed to the potential loss of control that we
would identify with hysterical or possession states,
the danger of being aroused and "carried away"
beyond the point of social accountability. The
first hazard defines the province of social
self-control; the second, which is the dimension of
identity crisis and mediumistic trance (Wagner
1977b) poses the fundamental dilemma of personal
control for the Daribi: a soul is not disciplined.
The interests and influences of this world are
themselves estranging, and their effects upon moral
man may be such as to excuse him from sanction.

"Talk" (*po*), meaning at once information,
speech, and language, the means of communicating and
also its content, is for Daribi the register of
morality. Public man is the speaker, and the public
is invoked by the act of speaking. Talk is the

product of the soul, and also the means through
which the soul is swayed or directed. It is through
its capacity for discernment, its ability to "hear,"
and respond to talk, that the presence of a soul is
detected. And so the soul is perhaps the *resonator*
of the moral, as it produces and resonates talk, and
the "public" is always an audience.

A person acting in the public eye may indeed be
disqualified -- the "talk" may be that of estranging
hysterical anger (*waro po*), of deception (*tibu po* or
iri po), or that of a possessing ghost (*ho po*) --
and the burden of shame lightened by the
disqualification. But I would argue that actions of
the aroused person are disqualified, and the onus of
shame mitigated, precisely because the talk is, so
to speak, qualified. What must be attended to is
not so much the person, an unwitting agent, perhaps,
but the talk. Talk illuminates, motivates,
discloses; it creates situations and audiences, and
so manifests the dimension in which public man, and
moral man, is found.

THE BAROK: NA KINIS KO ORONG

Talk, and communication generally, are quite
important to the Barok of New Ireland, as indeed
they are to every Melanesian people. But in one
significant respect the public sense of talk among
the Barok makes a perfect foil for that found among
the Daribi. This is the circumstance that, for
Barok, it is not the talk itself, or its content,
that is central to the public and the moral, but its
agents, and its occasions. A person is never
dismissed from accountability because of extenuating
circumstances; it is rather the talk that may be
disqualified, as "out of order." Although Daribi
might react to a hysterical performance with fear,
compassion, or admiration (in the case of a spirit
medium), the actor is not interfered with. Among
Barok, on the other hand, any suggestion of
"possession" provokes immediate public response and

interference; one of the few occasions on which I
was able to witness this, the performance of a
tranced "singsing" leader from some offshore
islands, concluded with the music drowned out by the
jeers of the spectators, who rushed in and mobbed
the dancers.

Although fewer in number than the Daribi (about
2,000 as opposed to over 5,000 Daribi), the Barok
exhibit far more local variation. The two major
dialects, Nabo and Usen, are in turn differentiated
into subdialects of a few hundred people each.
Barok villages, loose aggregates of the smaller
hamlets, total about 100 inhabitants each, and show
a greater historical continuity than the Daribi
settlements. Part-time fishermen, the Barok raise
their staples (yams in their view, sweet potatoes by
my observation) in a regime of swidden horticulture,
like the Daribi. Like neighboring peoples, the
Barok are organized into exogamous matrimoieties,
each of which is subdivided into clans that are
represented through localized lineages. Each of
these typically occupies a hamlet, centered upon the
hallowed, ceremonial space of its *taun*, or men's
house. Clans might be allied, at the local level,
by traditional relations of pooling *mis* (the
traditional shell-disc money), if of the same
moiety, and often, if of opposite moieties, by the
practice of marriage with classificatory cross-
cousins or paternal aunts. Patrilateral connection,
called *nat*, is important to the Barok, and it is
possible even to pass down a *taun* patrilaterally.

Barok have a concept of a soul, *a tanu*
(sometimes used interchangeably with *a tongon*, which
we might gloss as "spirit double" or body soul"),
which, although it is said to leave the body at
times, and turn into a ghost at death, is not used
an an objectifier for hysterical states, as is its
Daribi counterpart. And although the ghost or
double plays a significant part in certain
traditional activities, such a divination, it
provides a rather poor access to the image of public
man.

It is, however, remarkable that unlike the Daribi ghost, which is felt, heard, or spoken to, but rarely if ever glimpsed, such spirit apparitions among the Barok are only effective if *seen*. All ghost-accounts that I recorded were visual ones, and the complicated divination for a murderer (*kip sinibo*) is regarded as inconclusive unless the ghost of the victim *appears* to the crowd together with the *tongon* of the murderer!

Thus a Barok ghost is as little inferred as an esoteric cause of events as an imputed vulnerability of the soul is adduced as the source of social aberrations. Like its Baroque counterpart in Europe, Barok public life is a drama of self-evident signs of gestures, phrases, and sequences that are immediately recognizable in their public import and inseparable, in their outward form, from the intentionality of the actor. To act is to inscribe one's actions (and intentions), and the inscription is indelible: one may apologize or atone for an action, but neither apology nor atonement will erase or undo it.

The formality of public behavior is based on definition of personal demeanor involving pervasive protocols of constraint and avoidance, and expressed through the verb *yii* ("to respect") and the noun *a minenge* ("shame"). Almost any infringement of personal space or public decorum, any intimation of familiarity before or with others, is defined in terms of shame. Shame is "bought" (*kunu minenge*), or, as we might say, "bought off" by making determinate payments of money or traditional shell wealth (*a mangin*); bride-price is spoken of as "buying the shame" of the bride's mother, her brothers, etc., and is reciprocated by the bride's "buying the shame" of her husband's men's house. It should not be imagined that it is always the transgressor who "buys"; shame is not guilt, and as estrangement involves witnesses and those acted upon as much as the actor. A particularly humiliating form of redress is for a witness, or for the object,

of a transgression to "buy his shame" by presenting
mangin to the actor.

The cynosure of Barok public life, its "forum,"
so to speak, is the men's house, *a taun*, with its
stone walled enclosure and ordered, formal feasting
area. The *taun*, the objects within it, and the
spaces surrounding it are circumscribed with
restrictions and prohibitions, each of which
requires a "buying of shame" if violated. Ordinary
dwelling houses (*a gunun*) likewise partake to some
degree of the respect accorded the *taun*, and may not
be entered by non-residents. The fundamental
validating act in Barok culture, that which
legitimizes accession to status or succession (in
particular with regard to the lineality and property
of the dead), is the feast in the *taun*, *na kinis ko
orong*, "before the sitting down of the *orong* ('big
men')." The assembled group of feasters, which may
include all men of a given area, for absolutely any
man is welcome, and all *must* be feasted liberally
and treated with exact equality, is the ultimate,
focal "public." They sit quietly on benches
surrounding the enclosure, facing the center, or on
privileged seats with the *gunun*, the men's "house"
proper, at the rear of the feasting area, primarily
to *witness* the staging of the feast, in which they
then partake. All aspects of the feast, including
the buying of the (already cooked) pigs and the
areca nut (the purchase must take place openly, the
payment displayed, and the sum announced), the
statement of the reasons for the feast, and any
comment or criticism dealing with procedure or
protocol, must be *presented* to this "public."
Neither significant action or significant
transaction is permitted to be simply the actors'
own affair; to be legitimate it must undergo the
estrangement of publicity, must become, like the
Barok ghost, visible.

On the most general level, Usen Barok treat the
constraints upon public life in terms of two ethical
modalities, *malum* and *malili*. *Malum* is the ethic of
self-restraint or forebearance in respect of the

bereavement of another, a kind of ultimate tolerance
or respect. Epitomized in the obligation of members
of one moiety toward those of the other at a funeral
or mortuary feast of the latter, to undergo various
forms of ritualized humiliation, the ethic may be
generalized to an ideal of relations between the
moieties at all times, or to an overall realization
of consideration and self-control. *Malili*, the
"calm sea," implying that "the belly of the people
is serene, like the untroubled waters," is the
ethic of the feast in the men's house, and, beyond
that, of Barok public man. A kind of moral
communitas, it is the spirit of good fellowship, or
whole-hearted and emphatically equal participation
in the lavish bounty and focal publicality of the
taun. If *malum* measures the purchase of public
obligation over private interest, *malili*, like the
fraternite of the French Revolution, develops
publicality into a positive force or motivation.

Though they amount to ideal states, *malum* and
malili are hardly internal states: they must be
recognized and produced in the form of signs. *Malum*
is the "appropriate response" to a range of
aggressive hazing practices -- having the face
painted with soot and ashes, being thrown in the
sea, looted, sexually detained, publicly humiliated.
Malili is objectified in the presentation and use of
the areca nut (betel nut, Barok *a buo*) and its
condiment, the betel pepper (*a sie*), both of which
are distributed in generous but exactly equal
quantities to all participants at a feast. A
palpable, though non-addictive, narcotic, *buo*,
produces a kind of contained, intimate euphoria; one
might say that in New Ireland it gets everyone
through the day, and constitutes the "small change"
of everyday social encounters. At a feast, however,
its use is obligatory; a central figure, especially
someone to be honored, is enjoined to *tanga buo!*
("chew betel!") to hold the spirit, and perhaps to
break the tension of the occasion. Interestingly,
the same cry is used as a shout of approbation at a
particularly arresting *singsing* performance, to

commend the performers by attempting to "break the
spell" they cast over the audience, and return the
latter to the "calm sea" of public circumstance.

   Malum and *malili* demarcate ethical and social
boundaries, like the highly restrictive spaces that
surround the *taun*, and what they bound and
contextualize is the staging, so to speak, of public
man. Within the demarcated spaces, behavioral as
well as physical, all human action is a public sign,
and the image of public man so defined becomes the
exemplar and legitimator of morality and moral
decorum in general. Outside the boundaries of these
public contexts, the "publicness," and hence the
capacity for moral exemplification, of an act or
transaction is derivative and contingent -- a pale
reflection of the significance potential of the
truly public.

   The feast itself, which gives order and
protocol to public action -- which organizes *malum*,
malili, and the staging of actions within the *taun*,
is exemplified in the mortuary feast, the icon, par
excellence, of Barok life. Its organizer, in turn,
the socially marked status that is the counterpart
of the marked public spaces and behaviors, is the
orong. As with all such distinctions in Melanesian
cultures, the use of this term admits of a certain
relativity or ambiguity in practice. And yet it is
clear that the "traditional leader," as the Barok
gloss the status in English, is a consistent and
successful giver of feasts. By this very fact, the
orong is then the avatar of public man, the
resonator, as it were, of the moral. And the
central contingency of Barok public life is well
summed up in the formula by which the *kaba'*, the
culminating mortuary feast, is invoked: *asiwinarong*
(*a-siwin-na-orong*), "the need of a big-man."

                    COMPARISON

   The central incongruity in my comparison was
well summed up, on the occasion of a formal feast,

by some of my Barok hosts. They asked me what the
Daribi do when they have removed a pig from the
festive earth oven. I replied that they just stand
around eating it, whereupon my hosts rejoined:
"like dogs, eh?" (Daribi for their part, would
probably speculate that the Barok men need the
formal apparatus of a men's house to compensate for
their lack of residential contiguity.)

It is likely that in some Malinowskian
inventory of societal functions talk and feasting
would occupy different columns, or subheads, for a
utilitarian intuition would not see them as in any
sense homologous. Yet this is just the point of the
comparison: however incongruous their homology,
Daribi "talk" and Barok feasting are analogous in
that they serve to locate, for the respective
peoples, the image of public man. But since some of
the most important Daribi talk goes on at feasts,
and some of the most important parts of Barok
feasting protocol involve talking, the analogy wants
something in the way of sharpening. What is it that
distinguishes the two?

For Daribi, as we have seen the agents and
circumstances of talk may be disqualified so that
the talk itself may be qualified. For Barok, the
talk may be disqualified or not according to the
qualified nature of the circumstances. More simply,
the kind of talk is, in the end, more important to
the Daribi than the circumstances of the speakers,
whereas these circumstances are the significant
factor for Barok, whose talk is important as it
reflects them, and is situated among them. Context
marking is not simply more obvious among the Barok,
it is *the* designator of public man; among the Daribi
context demarcation is confirmed, and often enough
effected, by the talk.

All of this may be related to the moral person
via its relevance to the enactment of *sem*. The
circumstances for which *hare* is generically
described are characterized by the kinds of *talk*
appropriate to them: one "speaks carefully" in the
presence of the wife's father, "jokes lightly" with

the wife's brother, does not speak at all with the
wife's mother. The Barok *a minenge* may also be
generically defined in terms of kin protocals, but
is specifically expressed in terms of explicit
taboos relating to particular categories. The
taboos may involve qualifications of speech, but
largely as an adjunct to other -- especially spatial
-- implications of social presence (e.g., cross-sex
siblings may speak, respectfully but not so closely
as to "smell each other's skin"). Here too, it is
the marking of context by spatial and behavioral
constraints that is stressed. *Sem* is close to being
a shyness with respect to content among the Daribi,
and a shyness with respect to form among the Barok.

Daribi find public man, or perhaps Daribi
public man finds himself, within the dimension of
"talk" (*po*); the elicitation is aural rather than
visual. The true locus of action is in fact
visually obscure, sited in unseen internal organs or
in the numinal operations of invisible ghosts, and
herein lies the contrast with the masques,
theatricals, and public fora of Baroque London.
Morality must be allowed to flow from its inner
sources, the soul which, through the agencies of the
liver, heart, and lungs, articulates speech and
moral discernment. The body and its gestures are
merely symptomatic of this flow -- indices for the
perceptual elicitation of speech -- and it is to
that degree useless to constrain them. It is the
body, in this derivative sense, rather than the body
politic, that is the *theatrum mundi*, and it is no
surprise to find that the only real example of
ordered space in the Daribi interactional scene, the
longhouse, is in part terminologically identified
with the body -- it has a "face," a "back," and even
a kind of alimentary system (Wagner 1972:120-123).

Barok locate the object of their Diogenes-like
quest, the *orong* as the avatar of public man, amid
the world of public gesture and politesse in the
visual theater of the *taun* and its circumambient
spaces. So elemental is the force of visually
embodied meaning here that the speeches made *na*

kinis ko orong are largely commentaries on protocol and the staging of the feast. (Daribi speeches are most generally concerned with the revealing of information.) Morality and moral legitimation are inscribed and constituted in the production of visible signs,[5] according to a rigid decorum that modern Barok call *kastam*. The parallel with Sennett's historical evocation of Western public man is evident, though the circumstances, historical roots, and comparative scope of the two phenomena are markedly different. Although the everyday life of a Barok village should be suffused with something of the respect of *kastam*, Barok public man is not an image of street life and the ambience of urban promenades and theatricals, but a spatially and incidentally *focused* presentation -- a kind of social "noonday" -- like the fora and *acropoleis* of the Graeco-Roman world.

It is noteworthy that the elicitation of numinal "power" in each of these cultures is analogous, albeit dialectically, to the manner in which public man is "found." The power of Daribi mediumship is that of disembodied talk; that of the *habu* ritual and of numerous lesser manifestations is the intention or awareness of a soul that has come unstuck and "speaks" through afflication and omen, to be brought to heel by the "revealing speech" of a curer or ritual specialist. The most powerful numinal presence in the Barok world is the *tadak* ("*masalai*"), the tutelary spirit of a clan that habituates some focal natural feature(s) considered central to its holdings or origin. The traditional *orong* was expected to cultivate as intimate a rapport with his *tadak* as a Daribi medium with her ghost familiar. But in a world where visual signs speak with such authority, an invisible *tadak* would gain as little purchase as an invisible ghost. The power of the *tadak* is that of *changing shape* (*pire wuo*), of having more forms than ordinary beings, and of having, or rather *being*, the facility to change form at will.

Lest this comparison be mistaken for some sort
of sensory determinism, which is the farthest thing
from my thoughts, I should at least consider the
question of whether the Barok, however their
presentational forms may be oriented, are not simply
more "public" than the Daribi in any case. As in
some other points (hierarchy, or a tendency to it,
for instance) in which they appear to draw closer to
complex, centralized civilizations than the Daribi,
the Barok seem to have "differentiated out" their
public usages or subjected them to a greater degree
of specialization. This would seem to acknowledge a
tendency in this direction that is frequently seen
in Austronesian speaking peoples, as well as the
stereotype, found throughout Southeast Asia, of
subtle, sophisticated coastal dwellers as against
stolid, blunt inlanders.

But the issue is more complex than this. If we
admit to a more explicitly "public" emphasis in
Barok life (much of it attributable to the character
of visual sign), then it is clear that Daribi life
is more coherently communal, both in its domestic
ambience and in its moral character: Daribi public
man is in fact communal man, a hortatory, as opposed
to a formal leader.

If we accept Durkheim's definition of the moral
as the sum of things that force people to take
account of one another and regulate their conduct,
then communal man elicited through the rhetorical
imagery of Daribi speech, and public or ceremonial
man as evoked by Barok gesture and visual sign, are
certainly characteristic realizations of this ideal.
They are, to be sure, exemplary images rather than
comprehensive articulations of the moral person, as
indeed the tendency of these traditions is toward
evocative demonstration rather than fine
explication. Sennett's historical "public man," a
self-evident role in a world of self-evident signs,
bears a remarkable congruence with this evocation.

But what of this other, historical point of our
comparison? How does Western public man (or his
absence) affect our search for him in Melanesian

cultures? Sennett correlates the gradual, historical decline of public man and public life, and the corresponding rise of privatism and the image of the individual, from the seventeenth century, through the Enlightenment, Romanticism, the Victorian era, to the modern period, with a transmutation of focal, public expression from self-evident sign to codified, cryptic symbol. We are a culture of individuals, in this view, because person (and sign) no longer evidences the social, but merely references it (Sennett 1977).

What is left in the way of public man is perhaps "average man," a sort of retinal afterimage produced by the commodity fetishism of advertising. But what is signficant is the envelopment of the social and public side of things by the individual, which Sennett identifies with narcissism, and which can be delineated over broad parameters of contemporary obsession, from drug use to the drive for autonomy.

A society which has thus petitioned, and gained, the abdication of the absolute, which requires of its public officials not public examples, but private disclosures, can certainly afford the relative panoramas of anthropology. Indeed, having lost its "measure" in the collapse of social cynosure, Western society has relegated "measure" from the status of an asset, or possession, to that of a contingency -- something to be researched rather than owned. A qualitatively responsive -- a "symbolic" -- anthropology becomes virtually a function of a relativized culture. The need for measure, for perspective, for just relation may in some circumstances amount to a social problem, but for anthropology it is a ground of being. And in that respect we are entitled to ask just how far we really may be from the Melanesian contingency for moral measure -- from "the need of a big man."

FOOTNOTES

1. Fieldwork among the Daribi was supported by a grant from the Bollingen Foundation and the University of Washington, under the direction of Drs. K. E. Read and J. B. Watson, from November, 1963 to February, 1965, and by a Faculty Research Grant of the Social Science Research Council, from July, 1968, to May, 1969. Fieldwork among the Barok was supported by a Grant from the National Science Foundation from August, 1979, to March, 1980.

2. The Daribi share a great many cultural affinities with a continuum of peoples stretching westward to Mount Bosavi, though they are closely related linguistically only to the Polopa of the Southern Highlands, and to a lesser extent, to the Wiru of Mount Ialibu. The Barok share some features with the Mandak of central New Ireland, but seem to have strong cultural affinities with south New Ireland and with the Tolai of Rabaul and the Duke of York Islands.

3. This quotation is from R. Wagner (1981:98). The discussion in which it occurs likens the soul to a perspective, which, like a soul, may be truly "lost."

4. See Roy Wagner (1972:34). A superb example of this sort of rhetoric is reported in J. G. Hides (1938:87), as part of an interview with a Pawaian captive on the Purari River.

5. The remarkable *malanggan* and other art styles of traditional New Ireland bear witness to the aesthetic dimension of this production. *Malanggan* art is not historically characteristic of the Barok, whose aesthetic productions, done in a little-known "Southern New Ireland" style (Philip L. Lewis, personal

communication, 1980) do not seem to have survived the impact of external contact.

REFERENCES

DURKHEIM, EMILE. 1966. *The Division of Labor* (G. Simpson, trans.). New York: The Free Press.

GEERTZ, CLIFFORD. 1973. *The Interpretation of Cultures*. New York: Basic Books.

HIDES, J. G. 1938. *Savages in Serge*. Sydney: Angus and Robertson.

SENNETT, RICHARD. 1977. *The Fall of Public Man*. New York: Alfred A. Knopf.

STRATHERN, MARILYN. 1972. *Women in Between*. London and New York: Seminar Press.

WAGNER, ROY. 1972. *Habu: The Innovation of Meaning in Daribi Religion*. Chicago: University of Chicago Press.

WAGNER, ROY. 1977a. Analogic Kinship: A Daribi Example. *American Ethnologist* (4).

WAGNER, ROY. 1977b. Speaking for Others: Power and Identity as Factors in Daribi Mediumistic Hysteria. *Journal de la Societe des Oceanistes* 33:145–152.

WAGNER, ROY. 1981. *The Invention of Culture*. Chicago: University of Chicago Press.

Initiation as Experience: The Management of Emotional Responses by Ndumba Novices

Terence E. Hays

> There was no way of knowing what Asemo saw
> that afternoon as he trod the street
> carefully under the heavy ornaments of
> manhood, no way of sharing the private
> vision in the eyes that looked above the
> painted, feathered throng . . .
> —K.E. Read, *The High Valley* (1965:141).

Re-reading Kenneth Read's classic, *The High Valley* (1965), just prior to departure for my second field trip, his gift for evocative imagery took me back yet again to an afternoon in 1971 in Habi'ina ("Ndumba"), a community of Tairora-speakers on the southeastern fringe of the Eastern Highlands Province of Papua New Guinea. On that day, like Read twenty years earlier, I had just been witness to a male initiation ceremony, and was sitting in a courtyard awaiting the food distribution that would bring the events to a close. The five young boys who wandered casually about showed no outward signs of the terrifying and painful ordeals they had experienced over the preceding three days and nights. Instead, they presented images of proud, flamboyant warriors, disguising their children's bodies with new sporrans, bark cloth capes, cowrie shell bandoliers, and headbands of parrot feathers.

Three days before, I had sat on the bank of a forest stream watching these same boys scream in fear and pain and cry for their mothers, from whose arms they literally had been wrenched by the men who were now terrorizing them. Two decades previously, Kenneth Read had sat on a riverbank watching similar events among the Gahuku as the young boy Asemo and others were inducted into the *nama* cult. Then, Read "could only wonder with pain what Asemo felt, reaching out to him across a distance immeasurably greater than our respective years" (1965:127). And so I wondered, in the forest, later in the men's house, and finally in the courtyard: How and what did these boys *feel* about the experience of initiation?

The men had come for them in the morning, after their mothers had shaken them awake and led them out to the courtyard to be cleaned with pig grease and dressed in new sporrans and capes. In a cacophony of drum beats, shouts, and surprised squeals, the boys were then swept into a procession of men who pushed their way through the protesting women, up the hill, and into the male domain of the forest. With the women and children left behind in the *kunai*, the group threaded its way along a narrow forest path only to be "attacked" by lurking men as the wide-eyed boys straddled the backs of their "mothers' brothers" until, at last, a streambank was reached.

The men had selected a spot with a small waterfall and a shallow pool, into which the boys were led after first being stripped of their few garments. As they stood in the water, shivering, naked, and clutching their genitals, pain and humiliation now combined with fear and confusion to produce a sight at once pathetic and exhilarating. The boys repeatedly cried out for their mothers to rescue them from the ensuing trickery, beatings with stinging nettles, threats to their penes, and forced bleedings of their noses with bundles of sharp-edged

blades of sedge, but the only response was laughter
and derision from the men lining the banks of the
stream.

And then it was over, at least for the moment.
The boys were led out of the pool, told to dress,
and taken back out to the glare of the *kunai* amid
welcoming shouts and only half-serious attempts at
rescue by the waiting women.

The procession, still inviolate but grown
larger by the addition of the rest of the community,
now made its way back down to the hamlet until
finally it reached the palisade of a men's house.
With the women and children halted at the entrance,
the boys were escorted into the men's house
compound, their eyes darting at the wonders held
within this sacrosanct enclosure. Such secrets as
the existence of the men's latrine were soon
revealed, but always with a price -- ritual
tongue-bleeding and more beatings with nettles.
Such beatings would later be a frequent interruption
of the evening's events as the men gathered and told
stories, sang songs, and instructed the boys in
their new responsibilities and obligations. Only at
dawn the next day would there be brief respite from
the induction ceremonies, to be resumed the next
evening and night until finally, on the third
morning, the singular squeal of dying pigs heralded
the "coming-out." Decorated elaborately with
shells, feathers, and new garments, the boys were
led out of the compound, shown to the waiting
throngs, and celebrated and welcomed with gifts.

As food cooked in earth ovens, one more trip to
the forest was required. The boys were hazed and
instructed again and placed, serially, on a platform
above a smokey fire to be cleansed and strengthened
for their new lives that dawned with the day. Now
only one more ritual remained. The novices were led
to a nearby woman's house where a truly unusual
sight was waiting -- in blatant violation of Ndumba
men's concerns that women never be physically placed
above them, an unmarried girl stood on the roof of
the house. As the boys obediently passed through

the doorway in single file, she poured water on them
and switched them with branches, only to repeat the
process as they turned around and re-emerged. The
pecularity of the event was made even more striking
in contrast as all the males then returned to the
hamlet where they joined in the prosaic business of
eating the vegetable food from the earth oven. Only
on the next morning, the final day, would the pork
be distributed and eaten, with the boys receiving
some along with more gifts. Then daily life would
resume, albeit in an entirely different way for
these new *'ummanra*.[1]

     One of the major differences in their lives
would be that their relatively carefree days as
children were now ended forever. The life of a
Ndumba boy (*nraammwa*) is one of play and indulgence,
with virtually no explicit discipline and no
responsibilities (in contrast to a Ndumba girl,
whose child-care and gardening tasks begin early in
life). The transformation of *nraammwa* to *'ummanra*
('youth') status is sudden and drastic: leaving his
mother's house, a boy assumes residence in a men's
house or other domicile where he begins a lifetime
of association predominantly with males.[2] While few
tasks will be assigned to him for several years, his
male housemates (especially those of his patriclan)
are stern disciplinarians, imposing new food and
behavioral prohibitions and not hesitating to use
physical force to instill obedience and deference.

     The boys I watched in the courtyard had surely
received indications of the magnitude and scope of
these imminent changes during the hazing and
instruction included in the ceremony they had just
undergone. But how much of this did they realize at
the time, and how did they feel about it?

     Their proud, yet casual, appearances suggested
no clear answers to such questions, and I saw little
hope then of even being able to ask them. Only one
of the five initiates spoke Pidgin English, and he
soon left to return to the mission school from which
he had been summoned for the ceremony. Having been
in the field for only a few months, my rudimentary

ability in Tairora did little to supplement my
sympathetic (I hoped) smiles at the boys. I had
been a dutiful recorder of all that I had seen, but
felt that the *experience*, so far as these boys were
concerned, lay beyond a gulf I could not bridge.
And so I left the matter, turning to other demands
on my field time.

During the years since I left them in 1972,
after another opportunity to observe the ceremony
late in the field stay and with the subsequent help
of my co-researcher Patricia Hurley Hays, I have
reached a partial understanding of Ndumba initiation
ceremonies, at least in terms of conventional
anthropological concerns with the "functions" of
such rites (Hays and Hays 1982). When viewed as a
social phenomenon, the *'ummanra* ceremony lends
itself to a wide variety of complementary
interpretations. Sociologically, at least, it
appears to fit Whiting's characterization
(Harrington and Whiting 1972) of contexts that call
for rites to resolve conflicts created by boys'
(socially inappropriate) primary identification with
females. By shifting the boys' main frame of
reference from the household to the men's house
group and patrilineal clans, it also is consistent
with Cohen's (1964) discussion of the function of
such rites in "anchoring" the individual in wider
groups and lessening a child's emotional dependence
on his family of orientation. The induction and
socialization into the men's world, which includes a
whole cosmology as well as a new set of all-male
social groups, is compatible with Young's (1965)
argument that male initiation ceremonies are
centrally concerned with this ritualized change of
status, dramatization of sex roles, and enhancement
of male solidarity. In the Ndumba case, there are
also elements of explicit instruction in the local
gender ideology, which also is subliminally
communicated in the very structure of the ceremony,
as are relations of power and authority and
assertions of male control over life forces
(Langness 1974; Hays and Hays 1982).

Compelling as may be any or all of these ways
of understanding the social functions of the
'ummanra ceremony, my main concern that morning in
the courtyard was different and was not satisfied by
explanations that did not speak directly to the
perceptions of the participants themselves. I do
not refer here simply to "the native's point of
view" as that might be expressed in the exegesis
offered by elders -- indeed, for Ndumba, I would be
limited to men's reiterated statements that the
ceremony is carried out "because the ancestors did
it" and it is necessary if boys are "to grow
properly." What had nagged at me as I watched the
pain in the faces of the initiates and the apparent
glee of the men was: What thoughts and emotions were
the boys experiencing as they dealt with the
ceremony at a personal level -- with actual
individuals and not "descent groups," "social
structure," or even "the community of males?" How
did they view what was happening to them? To what
degree was their experience in fact personal, and to
what degree was it shaped and constrained by
culturally-constituted understandings of social
relationships?

Some scholars have raised these kinds of
questions recently, but few ethnographers have
included them in their field investigations (notable
exceptions include [Herdt 1981, 1982, and this
volume; Poole 1982, and this volume; Tuzin 1982]).
But, if we are to assess structural-functional
explanations on the basis of more than their
reasonableness and plausibility, we surely must
attempt to determine the meanings -- both personal
and social -- of the initiation experience for those
who undergo it.

At last, in 1981, my opportunity arose to
obtain the kind of materials that would enable me to
explore these sorts of questions by returning to
Habi'ina (coincidentally, within weeks of Read's own
revisit to Gahuku). The research project in which I
was then engaged allowed only a month's stay, but I
was able to sit down with four of the five boys who

had been initiated in 1971 (the fifth, the former
schoolboy, was again away at school) and we talked
as we never could before.   I conducted and taped
long interviews with each of the boys separately --
interviews that astounded me in both their content
and the ease with which they transpired.

   ₃All four of the boys, now grown to fine young
men, were fluent Pidgin-speakers.   Beyond that,
however, they showed a degree of sophistication and
even appreciation of my objectives such as I had
never known before with my "best" informants.   The
experience resembled Watson's among the Agarabi to
the north, where he worked first in 1954-55 and
returned ten years later (Watson 1972).   His early
attempts to elicit information about initiation
ceremonies, like my own, yielded little in the way
of clear or comprehensive accounts.   Later, however,
in talking with a seventeen-year-old young man, "the
impressive detail of ritual act and folk rationale
almost became secondary, so amazing was the feat of
detailing it coherently" (Watson 1972:178).   Such
were my experiences, in 1971 and then in 1981.
Whether because of a change in perspective on their
own lives that had come with acculturation (Watson
1972:179-181), or for some other reasons, the boys
poured forth their recollections in response to my
questions, verbalized at last.

   First, I asked each boy to recount the events
of the ceremony as he recalled them; these could
then be compared with my own notes and photographs
from 1971.   I learned in this way of some important
events I had not observed or fully comprehended
before, but my primary concern was with *how* the boys
remembered what had happened.   Not expecting their
memories to be either as complete or as objective as
were my camera and tape recorder, I was interested
in the boys' constructions of the ceremony -- what
was remembered clearly and what was not, and what
patterns might appear in their choices of emphasis,
omissions, distortions, or imagined occurrences.

   The second part of the interviews, and that
with which I am mainly concerned in this essay,

consisted of direct questions regarding their
recollections of how they *felt* at different stages
of the ceremony. Here, following a few pertinent
comments on the boys' versions of what happened, I
focus on their memories of their reactions to
certain major parts of the ceremony -- what they
remembered feeling at the time, and how they related
these feelings to the acts of other people,
especially their mothers, fathers, and mothers'
brothers, who were the key participants apart from
themselves. The results were surprising in the
light of my recollections and records of "what
really happened," but I believe they are
understandable when viewed as cultural constructions
of events, informed by social structural constraints
such as those Read (1955) has discussed in terms of
"distributive morality." Keesing (1982:31) has
raised the question: "How, if at all, can we
separate individual experience from the cultural
idioms in which it is cast?" One of the more
significant implications of the interviews is that
the social meaning of the initiation experience
(i.e, the "cultural idioms") may so overwhelm
"personal meanings" that the task of separating the
two may be futile or at least as difficult for the
individuals undergoing the experience as it is for
those who observe and analyze.

As they stood anxiously watching the men
approach on that morning in 1971, the five novices
-- (pseudonymously) Boraama, Honima, Seri, Toza, and
Unesa -- had no clear sense of what would happen to
them that day. My field notes indicate a continual
sense, on my part, that the boys were alternately
frightened, anxious, confused, dazed, surprised,
disoriented, and finally, exhilarated. During the
1981 interviews expressions like these were in fact
commonly used, in addition to "ashamed" and
"humiliated," as the boys recalled their *ummanra*
ceremony experiences.

On this point, Honima's account is
representative: "I didn't know [what they were

going to do]. I thought maybe they were going to
beat us, but I just didn't know . . . . I just
worried about it and I was afraid . . . . I wondered
what all of the commotion was about, and what they
were going to do. My heart pounded until I thought
it would burst. I saw their *saapwasa* arrows
[viciously barbed, with orchid fiber streamers that
break off beneath the skin and, it is hoped, result
in infections for the victim] and thought, 'Are they
going to shoot us with those, or what?'"

Throughout the three-day ordeal, the boys said,
they were warned repeatedly that they must never
disclose any of the details of the ceremony to their
mothers or sisters or younger brothers. The men
warned them that if such male secrets were revealed,
"they would beat us, and who knows what else? They
scared us" (*Honima*). Unesa was more graphic and
detailed in his conception of the punishments
awaiting disobedience: "They would get nettles and
tie us up with them. They would tie nettles to our
arms, legs, chests, and backs, and beat us with
firebrands too. They would say, 'Here's what you
get for being "blabbermouths,"' and it would really
hurt."[4]

It is possible, of course, that men's "secrets"
are not as well-kept as one is told; some men, for
example, have admitted to me that they have told
some of the particulars of male ceremonies to their
wives. Still, my attempts on various occasions to
elicit *candidates'* expectations about ceremonies
yielded results that lend a degree of credibility to
the boys' professions of a lack of foreknowledge of
their fates. In 1971-72, I had been unable to
obtain from *'ummanra* any clear notions as to what
the *'ia'vaati* rite (held for young men 18-20 years
old) would be like. Similarly, in 1981, the four
interviewees -- all of whom were *'ia'vaati* by then
-- had only vague expectations about their own
eventual marriage ceremonies, and these were quite
erroneous if one is to believe the accounts of men
who have experienced them.

If we grant, then, that the boys probably knew
little of what was about to happen to them, and
consider the traumatic nature of the ordeals they
suffered on that first morning, it is easier to
appreciate the appearance of confusion, anxiety, and
disorientation I noted repeatedly in my journal of
the day's events. Their state, as I perceived it
then, is well illustrated by Honima's remarks about
one minor deception among many enacted that day:
"They told us to look at [a *kapul* trap] and asked us
what was in there. We were so afraid, and we had
been tricked so often, we couldn't even answer
them."

What the boys told me in 1981 must be regarded,
then, as recollections of events that were initially
seen through eyes glazed with tears, confusion,
fear, helplessness, and a desperate wish to stop the
painful rush of uncontrollable assaults and remain
children. As Seri reports complaining at the time:
"I said, 'I just want to go on the way I was living,
but now you men have brought me here [to the forest]
and you're hurting me!' That's what I said to
them."

One cannot expect the boys' perceptions of
events under such circumstances to have been clear
and accurate, and their recollections ten years
later are bound to be affected by still more
factors, including their intervening observation of
other boys' initiations and, recently, their full
participation as *'ia'vaati*, which all of them were
by 1981. Thus I anticipated differences between
their accounts and my own of the events I had
witnessed earlier. What I did not expect was the
particular pattern that emerged regarding these
differences. To appreciate it fully, I must be
allowed a digression into my reflections of several
years ago on the possible emotional impact of the
ceremony whose experiential aspects still eluded me.

In 1978, as I was attempting to unravel the
allocation of roles for adult men in the *'ummanra*
ceremony, I was repeatedly troubled by what seemed a
reversal of what I expected. It makes sense, as

many initiation theorists have argued, to regard as
one of the principal functions of the ceremony a
redirection of boys' identities, dependence,
allegiance, and feelings of solidarity away from
their mothers and "the world of women" toward "the
world of men," which they will now enter fully.
Thus it is not surprising that the ceremony involves
the whole community, with men of all patriclans
assembling in the men's house and acting as a body
against the attacks and taunts of the women who
array themselves repeatedly (if unsuccessfully) in
both symbolic and physical barricades against the
men (Hays & Hays 1982).

However, in this society of patrilineal
corporate groups, not all men achieve an unequivocal
"victory" in this redirection of boys' identities.
Since each boy so initiated will now begin a
lifetime of primary affiliation with and allegiance
to his patriclan, it would seem that those who have
the most to gain by successful completion of the
ceremony are the boys' fathers and fathers' brothers
(all of whom are placed in the same kin category,
go). Conversely, their mothers' male clanmates
(*nau*) would stand to lose to some degree, if only
because of the other clans' increase in active
participants in clan-related affairs and disputes,
which are numerous in Ndumba. Thus I expected that
the boys' fathers and other patriclan members would
be the most vigorous promoters of the ceremony and
that their mothers' brothers would be less than
enthusiastic, if not actually opposed to the
initiation, and express such opposition either
symbolically or in fact.

The stage was then set, or so I supposed, for
the violent "attacks" by hidden men (mothers' clan
members) on the procession (of novices and fathers'
clan males) as it entered the forest, again as it
left, and finally -- as a "last stand" -- at the
revelation of the secret latrine in the men's house
compound.

However, it was the members of the boys'
fathers' clans who attacked the procession and

appeared to be hindering its progress at every step.
And those who withstood these attacks went on to
bleed the boys, beat them, disclose secrets to them,
and generally supervise their entry into the men's
world, were those who seemed to have the least to
gain -- (classificatory) mothers' brothers and, with
one exception, unrelated males.

As I pondered these role assignments, which
corresponded for the most part to professions that
the ideal situation would be to have the "mothers'
brothers" (*nau*) occupy the protagonist roles, it
seemed that they could be understood better by
shifting the focus away from the social dynamics of
the ceremony to its psychodynamics, or at least to
my speculations about the latter. In Ndumba, boys
not only need to be "weaned away" from
identification with and dependence on mothers and
the feminine world toward that of men. The aim of
identity redirection must be sharper -- toward the
boys' fathers and other males of their patriclans.
If the major disruption of their lives that is
entailed in the *'ummanra* ceremony were attributable
to fathers and male clan-mates, however,
identification and allegiance might be difficult to
establish and extract. The organization of the
ceremony, then, obviates this potential problem
since, to the dispassionate observer at least, if
anyone is to be blamed for the traumas induced, the
villains should be obvious.

If the ceremony proceeds according to the ideal
model, as a boy is carried into the forest on the
back of his mother's brother, he may feel the
security he has long associated with his mother,
especially as the procession is placed under attack.
But when the pain begins, and he cries out for his
mother to help him, not only do "her people" not
rescue him, but *they* are the perpetrators. As Toza
later recalled his shock of helplessness: "I cried
for my mother . . . (but) the men just hit us and
said, 'Your mothers won't come save you this time.'
. . . They just laughed at us and beat us some
more."

To the outside observer, the boys could hardly hold their fathers and clan-mates responsible for this suffering and betrayal. Not only were they not the principal initiators, but they have been part of the group apparently trying to prevent the initiation from taking place. Thus, if the *'ummanra* ceremony produces feelings of betrayal, resentment, or hostility on the part of the initiates, surely it is more likely that these would be directed at their matrilateral, rather than patrilateral, kinsmen, and the groundwork thus would be laid firmly for redirection of sentiments and bonds away from both the women's world and that of mother's kin toward their proper focus -- the world of men and especially that of one's male patriclan members.

Such was the understanding I felt I had reached -- until I sat down again with those boys in the summer of 1981.

"All the information you're ever told is a mixture of true facts and false facts floating on the surface of a great mass of wishes and fears and memories."
-Finbow, in C.P. Snow,
Death Under Sail (1932:185).

As far as the main events are concerned, the boys' narratives at the beginnings of the interviews were fairly complete and consistent with each other. What few differences appeared were resolved quickly and easily with focused questioning, e.g., when one or another boy did not initially mention a particular incident, such as the mother's prior preparation of the novices or the "smoking" ritual. Given the complexity of the ceremony and the passage of an intervening decade, it is remarkable that only one aspect of the boys' representations of the events differed significantly from my own records of how things had been. To my surprise, however, this concerned the parts played by various categories of people, especially during the first morning when the

reportedly and obviously painful nose-bleeding and
hazing took place.

My speculations regarding the emotional impact
of the initiation experience assumed an idealized
allocation of roles in the ceremony as this was
described in advance by various men, *viz.*, that the
novices' noses would be bled by their "mothers'
brothers" -- men whom the boys would call *nau* (a
category that includes both real and classificatory
mother's brothers) -- and that "under no
circumstances" could blood be shed or an active
initiatory role be assumed by a boy's father or male
clan-mate. I was prepared, of course, for various
contingencies to affect the actual allocation of
roles in the 1971 ceremony and, indeed, my records
indicate that only two of the boys, Toza and Unesa,
definitely had their noses bled by a member of their
mothers' clan (the same man in both instances).
Honima may also have been bled by this man -- a
distantly-related clan-mate of his mother -- but my
notes are unclear in his case, such was the
confusion in the stream on that morning and,
significantly, even in the minds of the men whom I
asked at that time. Seri, the fourth boy (Boraama
did not have his nose bled at all [Hays and Hays
1982]), was bled by a man who was his own clan-mate
(albeit distantly related), contrary to stated
ideals and for reasons still not clear to me.

For the present discussion, two points are most
relevant: first, that in the 1981 interviews, at
least two of the boys misidentified the men who had
subjected them to this painful experience; and
second, that their reported emotional reactions
indicate a very different affective legacy than I
had expected. With respect to the first point, Seri
insisted that his mother's brother had bled his nose
when it actually had been his own clan-mate, while
Unesa claimed that his initiator had been his own
clan-mate (FaBrSo) rather than, in fact, a distant
clan "brother" of his mother! Only Toza, and
possibly Honima, accurately reported "mothers'
brothers" as the men who had inflicted pain on them

that morning. I will return later to Unesa's
curious recollection but for now more important is
the second point regarding emotional reactions,
discussion of which will be enhanced by first
considering the overall emotional experience of the
ceremony as it was recalled by the boys.

The boys had displayed (and later reported) a
variety of affective responses to the ceremony,
especially to those parts that involved pain,
deception, and humiliation. Indeed, when I tried to
understand allocations of roles in the events, as
discussed earlier, it made sense to me that evoking
strong emotions was an important function of the
ceremony, particularly as anger and frustration
focused on the initiators (ideally, matriclan
members) might facilitate the transfer of identity,
dependence, and solidarity to the boys' fathers and
other patriclan members, the apparent "protectors"
of the novices.

On the one hand, this interpretation receives
support from the fact that even when the boys were
bled and hazed by men other than their mothers'
clan-mates, their recollections of the events
(except for Unesa's) were expressed in terms of the
ideal structure of role allocations. Thus, if
negative emotional reactions were processed in terms
of the boys' perceptions, the proposed purpose would
be served -- "mother's brother" appears as the
villain, with father and clan-mates untainted. On
the other hand, this was *not* the result if the boys'
reports of where they directed their affective
responses are to be believed. Rather than a clear
perception of "villains" and "saviors" emerging from
the reported deeds of particular individuals, the
boys seem to have been left with mixed and confused
feelings. If any simplification is legitimate, it
would have to be that the *fathers* were generally
perceived as the villians while mothers' brothers
were the saviors, with mothers occupying some median
emotional space.

With respect to mothers, the boys expressed
their (remembered) feelings in various, but fairly

consistent, ways. First, excerpts from Honima's
interview:

Q.   Were you angry with your father or mother?
R.   Yes, both of them.
Q.   You were angry with them?
R.   Yes.
Q.   When you were in pain, did you cry out for
     them?
R.   Yes, for my mother, but not for my father.
        . . .
Q.   So, you were angry with your mother
     because she got you ready and sent you off
     to have this done?
R.   Yes, she did that, but I still cried out
     for her.

And Seri, who also reported crying out for his
mother as his nose was bled:

R.   I was angry (with my father) and with my
     mother . . .
Q.   Your mother, too, huh? Why? She didn't
     hurt you.
R.   She was part of it.
Q.   Do you mean because she sent you off with
     the men for them to do these things?
R.   Yes, that's what I mean.

Toza (who also cried out for his mother):

R.   Then I was angry with my mother, too.
Q.   Your mother, too?
R.   Yes. She had sent me to have my nose
     bled, so I was angry with her.

Only Unesa denied assigning any blame to his mother:

Q.   At this time (in the forest), did you cry
     for your mother?
R.   Yes, I really bawled.
        . . .
Q.   Were you angry with your mother?
R.   No, just my father and this man.
Q.   Just your father and the man who bled your
     nose?
R.   Yes. They hurt me. My mother didn't hurt
     me, so I wasn't angry with her.

An outside observer might expect, given "what really happened," that the boys would have received mixed messages regarding their mothers on that first day of the ceremony. Accustomed to nurturance, support, and a generally close relationship with a woman whose few disciplinary attempts were often ignored with relative impunity, one might well hope for rescue from pain and hazing by calling out for her, as all of the boys reported doing. (They also reported crying out for their mothers years later when subjected to the even greater pain and discomfort of the *'ia'vaati* ceremony.) However, the boys' mothers could also be seen as accomplices, at least on the first morning. It was they who cleaned and dressed the boys and "set them up" for what followed. This participation was explicitly acknowledged in the interviews and was the reported basis for the anger at least three of the boys claim to have felt toward their mothers. The mixing of messages, at least for the observer, could come at two points: when the mothers and other women "attack" the procession, ostensibly trying to recapture the boys on their way back from the forest, and subsequently when they set up a wall of resistance -- with some women twanging bowstrings in defiance of the approaching male procession -- near the entrance to the men's house compound. Interestingly, however, none of the boys mentioned these "rescue attempts" in their narratives, apparently remembering only the duplicity of their mothers in sending them off to this painful experience.

If these selective recollections of events concerning mothers are curious, even more so are the reported perceptions and feelings regarding the male participants.

Consistent with men's stated ideals regarding ceremonial roles, the novices' fathers and close male clan-mates played minor parts on that first morning (but later they actively told stories and participated in other events in the men's house). According to my notes, they were bystanders, lined

up with other men on the streambank and fairly
inconspicuous; this is also the way they were
remembered in the boys' interviews. None of the
boys claimed to have been hurt or abused directly by
his father; instead, all explicitly mentioned their
fathers' bystander status. However, two of the boys
went further and asserted an antagonistic dimension
to their fathers' behavior. Honima characterized it
this way:

Q. Where was your father (during the
    nose-bleeding)?
R. He was there, watching.
Q. He just stood there watching? He didn't
    try to help you?
R. That's right. He just stood on the
    streambank and watched.

Later, in explaining why he was angry (then)
with his father, he added, "My father . . . egged
the others on to beat me more."

Toza's account was similar:

Q. While this (nose-bleeding) was going on,
    where was your father?
R. He was right there.
Q. Just watching?
R. He just watched and told the men to beat
    us, and they did.

. . .

Q. So you were angry with your father?
R. Yes.

These allegations of fathers encouraging others
to abuse the boys may have been true. What is most
significant is that these two boys remembered it
that way, just as Seri said, "I didn't want them to
bleed my nose, but they were insistent, so I had no
choice." When asked just who had been "insistent,"
he unhesitatingly laid the blame on his father.

Thus, in the eyes and memories of the boys,
their fathers, like their mothers, had been
duplicitous in arranging this painful experience --
preparing them for it, insisting that they go
through with it, and turning others' hands, if not
their own, against the helpless novices. Even

though it had been other men who had directly
inflicted the vividly-recalled pain, fathers (and
mothers) were remembered as betraying the boys and,
far from rescuing them from the onslaughts of
others, actually engineering the whole thing. It is
for these reasons, I suggest, that the boys
hesitated not a moment in saying that they felt
anger toward their fathers and mothers that morning,
although they all also claimed that they "got over"
this anger "later."

What, then, of the men who *had* inflicted the
real pain, according to my records and those
contained in the boys' memories? Curiously, while
anger was readily admitted toward those who had not
directly hurt them but who also did not help them,
for at least three of the boys the men who were said
to have inflicted the pain were also held up as
their saviors -- a paradox which appears to have
resulted in contradictory and confused management of
emotions.

I should repeat here that not all of the boys
in fact had their noses bled by their "mothers'
brothers"; even when that category is considered in
its widest sense. My documentation indicates that
Seri, at least, did not, yet he was among the three
who claimed their initiators had been their
"mothers' brothers." Conversely, Unesa claimed he
had been bled by his own clan-mate while, in fact,
his situation was in accord with the ideal pattern.
I will return to his case after considering the
other three boys' accounts in the interviews,
stressing again the point that they were presenting
their versions in terms of mothers' brothers
occupying the critical role of initiator.

None of the three boys -- Honima, Seri, and
Toza -- gave a simple account of his recalled
emotions toward the man who directly inflicted pain
on him in the forest stream. First, consider
Honima:

Q.   Who was it who bled your nose, your
     father?
R.   No, my *kandere*.

Q.   Your mother's brother?
R.   Yes .

. . .

Q.   When he bled your nose, were you angry
     with your *kandere* for doing this to you?
R.   Yes. As he did it, I shouted, *"Kandere*,
     let me go! That's enough!"

Such a reaction to the nose-bleeding is
understandable, of course, and it is consistent with
my recollections of struggle, resistance, and
screams on the part of the novices at the time.
What is significant here is that immediately after
Honima reported that he thus pleaded with his
mother's brother for release, I repeated the
question: "So you were angry with him?" to which he
instantly responded, "No, he's my *kandere*."

This kind of self-contradiction or at least
ambivalence was common to other boys who claimed
that their mothers' brothers had bled their noses.
For example, the account of Seri, whose nose was in
fact bled by his own distant clan-mate, went as
follows:

Q.   When you were in the water and your
     kandere bled your nose [according to his
     earlier claim], were you angry with him?
R.   No, he was my *kandere*.
Q.   How *did* you feel?
R.   I felt pain and I was a little angry with
     my *kandere*.
Q.   You were a little angry with him?
R.   Yes, I said, "I just want to go on the way
     I was living, but now you men have brought
     me here and you're hurting me!" That's
     what I said.[5]

Only Toza came close to a statement of
unqualified emotional reaction toward his mother's
brother for his part in the nose-bleeding:

Q.   At that time, were you angry with the men?
R.   I was angry!
Q.   But you weren't able to fight back?
R.   I couldn't fight back. I was afraid to
     even try! There were too many of them and

I was just a little boy. What chance
would I have had?

Q.   So you were angry with your *kandere*?

R.   No, I'm not angry with him!

Q.   I mean before, when he bled your nose.

R.   Yes, then I was angry with him and with my
mother, too . . . but later I wasn't angry
any more.

If Toza's testimony comes close to what one
might have expected as a reaction to the
nose-bleeding, Unesa's is perfectly on the mark:

Q.   When he bled your nose, how did you feel
about him?

R.   It was really painful and I cried and
cried.

Q.   Were you angry with this man?

R.   I cried and was very angry with him. I
wanted to escape and I was really angry
about the pain.

. . .

Q.   (Were you angry with) your mother, too?

R.   No, just my father and this man.

Q.   Just with your father and the man who bled
your nose?

R.   Yes, they hurt me. . . .

Here we have the single most reasonable account
of emotional reactions to a painful and harrowing
experience -- reasonable, that is, in terms of an
outside observer's view of how one might personally
react to such a situation. The remarkable aspect of
Unesa's report, however, is that he considered his
initiator to be a member of his own clan (FaBrSo),
rather than a man I identified as a distant
clan-mate of his mother. Thus the only boy who
expressed clear and straightforward anger toward his
initiator was the one who did not believe it had
been his mother's brother. One might go further and
suggest a pattern in this aspect of the boys'
accounts: those who (rightly or wrongly) considered
their initiators to be mothers' brothers were
reluctant, or at least ambivalent, about reporting
anger toward the men who bled their noses. A

similar pattern appears when we examine how the boys
presented their mothers' brothers, or others, as
their protectors or even saviors during the ordeal.

Honima, in recounting the procession's entry
into the forest when it was "attacked" by the
waiting men (including those of his own clan),
correctly recalled that "the men in hiding . . .
acted as if they were going to shoot us, and we
shook with fear. We didn't know whether they were
going to shoot us or not. Our mothers' clan-mates
escorted us and protected us, firing their arrows at
the bushes and the stream." (The latter events were
imagined, not real.) Later, in the men's house
compound, mothers' clan-mates "put us up on their
backs and carried us around the house. As we went
around, the men beat us with nettles." And, when
the men's secret latrine was revealed: "Men were
lined up in a corridor, and our *kandere* led us
through it, as the men beat us again with nettles
and threatened to shoot us with arrows. We were
terrified." Finally, regarding the pork
distribution on the final day: "We were given pork
to put away for our *kandere*, who came later to
collect it in return for their having helped us in
the ceremony."

These recollections, which were accurate,
appeared to overshadow completely for Honima the
pain his mother's brother had inflicted on him in
the forest stream. Indeed, in general discussion
later in the interview, I asked, "Your *kandere* look
out for you, huh?" to which he responded, "Yes.
Whenever others beat us, our *kandere* help us out.
They never beat us. In the men's house, our own
clan-mates would beat us a lot and discipline us."

Seri similarly characterized his mother's
clan-mates as helpful:

Q. Who showed you the (secret men's) latrine?
R. My *kandere*. He held me by the hand and
   showed it to me. My own clan-mates -- my
   brothers and father -- beat me severely!
Q. Men of your own clan (beat you)?

R.   Yes. They beat me, and my *kandere* stopped
     them and took me back to the men's house
     to sleep.

During the long nights of instruction and hazing in
the men's house, according to Seri, mothers'
clan-mates continued in a protective role: "Our
kandere only pretended to beat us with nettles and
we pretended to cry and try to fight them off. Our
fathers' clansmen *really* beat us!"   And, with
respect to the pork, "We took our shares and gave
some to our mothers' clan-mates because they had
helped us when we were being beaten by the others."

     Toza's account also stressed the same themes,
even at the expense of a curious self-contradiction.
First, "some men were holding nettles with their
bows and arrows [in the forest] and they beat us
with them.   I hurt a lot and we cried and cried.
Finally our *kandere* came and stopped it and rescued
us; they felt sorry for us because we were crying."
The contradiction then appeared in his account of
the nose-bleeding which was conducted, according to
his own claims, by his mothers' brother: "Blood
poured out and it hurt like hell.   We cried again
and our *kandere* came to rescue us again."

     Even Unesa credited his mothers' clan-mates
with a protective role in the men's house during the
night-long sessions: "They beat us and we cried and
cried.   Our *kandere* came and stopped them from
beating us."   But in subsequent questioning, he
attributed sympathetic behavior more broadly:

R.   When they beat me with nettles, I would
     get angry.   Some men helped me by trying
     to stop the others, but the ones who beat
     me made me mad.
Q.   Who tried to stop them?
R.   Most of the men.   But some said, "You
     can't tell me what to do.   It's my turn,"
     and they beat us some more.

     In addition to drawing attention to what could
be characterized as a sadistic element in the
behavior of at least some of the men -- commented on
several times during the interviews (Tuzin 1982) --

Unesa's account, uniquely, does not reserve the
"protector" role exclusively for mother's
clan-mates. The fact that he alone of the four boys
thought (incorrectly) that someone other than his
mother's brother had bled his nose is not, I
suggest, coincidence, but points to a main
conclusion I would draw about the boys' accounts of
their emotional responses to the events of the
'*ummanra* ceremony.

It is clear from the statements made in the
interviews and from the general tone of the boys'
stated recollections (although this latter cannot be
indicated satisfactorily in the excerpts provided
above) that the '*ummanra* ceremony entailed both
physical and emotional traumas for the initiates.
Also clear is the boys' organization of their
memories in terms of the "ideal" version of how the
ceremony is expected to proceed, even when they
misidentified the individuals who played certain
roles. Thus, with the curious exception of Unesa,
"mothers' brothers" were recalled as the initiators,
with fathers and other clan-mates occupying
secondary, but still significant, statuses.

If we grant the boys their versions of who
played the key roles of initiators in the forest
stream, and if we consider the events there --
including nose-bleeding and other acts both
manifestly and reportedly painful and humiliating --
as likely to be the most salient in terms of
emotional responses, we are faced with an unexpected
tendency in the interviews. For the most part, the
boys did not remember the ceremony as an occasion
full of traumas inflicted upon them by their
initiators (i.e., their "mothers' brothers," except
for Unesa), but one in which their "mothers'
brothers" (again, except for Unesa) tried, with
partial success, to *protect* them. Unqualified
expressions of blame and anger pertained to the
remembered actions of fathers, own clan-mates, and
mothers, but to the extent that negative feelings
were reported about the parts played by "mothers'
brothers," (again, and significantly, except for

Unesa) these were expressed hesitantly and ambivalently, or apparently outweighed by memories of help and protection from these men.

I cannot speak, of course, to the ways in which the boys perceived events and individuals as all of this was happening in 1971, but it is clear that a decade later both were remembered selectively and sometimes in conflict with my records. This, in itself, is not necessarily surprising; what was unexpected was the fairly consistent manner in which negative affect was organized around the recalled actions of mothers, fathers, and own clan-mates, with largely positive affect regarding the behavior of mothers' clan members. Given my earlier stated expectation that role allocation within the ceremony was consistent with an objective of breaking bonds of solidarity with mothers and "their people" and a shift in allegiance and solidarity toward fathers and "their people," we are left with an unexpected (apparent) emotional residue that calls for explanation in terms of both reasons why the boys would organize their recollections in such a way, and the implications of this result for our understanding of the initiation experience.

It is possible, of course, that the interview results are only unexpected and surprising because of misperceptions on the part of the ethnographer. Thus, it could be that the nose-bleeding and other forest stream events are only salient to the outside observer and carry little of the "experiential load" of the ceremony as a whole. In this case the boys' memories would be focused more directly on other initiation events, with the forest activities almost "forgotten" along with whatever pain and discomfort they entailed. This seems an unlikely explanation for two reasons. First, the *'ummanra* ceremony is invariably referred to in Pidgin English as *"sutim nus,"* suggesting a high degree of salience for that[6] particular aspect of a complex series of events. Second, the boys' own narratives were exceedingly detailed and vivid when it came to the nose-bleeding and other forest activities; indeed, no other parts

of the interviews were filled with so much precise
detail and emotional overtone in the telling.

Another possibility is that the boys
acknowledge the pain and agony inflicted upon them
at that time by their "mothers' brothers," but they
subsequently came to understand that it was all "for
their own good," in which case the perpetrators
would not be blamed but thanked, or at least
remembered favorably for having "helped" them in
this way, too. This also seems implausible since,
even a full decade later during which intervening
time they had had several opportunities to
participate in the ceremony in a wide range of
roles, the boys could provide little in the way of
rationale for the rite, in whole or in part.
Instead, they expressed only regret that they had
been forced to experience it at all; it was their
reported hope and expectation that "once the older
men have all died," such customs would be abandoned
quickly.

I suggest that the clearest understanding of
the boys' reported emotional responses to the events
of the 'ummanra ceremony might be obtained by first
recognizing that when we investigate the assignment
of "blame," expressions of "anger," a sense of
"humiliation" and "betrayal," and perceptions of
others as "protectors" or "villains," we are, after
all, dealing with the *moral* dimension of the
ceremony. We are, essentially, inquiring into the
moral judgements that the boys made at the time of
the experience or, more accurately in this instance,
the moral judgements they are prepared to make when
they are asked to do so. In this realm of
anthropological inquiry, Read long ago (1955)
cleared a fruitful path in his discussion of
"distributive morality" among the Gahuku-Gama.

Among the parallels between Read's experience
with the Gahuku and mine with Ndumba, one which
stands out vividly is the frequent reluctance of our
respective hosts to evaluate and criticize or
support the acts of their fellows in terms of neat

and simple abstract moral principles (Langness, this volume). Frustrating attempts by their ethnographers to infer clear and consistent attitudes towards particular acts as "wrong" or "right," Gahuku and Ndumba repeatedly employed what might best be called "relational ethics," to use an expression suggested by Edward Schieffelin (personal communication). That is, with respect to the likely or most appropriate reaction on the part of a given individual to the act(s) of another, the act had to be viewed in terms of the parties involved and the social relationships that existed between them. As Read summarized the situation for Gahuku (1955:260):

> Stated as sharply as possible, moral obligations are primarily contingent on the social positioning of individuals. They are not derived from, neither do they refer to anything which is intrinsic to the nature of the agent himself or to the nature of other human beings as such.

Nor, with respect to Ndumba at least, do they refer to or derive from moral qualities intrinsic to acts as such. Thus, stealing a pig, physical assault on another person, or issuance of an insulting remark might properly evoke either involvement at some level or aloof observation of the involvement of others. The meaning of the act and its moral implications must be calculated in terms of the culturally constituted social relationships between the persons involved, including such considerations as relations of power, authority, nurturance, and the like. Thus, in Read's terms (1955:257), predicting whether and how a given individual will appropriately respond to a particular act requires considerations of "a 'distributive' recognition of moral obligation":

> As a moral agent his responsibilities vary considerably according to the positioning of other individuals within the system of inter-personal and inter-group relationships . . . (Each) agent

recognizes that his moral obligations to others are differentially apportioned.

The significance and utility of this view of moral responsibilities in terms of the current inquiry into the Ndumba boys' organization of their emotional responses to the traumatic events of *'ummanra* initiation become clear when we realize that asking a boy whether he felt "anger" at the time and toward whom is asking him to perform calculations resulting in moral evaluation of the behavior of others with respect to him. If morality is "distributive" in a way such as Read has argued, or if ethics are *relational*, then the boy cannot simply respond to "the act" (e.g., having his nose bled), but he must take into consideration *who* performed the act and who, in fact, he *himself* was *in relation to* that man. That is, the act must not only be seen in the context of other acts, but also in the context of a whole network of rights and obligations that exist between the parties involved. Thus, the event in question was not a man forcing a boy's nose to bleed, but a "mother's brother" forcing "a sister's son's" nose to bleed. It is of critical importance to an understanding of the boys' stated reactions to that event that we realize the actual identity of the initiator was less significant in calculating how to respond to it than was his perceived *social identity*. As Read has argued for the Gahuku, rather than in terms of abstract, generalized concepts of "persons," such calculations must be conducted in terms of social identities: "To his fellows, the social role is an intrinsic component of each man's identity and, as such, it constitutes an essential element to their awareness of him; it becomes, as it were, an inseparable component of his individuality" (1955:278).

It is in light of this view of "distributive morality" or "relational ethics" that we begin to gain insight into the Ndumba boys' processing of the emotional (i.e., evaluative) aspects of the initiation experience. Just as Ndumba men, in

describing the *'ummanra* ceremony, characterize the
participation of various individuals in "ideal"
terms, with specific roles allocated according to
social identities, the boys themselves (excepting
Unesa) remembered the events as proceeding according
to that ideal pattern, with "mothers' brothers" as
initiators, etc. Whether or not they actually
perceived their initiators at the time to have been
their "mothers' brothers," this is the way that
three of the four boys structured their memories (or
at least their reported memories) of the events.
Thus, when called upon to express affective
dimensions of the experience, we should not be
surprised if judgemental statements (e.g., "I was
angry with him," implying that some "wrong" had been
committed) are informed by rules of morality that
pertain to the *social identities* in question. We
must ask, then, not whether a boy would "reasonably"
be angry with "someone" who inflicted pain and
humiliation on him, but whether a Ndumba "sister's
son" would "reasonably" be angry with a "mother's
brother" who inflicted pain and humiliation on him.
Correspondingly, would a Ndumba "son" reasonably be
angry with a "father" and/or "mother" for their
remembered acts, and would a Ndumba "junior
clan-mate" reasonably be angry with a "senior
clan-mate" who behaved in a particular recalled
manner? If we consider the boys' memories and
judgemental statements to be structured primarily in
terms of the rules governing behavior between these
various social identities, not only can we
understand better why three of them said what they
did but also why Unesa's testimony frequently
contained exceptions to the general pattern.

Before proceeding with a brief consideration of
the three relevant dyads of "mother-son,"
"father-son," and "mother's brother-sister's son,"
it must be made clear what is at issue in this
inquiry. Since the interviews in question were
conducted when the boys were late adolescents and
they were being asked to recall feelings and
perceptions from a decade earlier, we cannot assume

that we are necessarily learning anything about how
the boys actually felt in 1971. It is entirely
possible that when a nineteen-year-old boy reports
that he "felt angry" with someone when he was nine
or ten, he is in fact projecting onto the past what
his *current* evaluation of such a situation would be.
It should be stressed, however, that all four of the
boys affirmed in the interviews that they had
"gotten over" their anger and other feelings and it
would be, I believe, a mistake to assert that
selective memories and possible projection render
the results of the interviews without value. What
is of value, I submit, is that from the boys'
statements we are at least in the position of
learning how a late adolescent Ndumba male thinks a
young boy *would have* appropriately directed his
emotions in the context of the initiation ceremony.
What can emerge from the inquiry, then, is a sense
of the degree to which *imputed* feelings and emotions
can be understood in terms of the social identities
imputed to have been involved in the events. Such a
discovery would help us toward an answer to the
question of why the boys organized their accounts of
emotions and feelings in the ways that they did.

As earlier discussed, three of the four
interviewees freely recalled having felt anger
toward their mothers when their noses were bled; the
fourth, Unesa, reported anger toward the immediate
inflictors of his pain (in his view, men of his own
clan) but none toward his mother since she had
played no direct part in his suffering. When asked
why they were angry with their mothers at that time,
Honima, Seri, and Toza all indicated that their
mothers shared in the responsibility for their
misery since they had prepared the boys that morning
and sent them off with the men to have these things
done to them. Interestingly, all three of the boys
(but not Unesa) claimed to have cried out for their
mothers despite their anger. The interviews,
unfortunately, did not disclose whether reported
feelings of anger were precipitated by subsequent
realizations that their calls for help had gone

unanswered (except by "mothers' brothers"; see below) or whether they took shape during the actual experience. In either case, the boys' comments about their mothers resonate well with the general relationship between a Ndumba mother and young son.

Since, in 1971, virtually every Ndumba man lived in one of the several men's houses, a boy spent his childhood years in a household comprised entirely of females and male children. Sexual segregation, based largely on an ideology of male fears of female pollution as elsewhere in the Eastern Highlands (Hays and Hays 1982; Read 1954; Langness 1974), resulted in two basic interaction patterns for boys with respect to adults. Until the age of three or four, a boy would seldom be far from his mother, following her to gardens and even to women's seclusion houses, and eating all of his meals with her (or with other women in their similarly-composed households) and sleeping next to her in her house. The mother's role with respect to her son(s) was predominantly nurturant, as the main source of satisfaction of both physical and emotional needs. With older males (including, especially, fathers and mother's brothers) in the household only on an occasional visiting basis, what discipline was imposed (distraction rather than physical punishment) derived primarily from the mother. One could not, I believe, accurately characterize mothers as objects of fear on the part of sons since maternal discipline was usually mild, and certainly often ignored by young boys. Admonitions, shouts, and reproving looks supplemented the earlier strategy of distraction but carried little force, and were backed up with even less. By the time a boy was six or seven years old, his relationship with his mother would become less dependent, if not less close, as his mobility increased and "gangs" of male agemates became his primary interaction and reference group. A son of this age range might or might not assist his mother in gardens or at household tasks and otherwise comply with her wishes, depending largely on the

immediate   availability   of   more   attractive
alternatives of play or mischief.

The *'ummanra* ceremony takes place for a given
boy when he is about eight to ten years old, i.e.,
at a time when he has largely achieved a degree of
independence from his mother except for subsistence
needs, and these latter may be met by a wide range
of female kin or neighbors. (It is precisely this
state of independence and "wildness" that men focus
on in their chastisement and physical abuse of boys
as being *"bikhet"* during the *'ummanra* ceremony and
subsequently in the men's houses.) A mother will
have always been a source of other kinds of support,
however, should a son choose to request or demand it
(as she will continue to be into his adult life as
well), and it is in this light that we can
understand why three of the novices reportedly cried
out in their pain for their mothers to come rescue
them, since mothers had always been "on call" for
such purposes. When the cries failed to yield a
response, perhaps for the first time ever, a sense
of betrayal might be a logical outcome. Seen
through a son's eyes (especially, a son still at
this young age), such betrayal would be proper
grounds for resentment and anger. The free
expression of such anger, at least in later
interviews, is simply a continuation of a long-term
pattern of disobedience, refusal to cooperate,
tantrums and "sassiness" in response to mothers'
requests, demands, and acts in the past -- responses
which sons have always given with relative impunity.

All four of the boys unhesitatingly admitted
having felt anger toward their fathers (and other
male   clan-mates),   with   Unesa   (erroneously)
identifying his father's brother's son as his
initiator and the others attributing to their
fathers the "egging on" of others to beat and harass
them. None of the boys reported having cried out
for their fathers to help them from their streambank
perches. Comments in the interviews consistently
portrayed unqualified attitudes of resentment and
anger   toward   fathers,   not   for   their   lack   of

assistance as with mothers, but for their alleged part in making a bad situation even worse.

Again, insights are to be gained by considering the household and other interaction patterns of young Ndumba boys in 1971. Motivated in part by fears of the dangers inherent in "too much" contact with adult females and also the dangers attending contact with those who spend most of their time with women (i.e., children of both sexes), Ndumba men spent relatively little time with their sons prior to the latters' initiation and entry into the world of the men's house and men's activities. Depending on the particular relationship between a given husband and wife, men might be daily but often less frequent visitors to their wives' houses. Such visits mostly took place in the early evening hours as men would stop by to collect food for the evening meal and, perhaps, to talk about the day's events until mid-evening, when they would retire to the men's house to actually eat the food, talk of "more serious" matters, and sleep. During these evening visits, it is my impression, interaction between fathers and young sons (excepting infants and toddlers) was slight; the two, after all, would have little in common, with young boys representing far more of the world of women (and, later, the world of boys) than that of men. Contact between fathers and sons was even more limited in the hamlet environs, with children associating primarily with their peers or with women at public gatherings. In the gardens, if a man happened to be working on a fence, e.g., with his wife and young son engaged nearby in other tasks, there might be more opportunities for interaction, but by the time a boy was six or seven, such assistance in his mother's gardens became less and less common, decreasing even further the chances of father-son relationships becoming multidimensional.

In the interviews boys did not always clearly distinguish between their fathers and "fathers' brothers" (all of whom are designated ǥo), and it is my impression that this blurring of identities is a

reflection of the lack of any clear cut character of
father-son relationships. It is true that fathers
would often show interest in playing with sons in
their infant and toddler stages but subsequently, in
my view, they blended into the background of older
male members of one's clan. Commands and
remonstrances might be issued by fathers or other *go*
more forcefully than were admonitions from mothers,
but they were accompanied, as yet, by no other
disciplinary measures. Men frequently expressed
disgust with boys in their clans as *"bikhet"* and
this attitude came though clearly, I believe, to the
boys. Even if such men did not back up their dark
reproving stares with physical force, there was a
frequent undertone in their exhortations that more
tangible sanctions might be forthcoming. Continuing
disobedience and "big-headedness," then, was likely
perceived as tinged with an element of risk, unlike
the situation with one's mother, who "would always
be there when you needed her" regardless of how you
treated her now. Nor did compliance with the
requests or orders of one's "father" necessarily
entail any clear rewards. To be sure, one learned
early that one's clan-mates would be an important
support group in the future, but such support was
largely a vague kind of solidarity, more jural than
personal. Moreover, in future disputes as well as
more positively-framed group activities, one's
agemates were far more evident sources of support --
both physical and emotional -- than were senior
clan-mates. In sum, my impression is that for young
boys their fathers and fathers' brothers were
somewhat distant figures, appearing as formidable
forces perhaps to be reckoned with some day.

    For the interviewees, that day arrived with the
'ummanra ceremony and the beginning of life in the
men's house. With respect to post-initiatory males,
fathers and "fathers' brothers" were often said to
be stern disciplinarians who backed up their
accusations of "big-headedness" with physical force
and deprivation. Illustrative of early adolescents'
alleged experiences is an account by Honima:

Once when I was a new *'ummanra*, I was playing around shooting arrows. One of my arrows went into the wall of a woman's house, that of Seri's mother. She was in there and came running out, shouting 'Hey! Who's shooting arrows at my house?'

(My father's brother) was nearby scraping bananas and he heard the commotion. He told me to go with him. I was still wearing my *'ummanra* decorations and he told me to take them all off. Then he got a big bunch of nettle branches and leaves and made me lie down on them. Then he tied me down with a vine. He untied me later, but I just rolled around on the ground in pain from the nettles.

. . . He told me that the government [i.e., the Australian administration] had come, making lots of new laws, so the men take it easy on us boys. He said that we're too *'bikhet'*. Before (the government came) they beat the boys a lot. He said they used to tie boys down on bundles of nettles and then beat them with sticks. But now they're easy on us and we're *'bikhet'*.

This account is typical of many young and older men's testimony regarding the discipline imposed in the men's house. Invariably it is the men of one's own clan, if not one's actual father, who were alleged to administer punishments. Also, in the interviews, several times the boys claimed a "day of reckoning" aspect to the hazing of the *'ummanra* ceremony. According to Seri, as he cried for release from the nose-bleeding and other inflictions of pain, "they said we hadn't been obedient; now maybe we would think about that and obey them in the future." And Unesa: "The men just laughed. They said, 'You thought you were really something when you were little boys. Now we'll show you!' and they laughed and laughed." Such accounts gain credibility, as does attribution of revenge behavior

to fathers and other clan-mates, from comparable
testimony from adult males about their parts in
'ummanra ceremonies and subsequent life in the men's
houses. On many occasions men laughed as they told
me how they punished *"bikhet"* boys -- their own sons
and other boys of their own clans, finally "getting
back" at youths who had allegedly thought for years
of nothing but play. Nor did the boys themselves
consider the revenge unwarranted; all whom I
questioned admitted, with chuckles, that as little
boys they had "run wild" with no regard for what
elders said or wanted.

We must acknowledge, then, this "punishment"
aspect of the violence in the forest stream and
later in the men's house. It is reasonable, I
submit, to think that the boys realized, possibly as
it was happening and certainly later, that this was
the "day of reckoning" that had been presaged by
their fathers' and other clan-mates' angry but
seemingly-empty threats. After such a long period
of apparent immunity, the boys might have been
surprised that "they really meant it after all" and
responded with anger and resentment that such fears
had become reality at last. The fact that such
emotions could be so easily expressed directly
against fathers and other clan-mates (whose support,
as clan-mates, was "guaranteed" in any event) would
not, by the evidence, surprise those men themselves.
According to men's conversations with me, fathers
and own clan-mates *are* the disciplinarians of boys
(indeed, the only permissible ones as far as
physical punishment is concerned) and, *of course*, it
makes boys angry to be punished. But, the sequel
goes in stated or unstated form, "what can they do
about it?"

If fathers represent the inevitable authority
and power of the clan, the resentment of which is to
be expected and need not be suppressed, we can
appreciate better the relationship between a boy and
his "mother's brothers" (*nau*) that lends a very
different tone to the interviewees' recollections of
their initiation. All three of the boys who

believed their initiators to have been their *nau*
recalled confused and ambivalent emotional responses
to their pain and humiliation. Even when they
admitted that their *nau* had bled their noses and
otherwise hazed them, they seemingly could not admit
anger with them without denying such feelings in the
next breath or emphasizing repeatedly how much and
how often their *nau* had rescued them from the
attacks by their fathers and other clan-mates.
Significantly only Unesa attributed solely helpful
behavior to his mother's brother, but he had
(erroneously) *not* identified this kinsman as his
initiator.

If the boys' emotional reactions were not
simple, neither was the relationship between a
"mother's brother" (*nau*) and a "sister's son"
(*nondi*). On the one hand, as a representative of
mother's clan, a *nau* was a figure demanding respect
with his name being forbidden to say aloud on pain
of payment of compensation for such an "insult."
This status was accompanied by expectations of
obedience, should he choose to make a request or
speak on behalf of a request issued by his "sister,"
i.e., one's mother. If compliance were not
forthcoming, however, no physical or other obvious
punishment was used as a sanction, but future
support from him might be thus jeopardized. For a
young boy, obedience to one's *nau* would elicit
generosity in return, perhaps with food or gifts in
the immediate future but also with later sanctuary
in the event of trouble with one's patrikin. As an
adult, a man faced with sorcery-based troubles or
other difficulties that were making life with his
own clan-mates problematic could always seek
temporary or even permanent refuge with his mother's
kin. He also had claims on his mother's clan's land
for gardening, hunting, or other purposes, so long
as the request was approved by the adult male
representatives of that clan, i.e., his "mother's
brothers."

These kinds of support were by no means
guaranteed, however, but depended on the

relationship between a particular *nau* and *nondi*, and
that relationship began to take shape very early in
a boy's life. From early childhood a boy would very
possibly have more face-to-face contact with
his *nau* (especially, his true mother's brothers)
than with his father. While any man would be
reluctant to spend much time in the company of
women, dangers from such contact were far fewer or
less severe with respect to one's mother or sister
than one's wife. Thus, male visitors to one's
mother's house would include her brothers, accepting
food from her (less risky than accepting it from his
wife, especially in the early years of marriage) and
engaging in relatively unstressful conversation. If
any adult male was likely to be viewed by a young
boy as largely supportive, at least potentially, it
was his *nau* rather than his father.

When one views the *'ummanra* ceremony in its
entirety, and does not focus only on those events
that strike the outside observer (as well as,
apparently, the interviewees) as most traumatic, the
parts played by "mothers' brothers" are mainly of
this supportive kind. That is, the boys were
correct in remembering the assistance of their *nau*
in showing them the secret latrine in the men's
house compound against resistance mounted by the
boys' own clan-mates. Moreover, testimony by the
ritual elder who had supervised the 1971 ceremony
corroborated the boys' versions of events when I
interviewed him in 1981. For example, as the
procession entered the forest, he said, "the boys'
kandere stret [i.e., their true mothers' brothers]
protected them by shooting at the others," and, with
respect to the beatings with nettles in the men's
house, "the boys cried and their *kandere* helped
them. They would get the men [fathers and other
clan-mates] to stop beating on one, but then they
would just start in on another."

If this image of mothers' brothers coming to
the rescue of sisters' sons being harassed by their
own clansmen is a fiction, it is a widely-shared one
and it recurs in many contexts. As one final

example, after Honima recounted the story quoted
earlier about his punishment for a carelessly-shot
arrow, he speculated that, "if my mother's brother
had been there, he would have untied me." To that,
I responded with a direct question:

Q.   Your *kandere* look out for you, don't they?
R.   Yes. Whenever others beat us our *kandere*
     help us out. They never beat us. In the
     men's house our own clan-mates would beat
     us a lot and discipline us.

One should not conceive of the mother's
brother/sister's son relationship in Ndumba as
entirely amicable. It could happen, e.g., that the
two as adult men (or, more likely, the "sister's
son" and his "mother's brother's son," who is also
nau) would find themselves on opposite sides in
disputes or even warfare since, after all, they
represent different and sometimes competing clans.
(At least one adult male informant, however,
reported that in battle one would try to avoid
firing at one's mother's clan-mates.) However, to
whatever degree actual behavior conforms to the
expected pattern of obligations such kinsmen have to
each other, it seems clear that the relationship is
viewed as one of respect toward "mothers' brothers"
and generosity, assistance, and emotional support
for "sisters' sons." In this regard, then, the
"mother's brother" could be seen as the complement
of the eventually stern disciplinarian "father."

It is with respect to the social roles of
"mother's brother" and "sister's son," *as ideally
conceptualized*, that Read's injunctions help us the
most. When we assess the boys' reported feelings
about the men who allegedly inflicted pain and
humiliation on them in the forest stream (but not
subsequently), we must remember that "the social
role is an intrinsic component of each man's
identity and, as such, it contributes an essential
element to *their awareness of him*; it becomes, as it
were, an inseparable component of his individuality"
[1955:278; emphasis added]. When viewed in this
way, the events in the forest stream no longer

appear as a variety of traumas being inflicted by
men upon boys, but "fathers and own clansmen"
inflicting pain and stress on "sons and junior
clansmen" as they have long threatened to do, and
"mothers' brothers" inflicting pain and stress on
"sisters' sons" as one has never expected them to
do, *but* following it with the kinds of support one
has always looked to them to provide, whereas
fathers and clan-mates go on to incorporate
punishment and discipline in their daily life in the
men's house. The situation is, thus, complicated,
and not surprisingly evoked confused and ambivalent
emotional responses. *Yet*, the responses *were*
patterned, at least in hindsight, deriving order
more from their social rather than personal
meanings.

We might interpret Unesa's account as an
extreme reaction to this state of affairs, but one
that illustrates clearly the social constraints on
the channeling of emotions -- he simply *denied* that
his "mother's brother" had been his initiator. The
others, including one boy who probably mistakenly
believed his "mothers' brother" to have played such
a role, admitted feeling anger, but also denied it.
I suggest that the admissions reflect a frank
recognition of what was believed to have happened,
but to admit that alone would be unacceptable for
two reasons: first, the expression of unmitigated
anger or resentment could be construed as
disrespectful to the most demanding respect figure
of all; and second, such an emphasis would
improperly underplay the supportive roles that
"mothers' brothers" had also performed, roles that
were perfectly in keeping with one's expectations
and other experiences.

In this paper I have tried to show how we can
gain an understanding of Ndumba boys' renderings of
their emotional responses to the initiation
experience when we examine that experience not
simply as objectively describable happenings to
individuals (although, at one level, they are such),

but also as culturally-constituted happenings to
personae engaged in a drama peopled by social
identities -- a drama that had a script in more
senses of the word than just the assignment of
roles. The reported reactions (including those
based on "erroneous" perceptions of just who played
which roles) can be viewed usefully as the results
of moral calculations performed by boys who brought
to the experience, and later interpreted it in terms
of, certain expectations regarding the players in
the drama. These expectations did not have to do
with the actual events that would occur; indeed,
these could not be anticipated in any clear sense by
the boys given the prescribed (if not actual)
secrecy surrounding initiation ceremonies. The
"script" furnished to them included, instead,
directions regarding what kinds of behavior, in
general, to expect from certain categories of
persons; how to interpret the experience in terms of
those directions; and how to organize and direct
their feelings about the experience including, if
necessary, rationalization and selective perception
or recall in the face of apparent dissonance.

To some degree, this script was transmitted in
the course of socially-structured early
socialization, as I have tried to indicate by
sketching some of the more important interaction
patterns in a young Ndumba boy's life. Many others
have developed this kind of analysis more fully in
other ethnographic contexts. For example, in
addressing the question of how Ifaluk children come
to "believe in" malevolent ghosts, Spiro (1953:379)
has argued that they are taught (through the
employment of various sanctions) to selectively
perceive (or, perhaps better, to cognize) the world
in terms of "frames of reference" that "are learned
in the process of interaction with other
individuals, in which the nature of one's world is
inferred from the [socially-constrained] perception
of it." More than simply a "world view" is implied
here, for Spiro is concerned with how Ifaluk
children learn to channel their emotions --

including not only their expression but also their
very internal processing -- in "socially acceptable"
ways.

Hildred Geertz has made much the same point in
her discussion of the Javanese "vocabulary of
emotion" (1959:249):

> Every cultural system includes patterned
> ideas regarding certain interpersonal
> relationships and certain affective states
> . . . The child, growing up within the
> culture and gradually internalizing these
> premises, undergoes a process of socially
> guided emotional specialization . . .
> (The) adults around him provide not only
> the situation for his learning about
> himself and his world, but also
> definitions and interpretations of this
> situation, and conceptualizations of their
> feelings and his feelings within it.

The present analysis follows clearly in the
tradition of Spiro, Geertz, and others who have
focused on the cultural shaping, channeling, or
canalizing of emotions. They have properly
recognized, as did Read in his pioneering
exploration of morality and personhood (1955), that
here we find a critically important and illuminating
articulation of the social and individual dimensions
of the person as a social being.[8] I have tried to
advance this tradition by supplementing a plausible
scenario of the early cultural shaping of
expectations regarding others with evidence, through
the interviews, that "reality" does, in fact, get
processed in a manner consistent with those
expectations, at least with respect to its affective
dimensions.

It appears that an examination of the
initiation experience is a particularly felicitous
choice of routes toward these destinations, for here
we see not only a good example of the affective
results of earlier socialization but also a special
case of the intensification of the channelling
process. Socialization into both cognitive and

affective rules for understanding, dealing with, and feeling about others consists, as it must, of far more than (guided) absorption and inference from everyday interaction, since there are always some chance elements involved. Thus, while it may be true that "in the relatively random experiences of children with others within a culture, a great variety of relational lessons are learned," it is also true that social groups at some point(s) systematize and intensify this learning "to modify and control this primary knowledge" (Levy 1982:520). For the child, "transitions brought about both by the maturational sequence of his body, and by the progressive enlargement of his social sphere of action" (Geertz 1959:262) may be especially appropriate opportunities for this intensification to occur.

While the point is seldom remarked, Ndumba are not alone among highlands peoples in their timing of initiation ceremonies. Even when a boy must undergo a long-term series of rites, the age range of 8-10 years is often chosen for a major rite of passage, as it is in Ndumba (Herdt 1982b). It is unlikely to be mere coincidence that this is precisely the maturational period which Cohen (1964:45-46) has called "the first stage of puberty," a time of significant biochemical and hormonal development:

> The external appearances of the body remain superficially unchanged for a time but there is no longer the earlier congruence between external appearances and internal experiences and feelings . . . . The individual . . . experiences confusion and great emotional and psychological vulnerability; for the society, this event provides a non-recurring opportunity to make a permanent imprint on the personality.

If Cohen is correct, the timing of the 'ummanra ceremony is ideal for the intensification of the learning of "relational lessons" (including

relational ethics) since, through both the structure
and the content of the rite

> The cultural system . . . provides a
> series of interpretations of the meanings
> of these transition points, and recipes
> for the child's reactions to them. The
> culture presents not only a set of
> suggested answers on *how to behave* in
> these situations, but also clues to *how to
> feel* about his actions . . . which as he
> grows older (provide) meaning, form, and
> apparent predictability to his inner
> experience (Geertz 1959:262-263).

As if to remove even more chances of "noioc,"
the emotionally vulnerable boy is put through a
ceremony that is itself highly emotionally charged,
another feature (together with highly elaborated
symbolic content) that distinguishes initiation
ceremonies from non-ritual socialization
experiences. "Once the intense and compelling
feeling of emotion arises [in the initiate] the
processes of secondary evaluation, of cognition per
se, begin. Here cultural systems and their private
components and versions . . . are centrally
influential in naming, classifying, interpreting,
directing" (Levy 1982:520-521).

Thus we come to see the initiation experience
as one which embeds its lessons in a highly
emotional context and at a maturational stage in
which emotional receptivity and malleability may be
at its highest, with a certain foundation already
having been laid in previous socialization for the
socially appropriate organization and channelling of
feelings. Among these lessons are the very
relational ethics which have been the focus of this
analysis -- ethics which are both the subject and
organizing frame of the experience. In addition to
further reinforcement of notions regarding
particular kin categories ("mothers," "fathers," and
"mothers' brothers") and the explicit teachings
included in the ceremony, we can see glimpses of

other likely lessons of special significance in
societies like Ndumba:

-- in a relatively egalitarian society, the
intolerability of self-centeredness and
uncooperativeness, i.e., being *"bikhet"*;

-- in a society chronically engaged in
warfare, the possibility that pain and
betrayal can also be inflicted by those
nearby, and these can hurt as much as an
enemy's arrow;

-- in a society organized in terms of
kin-based groupings, rights and
obligations are not always coincident with
supportive, personally-gratifying
relationships, nor are they mutually
exclusive; life and "kinship" are, after
all, more complicated than that.

With this last point, we might also see hints
of lessons for ourselves as we move past the
simplistic structural-functional approaches of the
past and try to delineate just how, and how deeply,
"cultural codes" penetrate and inform both social
action and individual experience. The dilemma faced
by Ndumba initiates in coming to terms with an
intense personal experience that must, to some
degree, be reconciled with and ordered by social
meanings may derive much of its problematic
character from, as Read (1955:256) attributed to the
Gahuku, "a particular conception of man which does
not allow for any clearly recognized distinction
between the individual and the status which he
occupies." This does not mean, however, that there
is no such distinction.

I did not need the 1981 interviews to convince
me that the initiates had experienced and struggled
with real feelings as they tried to make sense of
what was happening to them. As an anthropologist
and as a person I, too, was torn between intense
emotions evoked by witnessing the ceremony and an
obligation to render it in appropriate idioms -- for
my reference group, these included notions such as
"functions," "clan solidarity," "sexual antagonism,"

and the like. What I did need that was supplied by
the interviews was correction of erroneous
speculations and, more importantly, an increased
awareness of the difficulty -- for those we study as
well as for ourselves -- in sorting out the
relationships among the individual, society, and
culture. The analysis offered here is only a
beginning effort in the task, but I am heartened by
the legacy of Kenneth Read who has shown us the
possibilities that emerge when we turn a sensitive
ear to what even boys can tell us in their "other
voices."

FOOTNOTES

1. The preceding sketch is based on two separate
    observations of the Ndumba *'ummanra* ceremony in
    1971 and 1972 during field research generously
    supported by the National Institute of Mental
    Health.   The "smoking ritual" and related
    events were not observed on those occasions,
    but were agreed-upon by the initiates and
    several adult males questioned in 1981 in the
    course of research supported by the National
    Endowment for the Humanities and the Institute
    of Papua New Guinea Studies.   I am deeply
    grateful to these sources of support and, above
    all, to the people of Habi'ina for making this
    essay possible.   In addition to the stimulation
    provided by Kenneth Read's work, I have
    benefitted greatly from criticism of an earlier
    draft of this paper by Patricia Hurley Hays,
    Lew Langness, Edward Schieffelin, and Fitz
    Poole, to whom my thanks go and an apology for
    not having developed even more of their many
    insightful suggestions.

2. In 1971-72, only two or three men were
    conducting the bold experiment of residing in
    the same houses as their wives.   The number of
    such trials in 1981 was much higher, but not an
    entirely comfortable alternative as yet to the
    traditional sex-segregated residence patterns.

3. In 1981 the interviewees were young men of
    nineteen or twenty. I refer to them here as
    "boys" solely for clarity of reference.

4. Interestingly, Unesa's speculations may be more
    than that since he insisted that he and others
    actually suffered these punishments when one of
    their number disclosed the details of the
    ceremony to his younger brother. When this was
    discovered by the men, according to Unesa, all
    five of the boys were abused in these ways in

the men's house. The other three boys interviewed, however, denied that they had had any personal experience of this kind and denied that anyone had ever broken the rules of secrecy within their lifetimes.

5. It is of interest to note here Seri's testimony regarding the *'ia'vaati* ceremony, which he had undergone just a few years prior to the interview:

> Q. When you became *'ia'vaati*, did you get angry again with your *kandere*?
> R. No.
> Q. It wasn't really painful (like the *'ummanra* ceremony)?
> R. When they cut my penis, it was very painful.
> Q. And that made you angry with whom?
> R. I was angry that my penis was cut.
> Q. But with whom?
> R. With my *kandere* [who was said to have done the penis-cutting].
> Q. And your father, too?
> R. Yes, my father, too.
> Q. Your mother, too?
> R. My mother, too.
> Q. So you were angry with all of them?
> R. Yes, all of them. We wanted to stay *'ummanra*, but they overpowered us and cut our penes. We said we didn't want it done, but our fathers insisted, and they cut them. They said it would be good for us.

In addition to expressing freely his anger with his father and mother, as with the *'ummanra* ceremony, Seri here again betrays some ambivalence toward admitting, if not experiencing, anger toward his "mother's brother," whose behavior, after all, could not be denied completely.

6.   The significance of this Tok Pisin expression
     might be qualified by the acknowledgement that
     the ceremony is referred to in the Ndumba
     dialect of Tairora simply as *'ummanraaru'waare*,
     glossed as "making *'ummanra*." However, this
     vernacular expression was elicited only with
     great difficulty and I have no reason to
     believe that it was used commonly. Moreover,
     even non-Pidgin-speakers would use the phrase
     "sutim nus" or use non-verbal gestures to
     indicate the nose when the ceremony was
     discussed.

7.   Again it must be stressed that the boys'
     accounts of how they felt when they experienced
     the events described may not be accurate, but
     simply projections onto their own pasts of
     feelings and attitudes they would, or perhaps
     only *should*, have possessed at the time. In
     either case, what requires examination is why
     they chose, in 1971 or 1981, to consciously
     organize those emotions in the ways they
     reported in response to my questions.

8.   At issue here is more than just the matter of
     identifying culturally variable "display rules"
     for innate, universal emotions (Izard 1980).
     My concern and that, I believe, of the others
     cited is with cultural influences on the very
     experiencing of emotional states in the sense
     of cognitively organizing them.

REFERENCES

COHEN, YEHUDI. 1964. *The Transition from Childhood to Adolescence: Cross-Cultural Studies of Initiation Ceremonies, Legal Systems, and Incest Taboos.* Chicago: Aldine.

GEERTZ, HILDRED. 1959. The Vocabulary of Emotion: A study of Javanese Socialization Processes. *Psychiatry* 22:225-237. (Reprinted 1974 in *Culture and Personality: Contemporary Readings.* [Robert A. LeVine, ed.], pp. 249-264. Chicago: Aldine.)

HARRINGTON, CHARLES AND JOHN W. M. WHITING. 1972. Socialization Process and Personality. *Psychological Anthropology.* New Edition (Francis L. K. Hsu, ed.), pp. 469-507. Cambridge: Schenkman.

HAYS, TERENCE E. AND PATRICIA H. HAYS. 1982. Opposition and Complementarity of the Sexes in Ndumba Initiation. *Rituals of Manhood: Male Initiation in Papua New Guinea.* (Gilbert H. Herdt, ed.), pp. 201-238. Berkeley: University of California Press.

HERDT, GILBERT H. 1981. *Guardians of the Flutes: Idioms of Masculinity.* New York: McGraw-Hill.

HERDT, GILBERT H. 1982a. Fetish and Fantasy in Sambia Initiation. *Rituals of Manhood: Male Initiation in Papua New Guinea.* (Gilbert H. Herdt, ed.), pp. 44-98. Berkeley: University of California Press.

HERDT, GILBERT H. 1982b. (Editor) *Rituals of Manhood: Male Initiation in Papua New Guinea.* Berkeley: University of California Press.

IZARD, CARROLL E. 1980. Cross-Cultural Perspectives on Emotion and Emotion Communication. *Handbook of Cross-Cultural Psychology, Vol. 3, Basic Processes.* Harry C. Triandis and Walter Lonner, eds.), pp. 185-221. Boston: Allyn and Bacon.

KEESING, ROGER M. 1982. Introduction. *Rituals of Manhood: Male Initiation in Papau New Guinea.* (Gilbert H. Herdt, ed.), pp. 1-43. Berkeley: University of California Press.

LANGNESS, LEWIS L. 1974. Ritual, Power, and Male Dominance in the New Guinea Highlands. *Ethos* 2:189-212.

LEVY, ROBERT I. 1982. On the Nature and Functions of the Emotions: An Anthropological Perspective. *Social Science Information* 21:511-528.

POOLE, FITZ JOHN PORTER. 1982. The Ritual Forging of Identity: Aspects of Person and Self in Bimin-Kuskusmin Male Initiation. *Rituals of Manhood: Male Initiation in Papua New Guinea.* (Gilbert H. Herdt, ed.), pp. 99-154. Berkeley: University of California Press.

READ, KENNETH E. 1954. Cultures of the Central Highlands, New Guinea. *Southwestern Journal of Anthropology* 10:1-43.

READ, KENNETH E. 1955. Morality and the Concept of the Person Among the Gahuku-Gama. *Oceania* 25:233-282.

READ, KENNETH E. 1965. *The High Valley.* New York: Charles Scribner's Sons.

SPIRO, MELFORD E. 1953. Ghosts: An Anthropological Inquiry into Learning and Perception. *Journal of Abnormal and Social Psychology* 48:376-382.

TUZIN, DONALD F. 1982. Ritual Violence among the Ilahita Arapesh: The Dynamics of Moral and Religious Uncertainty. *Rituals of Manhood: Male Initiation in Papau New Guinea.* (Gilbert H. Herdt, ed.), pp. 321-355. Berkeley: University of California Press.

WATSON, JAMES B. 1972. Talking to Strangers. *Crossing Cultural Boundaries: The Anthropological Experience.* (Solon T. Kimball and James B. Watson, eds.), pp. 172-181. San Francisco: Chandler.

YOUNG, FRANK. 1965. *Initiation Ceremonies: A Cross-Cultural Study of Status Dramatization.* Indianapolis: Bobbs-Merrill.

The Accountability of Sambia Initiates

Gilbert H. Herdt

INTRODUCTION

What are the processes through which moral personhood develops and how shall we anthropologists understand the human consequences of such for individual and societal adaptation? This theme underlies the seminal works of K.E. Read and, in this essay, I wish to pay him tribute by studying one of its Melanesian forms: the moral accountability of ritual initiates among the Sambia, a hunting and horticultural people of the Eastern Highlands, Papua New Guinea.[1]

Usually we think of moral behavior as a product of developmental continuity. Children learn moral precepts and conduct from parents and other caretakers within the total "environmental conditions" (Mead 1930:205) of early socialization. Later social learning merely builds upon the early core. What one sees in adult morality is a florescence of the good and bad found in impoverished rendition in children. Moral development in tribal societies has thus been stereotyped as a steady progression of social transitions into adult social relationships, with their networks of rights and duties. Indeed, the

personhood, in the Maussian sense, is synonymous
with the moral agent acting in concert with custom
albeit supported by social sanctions. Being moral
is therefore isomorphic with customary social
development: there can be no contradiction between
them.[2]

When attuned to questions more specifically
concerned with social learning, not morality, this
paradigm has fared rather badly the last 40 years,
at least in anthropology (reviewed in Spindler and
Spindler [1982]). One need only mention their
advertisements -- "the famous studies purporting to
show that the Oedipus complex was backwards in the
Trobriands, sex roles were upside down in Tchambuli,
and the Pueblo Indians lacked aggression (it is
characteristic that they were all negative -- 'but
not in the South')" -- as Geertz (1972:23) put it,
to recall old nature/nurture controversies, complex
issues over-simplified and which still haunt us,
that anthropology had ruled on in favor of simple
social learning. In the same period, however,
Bateson (1958:133ff.) showed how initiation made
novices "contra-suggestible to the female ethos" in
Iatmul culture; Sapir (1938) reminded us that
cultural patterning does not rule out individual
variation and, indeed, suggests individual
creativity; and, more importantly, Ruth Benedict
(1938) -- who made this behaviorist paradigm happen
-- argued for recognition of basic *discontinuties* in
socialization, from childhood to adulthood, both
among tribal and Western groups. Many later
studies[3] could be adduced to make the same point:
adult social behavior is neither merely nor always
the product of steady, accumulating, social
learning.

For tribal societies, ritual initiation is a
particularly striking example of discontinuity in
socialization and cultural training. Since the
early studies of Margaret Mead, Gregory Bateson, and
John Whiting, New Guinea cultures have emerged as a
kaleidoscope of ways through which traumatic rituals
produce adult persons in the context of discordant

social development (Herdt 1982a). Male gender identity and sex role dramatization are two areas in which extreme discontinuity between childhood and adult experience have long been recognized (Whiting et al. 1958; Young 1965). More recently I have reviewed male initiation as a psychocultural mechanism for "radical resocialization" in the emergence of gender identity and social behavior among Sambia (Herdt 1981).

But what about morality? To return to my original point: if social development can be the product of cultural discontinuities, as instanced in the case of male initiation, can a people's morality be likewise understood? Can the things people see as good and bad be turned around, even inverted, for children versus adults *because* of a social institution like initiation? Indeed, can the radical transformation of personhood in boys -- requiring concomitant changes in their moral obligations -- be the very object of men's efforts to initiate them? For Sambia the answer to these questions is emphatically yes.

It was Read's (1952, 1955) work that first raised such questions in Highlands studies. His classic essay, "Morality and the Concept of the Person," showed us a logic of situational morality pervasive in Gahuku-Gama culture. He argued also that the men's moral reasoning was, like the contradictions in their ideas about maleness and femaleness, strongly related to ritual experience and their social identities as ritual personae. Elsewhere, Van Baal (1966) examined similar contradictions between Marind-anim men's ritual repudiation of, but dependence upon, women. Tuzin's (1982) recent essay on ritual violence takes seriously a study of related moral issues. Tuzin reviewed the evidence for a moral contradiction between images of ritual violence versus domestic harmony among the Ilahita Arapesh. He persuasively documented, in effect, the personal signs of men's guilt in coping with an institutionally imported system that increasingly troubles them as they

discover the ultimate truth of initiation: that it
is what men, not what their gods, do.   The Ilahita
elder lives with responsibility for this secret.
These scholars' works have made possible the
construction of the problem of my essay; I believe
their viewpoints encompass other Melanesian
societies -- including the Sambia.

                        THE PROBLEM

    How shall we understand the cultural and
psychodynamic transformation through which Sambia
boys -- reared in a domestic world of profane women
-- become self-accountable to the ritual-based
moral norms of the men's secret cult?   What are the
mechanisms that produce this transformation?   What
kind of personhood do they produce?[4]   These problems
inform my essay, though, for lack of space, I only
allude to them here.   Sambia themselves see the
nature, morality, and personhood of boys (and girls)
as being fundamentally different from, and, in some
respects, antithethical to, that of adults.   And
only initiation bestows upon males the good things
in life and makes them moral.   This view is our
departure-point.
    Since the earliest period of living among
Sambia I have been impressed by an interpersonal
phenomenon I shall refer to as "accountability."
Though ellusive, its effects reach into virtually
every cultural domain and social arena in Sambia
life, from rhetoric to eating.   I believe
furthermore that its systemic centrality is in large
measure due to warfare and the institutionalization
of secrecy in Sambia society.   The totality of its
elements have no ready counterpart in Western
urbanized life.   (But spend a month in any American
farm town and see how accountability is laced into
everyday existence.)   Nevertheless, living with
Sambia has taught me some rudiments of being
accountable.

A common example: Moondi -- a young bachelor friend -- once said to me, "We [Sambia] ask a lot of questions . . . [of each other]: 'What are you doing?' We want to know: 'What is he [person] doing? Where is she going? [or] Where have they been?' That's our fashion [*pasendu*: custom and interpersonal style]."

But there also is an inner dimension of accountability. Again, Moondi: "You've got to think about [pay notice to] all the others -- what do they think of you?" So being accountable can mean, among other things, knowing that someone knows you know he can at any moment ask you to make account of your actions. Thus, being accountable involves also a "desire" to construe one's experience as if it had to be accounted for to significant others. (This intersubjective idea has no cover term in the vernacular, and it is not fully conscious in social thought.)

Sambia expect one another to make account of themselves. Such expectations take two forms: "outside" behavior and "inside" experience. Stated simply, being accountable for adult men means knowing one must always be prepared to show (i.e., candidly express, rationalize, disguise, hide, or lie) that one's behavior *conforms to ritual directives*. In other words accountability, begun in infancy and nourished in childhood, takes its adult forms directly from ritual initiation. (This generalization holds for both males and females; however, I[5] shall here speak mainly to male experience.) The trick is that many of these ritual directives are secret: they are hidden from women and children. Other directives (especially related to sexual activity) are not secret but they are kept private, and men and women mutually hide these things from children. Therefore, children are not -- and cannot be -- accountable persons in certain arenas of social life. How do we interpret these "nots" and the awareness that later replaces them in adulthood?

The hermeneutic issues involved in the notion
of accountability, as an object of interpretation,
lay at the heart of many great debates in the human
sciences about the[6] relations between the individual
and social order. In ordinary language the Oxford
dictionary defines accountability as "being liable
to be called to account," "to be counted on," and
"to be attributed to." What is essential is the
theoretical recognition of the cybernetic
interaction between experiencing the "desire" to
account for, and the behavioral self-control of,
one's communications as a product of subjective
"reference values" (Powers 1973:45). As an
interpersonal process, accounting behavior consists
of forming and testing "hypotheses" about customs
and interpersonal behavior *vis-a-vis* perceptual
feedback from within the person's symbolic
environment. Thus, accountability is best
understood in terms of what Bateson (1972) calls a
"psychological frame" -- a complex set of premises
for coding discrepant contexts and therein
articulating the pieces of identity we call the
self. Achieving personal accountability to the
norms of masculine personhood must be counted as a
key function and outcome of final initiation into
adulthood. But even then the need to be accountable
remains so powerful that for the top ranking elder,
too, it would difficult to boast (like the poet
Steele): "I am accountable to no man."

What is remarkable about the emergence of
accountability in Sambia boys is not that it occurs,
but rather that it is so diffuse in children, so
sharp and focused so quickly in ritual initiates; so
much so that within the space of a few months after
initiation they are able to switch "frames" --
between the norms of public situations and the
negotiation of secret domains -- like any competent
cult member. And this capacity requires some rather
dramatic transformations and moral contradictions in
a boys' experience and social behavior. I shall
study these developmental discontinuities in terms
of the question: What are the underlying moral

premises to which boys, through first-stage initiation, are being made accountable as ritual initiates?

THE SETTING

Sambia are a forest people numbering some 2,000 individuals inhabiting scattered hamlets in part of New Guinea's most rugged terrain -- the southern fringes of the great Eastern Highlands. Their hamlets are small enclosures built atop mountain ridges for defense and proximity to the forest. Before pacification (1964-1965) they were pallisaded against attack, for warfare was chronic and destructive, such that no aspects of individual or group existence were unaffected. Hamlets cluster in several river valleys, within which neighboring hamlets are in earshot of one another. Historically these local groups engaged in bowfights with one another; at other times they united to form war parties in raiding neighboring enemies. But these hamlets also intermarried and staged joint initiations. Thus, men became age-mates and members of the men's secret cult, while also being potential and real affines and enemies.

Hamlet social organization is based on principles of patriclanship and patrivirilocal residence after marriage. Marriages are arranged between exogamous clans, resulting in the common Highlands pattern of women moving into the hostile hamlets of their husbands (Meggitt 1964). Relationships between the sexes are markedly polarized alongside of a strict sexual devision of labor, men being hunters, men and women gardeners. Men, their wives and children, reside in "women's houses," whereas all unmarried initiated males live in a hamlet's men's clubhouse, which is strictly tabooed to all females. But married men, too, look to the clubhouse for social recognition and esteem, and they sleep there in times of ritual activity (as they did before, prior to war raids). The clubhouse

is the center of all secret and ritual plans and
discourse. Furthermore, the entire hamlet is
spatially divided into "male" and "female" spheres,
with pathways and spaces off limits to the opposite
sex. Every Sambia hamlet has, therefore, distinct
spheres which are defined either as "public" or
"private" or "secret." And this institutionalized
segregation is remarkable in such small worlds.

The regionally organized male initiatory cult
is the chief institution through which this
ritualized sexual polarity is constructed and
maintained. Like any complex institution it has
many facets; yet it is instrumental in training boys
to be warriors as well as economic producers, and it
is ultimately charged with the psychosocial
production of masculine persons and the social
reproduction of Sambia society. Through its social
controls the men's cult perpetuates a ritualized
hierarchy: first come elders, then married men,
bachelors, and lastly, prepubescent initiates.
Elders manage public affairs and hold political (and
some supernatural) power over women and children.
The male ideology surrounding this cult disparages
women as contaminating and depleting beings,
inferior to men in every sense -- except the
reproductive one. Women are seen as antithetical to
biologic maleness, masculine social performance, and
to the secret cult. Moreover, secrecy -- which is
intricate and which the Sambia have virtually made
into an art form -- so completely entangles
male/female relationship that its political and
magical embellishments are everywhere, painstakingly
etched into male identity, ritually appropriating
whole domains of cultural knowledge and experience.
Their twin effects color all heterosexual
relationships, strain families, and sour some
aspects of marriage. The women's world is also
mysterious and in some ways secret *vis-a-vis* men.
The structural effect of the male cult, then, as I
have argued elsewhere, is the existence of distinct
male and female subcultures (Herdt 1981, 1982a,
1982c).

To understand the effects of sexual polarity on male accountability it is necessary to take a twofold view of ritual-based social controls: *internal* social order and hierarchy inside the male cult versus the *external* controls of the cult exerted within the public domain of hamlet and family life.

The initiatory cult thoroughly regulates male development from late childhood into old age. Every male is initiated without exception; firststage initiation makes one a member of a fixed regional age-set, and there are six stages of initiation corresponding to six distinct age-grades. An elaborate belief system underlies and rationalizes male initiation according to the conviction that males, unlike females, are not "naturally" (biologically and socially) complete at birth; extensive ritual treatment -- including years'-long ritualized homosexual contact -- is needed for a boy to achieve biological reproductive competence. The collective initiatory cycle occurs every 3 or 4 years during which first-, second-, and third-stage rites are held. First-stage initiation comes when boys are 7-10 years old. It is a traumatic break with mother, children, the female subculture, and, in general, it brings an end to social irresponsibility. Second-stage initiation is held for boys 10-13 years old. Third stage initiation (a puberty rite) recognizes youths' (14-16 years old) competence: sexually, making them fellateds in secret homosexual contacts with younger initiates (insertees); and socially, making them economic producers and soldiers in the front ranks of the warriorhood. Again, these collective initiations are jointly performed in times of peace by the loose knit confederation of neighboring hamlets. The final three initiations, on the other hand, are organized by single hamlets for particular youths, underlining their individualized character as celebrations of "life-crisis events for youths and their prospective brides." After the birth of two

children, a man is accorded full adult status
(*aatmwunu*), as is his wife.

Initiation thus perpetuates a hierarchical set
of ritual categories of male personhood involving
social statuses, roles, and their attendant rights
and duties in male/male relationships. At the most
basic level of contrast these categories distinguish
all males (*aatmwol*) from all females (*aambelu*).
There are four major categories of ritual-based
personhood. (1) All first-stage and second-stage
initiates are categorized as *kuwatni'u*, which I
shall refer to as "initiate." *Kuwatni'u* are
subordinates of all older males, who exercise
political and sexual control over them. As
age-mates, though, they are peers and competitors.
(2) Third-stage initiates are classed as *aatmwol
nungenyu* (literally "male bamboo"), or
bachelor-youths. They are prototypic "bachelors"
because they are sexually mature insertors who are
seen as being eligible for marriage. Fourth-stage
initiates are anomalous in some ways, for they are
married but not cohabiting with their wives. They
live in the clubhouse and engage in homosexual
practices. So they are often referred to as
nuposha, their ritual status title. (3) However,
nuposha are sometimes situationally categorized with
fifth-stage and sixth-stage initiates as *aatmul
chenchorai*, a term best translated as "newlywed."
(Their wives have corresponding social statuses.)
(4) The final category, *aatmwunu*, is bestowed upon
men who have fathered children. *Aatmwunu* means for
them reproductive competence and jural/moral
authority over younger initiates, women and
children. In this essay, though, I am mainly
concerned with the category of *kuwatni'u* --
initiates.

The ritual cult powerfully influences
relationships between the sexes in the public domain
of the hamlet, some of which controls directly
follow from the cultural definitions of male persons
noted above. Examples: all initiates must
stringently avoid all females; initiates and

bachelors are expressly forbidden to engage in any premarital heterosexual contacts; women are answerable to their husbands for many of their actions since they are under constant suspicion of adultery and sorcery; each sex is expected to play its ascribed part in social activities: initiates are shamed if they fail to do so; and all initiated males must uphold the secrecy of ritual traditions *vis-a-vis* women or be punished (ultimately with death). The dynamics of these ritual directives are reducible to a few principles: elders and men are superordinates over all other persons; men are in complementary relationships to women, who are defined as their subordinates; older males dominate younger initiates in complementary relationships; age-mates are a cohort in symmetrical relationships to one other; yet all males are ultimately accountable to the *secret directives of the male cult*, to which they (and indirectly women) are subordinated (Bateson, 1958). While these controls draw their power from male ritual, their effects protectively ensure the maintenance of the hamlet as a whole community.

I will examine these ritual directives in some detail below. What matters here is analytic recognition of their dual nature. Having sketched how the ritual cult orders social behavior in ways that intrude into public life, I should also establish the reverse perspective: the effects of certain domestic patterns upon ritual behavior. My concern is with the young initiates' accountability to ritual-based moral directives. The fact is: domestic influences cut across these moral directives in three important respects.

First, in spite of the divisive intrusions of the ritual cult, Sambia are a gregarious people with a strong sense of sociality and notions about what constitute "good" (*singundu*) and "bad" (*maatnu-maatnu*) behavior in everyday life. For children and adults alike, the list of these moral norms is simple and sensible: one should be hospitable and share food (or consumables like

tobacco); one should not steal or destroy others'
property; one should not physically harm others or
shame them; one should provide for self and family
and not be lazy; and one should converse with
others, follow parents' instructions, be good to
one's word, but not meddle too much in others'
affairs. For adults, moreover, the list would
include more serious injunctions pertaining to
ritual, fighting with or killing (except in
self-defense) one's kin or affines, and never
engaging in heterosexually promiscuous or adulterous
behavior. All of these norms, incidentally, apply
only to one's social world (from one's village to
close neighbors) in successively weaker degrees.
Enemies are not human; therefore killing, raping, or
looting among them are not moral violations (Read
1955). All Sambia share in these morals; that is
what makes them Sambia. Thus, in childhood before
initiation, boys are exposed to a moral system to
which they are always bound in certain ways. The
men's ritual rhetoric may belie these shared roots
planted in the same soil of public life and the
women's subculture, but it cannot erase them.

Sambia definitely recognize, though, moral and
personality differences among individuals. Common
expressions of this recognition can be found in
unelicited remarks that so-and-so is a good
story-teller or a sayer of funny things; that some
men are great hunters and fearless warriors, while
others are rubbishy; or that some women are
industrious gardeners and really generous with their
food, while others are lazy or stingy. Why are
people this way? Eccentricity, biological
inheritance, clan differences, bad spirit
influences; the accounts offered in response may
vary, but the principles are the same, which leads
to the second domestic influence.

It is ultimately one's thought (*koontu*)[8] which
is responsible for individual traits. (And this
form is the syntactical construction these accounts
take.) When saying why so-and-so has a particular
habitualized behavior pattern people say: "That's

just his fashion" or "that's his thought."
Sometimes spontaneously, and at other times after
being asked, people will say: "That was the fashion
of his father" (or "of her mother"). Many behaviors
are alternatively attributed either to custom,
ritual teachings, ancestral ways, or myth. Moral
and personality nuances are products of one's
koontu. In dream reports, moreover, *koontu* is a
signifier of one's conscious waking personality.
Indeed, the category term which comes closest to the
Western idea of self is *koontu*: one's thought *is*
oneself. Furthermore one's *koontu* should reflect
customary moral norms that define the "good person."
These normative definitions of self, I claim, are
introduced and firmly set in childhood before
initiation. This idea points to the last domestic
influence on morals.

If thought, and hence self, have origins in
childhood, then what is left to conclude but that
selfhood includes aspects of the secular -- that is,
profane -- world of mother and women? This view,
which is implicit in men's ad hoc statements, is
counter to male ritual dogma, though, and both
initiates and men are ambivalent about it. They do,
however, believe that one's soul (*koogu*) is purely
bestowed by one's father, is nourished and matured
through initiation. In private interviews some men
and initiates say they did learn things from their
mothers, although others flatly deny such an idea.
Yet such personal statements are never expressed in
public rhetoric. Even so, no Sambian ever denies
the facts of their biological heritage or subsequent
maternal ministrations. This maternal bond and the
profane world it represents signify the mundane
morals and selfhood noted above, but men are loathe
to acknowledge it. To be polarized against the
women's world and reject it is no less a feat than
the rejection of a part of one's own morality and
selfhood.

To sum up: it is precisely the difference
between childhood *koontu* and ritual custom, in boys,
that is registered in the imperative to initiate

them; following which ritual morals must be
instilled for them to become masculine persons. In
the Sambia world the recalcitrant adults'
idiosyncracies can be indulged, so long as they do
not disrupt the social order. Jural wrongs can be
settled through moots. Some wrongs are
supernaturally punished; but make no mistake that
dangerous trouble-makers are eventually killed.
Sickness and social malaise are dealt with by
shamans in healing cermonies. In these contexts
Sambia believe that the individual's *koontu* has
become "opposed" to customary behavior. Yet the
societal dilemma of how to handle uninitiated boys
is inevitable and of far greater magnitude. Boys as
a cohort are viewed as socially unproductive and
irresponsible: they are a part of the women's world,
yet the women cannot control them. In order for
boys to be made accountable to elders, then, they
require initiation -- to bring their *koontu* into
line with ritual directives. Thus the male cult
conscripts them. Nevertheless, the outcome is a
personally problematic discontinuity between the
koontu -- and selfhood -- they experienced as
children, and the ritual personhood that makes them
opposed to unsufferable moral images of mother and
their childhood world.

TWO IMAGES OF MALENESS

The psychosocial transformation of boys
involves first removing them from the women's
secular domain, wherein they have relative freedom,
and then conscripting them into the ritual cult, the
moral norms of which are obligatory. This dramatic
change is informed by problems of great magnitude in
Sambia society. There is for men an administrative
problem that dove-tails into domestic politics: how
to convert puny and irresponsible *kwulai'u* into
controllable initiates. There is also the
transmission of ritual ideology: how to coerce
initiates into conforming to ritual cult ideals and

their secret directives, social and sexual divisions, and relations of production -- which rationalize the *status quo* social system and reproduce it in the next generation. Hence, boys -- who are "childish" and have "no thought," no moral selfhood -- must be made into ritual persons who not only identify with but have internalized the rhetorical images of good and bad (especially concerning women) perpetuated by the cult. These shifts from coercion to conformity to internalization (Kelman 1958) demand not only the learning of new, even revolutionary principles, but the negation of old ones.

Even a cursory glance reveals the relative lack of discipline and domestic control parents exercise over children, especially uninitiated boys. As boys grow older they become more unmanageable. They have a good deal of social freedom in Sambia life: too small and untrained to be involved in warfare, they are left in the women's care. They are well protected and fed, inside the security circle of the hamlet; hence, life's hardships fall mostly on adults. Sometimes they can be dragged into garden chores by their mothers, or sent to fetch things like water or betel-nut by their fathers. They are notoriously bad babysitters. Girls, however, are much better garden producers, and far better babysitters. Indeed, in general it is considered a chore to get boys to do the little they do, and they are undependable in getting it done. Only when older, near initiation, do they contribute much to their families' resources by helping garden and by trapping rats, frogs, and tadpoles (female foods). Yet they remain unruly: boys disobey orders, quarrel with smaller children, make fun of the men's cult (for instance, by imitating the sounds of the secret flutes), take food, spoil traps, and generally evince a genius for finding exciting ways to make mischief.

In spite of their misdoings, however, parents loathe and virtually refuse to punish boys, at least physically. Mothers more than fathers are involved

in controlling children. Mothers will gripe and
holler at their children if necessary. Shaming is
also used to control children; in my experience,
though, it is more effective with girls than boys.
Teasing and various threats are also used: "Don't
act like a baby;" "I won't give you any food tonight
unless you . . . ;" "It's almost dark, don't go far
or the ghosts will get you," etc, etc. What boys
use as the ultimate weapon of revenge is the temper
tantrum. It is quite effective. They howl and
bawl, literally for hours screaming and rolling
around in the dirt, until they get their way, or
exhaust themselves -- in which case they resort to
sulking. And, indeed, adults hate for children to
cry -- among other things it is socially
embarrassing -- so they often "give in" to a child's
demands, giving them food to shut them up.

Why don't parents better discipline their
children? The key issue is how Sambia view the
punishment of children. In native belief the
physical punishment of children "stunts their
growth," keeps them from "maturing quickly." Even
verbal reprimands are actually frowned upon for the
same reason (see men's bitter castigations of women
for cursing boys, and the nosebleeding of boys in
initiation to expel these "bad words" Herdt (1982c).
Similiar beliefs are apparently widespread in New
Guinea (Forge 1970:273; Langness 1981). Second in
importance is the idea that children have "no
thought," and are incapable of really taking
responsibility in many areas; so it is cruel, and
really foolish, to punish them for what they cannot
do. (I shall return to this point below.)
Children's familial manipulations feed upon sexual
polarity by pitting their fathers against their
mothers over the issue of discipline. A mother will
scold or even hit a child during some conflict while
the father tends to side with the child, and *vice
versa.* The parents then squabble or fight, so the
child goes undisciplined. Children are clever at
this manipulating game, and adults (who were, after
all, once themselves children) know that it goes on.

There is the additional fact that some mothers
pamper and favor their sons over their daughters for
a variety of reasons -- but chief among them is the
(reality-oriented) attitude that one day sons will
replace husbands as their main economic supporters
in old age.

The uninitiated boy, therefore, is seen as a
special and problematic category of personhood. He
is male but not socially or psychologically
masculine. Although an object of paternal pride and
a valuable maternal asset, a boy is a consumer, not
a producer, and he is useless for village defense.
He does not contribute much economically, at least
not as much as his sisters do; and, unlike them,
hard work is required to culturally ensure through
initiation a boy's achievement of adult reproductive
competence. Moreover, boys are lumped together with
women in many ways, and because they run virtually
free through the hamlet (excepting the men's
clubhouse), they are potentially naive transmitters
of female contaminants and thus cannot be trusted to
help preserve masculine ritual purity. The older
boys pose threats to the men's maintenance of
authority over public affairs and the maintenance of
ritual secrets. The unmanageability of a whole gang
of boys in the village eventually plays a role in
the decision to stage a new initiation (Turner
1968). In sum, initiation can be viewed as a
collective measure to place boys under ritual
control, structurally removing them from the public
domain -- whose social hierarchy they increasingly
threaten as they age and sexually mature, becoming
consequential social agents dangerously unrestricted
by adult ethics.

It is this image of childish maleness which is
played off against the other image of manly ritual
responsibility in the rhetoric and ceremonial
symbolism of cult initiation. Men constantly point
to the fine and shining example of older initiates
and bachelors in lecturing boys. The former, cult
members, are strong, virile, and good hunters and
fighters who help their parents in economic tasks

and follow their elders' directives -- as can be
seen from how fast they have grown and how healthy
they are -- despite the dangers of war, sickness,
the forest, and the seductive, contaminating
presence of women. What better rationale for
radical resocialization?

INITIATION PRINCIPLES

The ritual resocialization of first-stage
initiation concerns the production of a new person
and selfhood in a boy. Final success is measured by
outcomes (i.e., body physique, male personality
traits, e.g., prowess, and masculine achievements in
war and hunting) which are dictated by ritual
conventions and defined as "purely masculine, not
feminine."
The first step in this process is the
separation of boys from the profane world of women
and children. Then, through various painful
ordeals, they are slowly "stripped" of the feminine
trappings of that world, a phase often harsh and
violent in Highlands' cultures compared to other
culture-areas (Whiting et al. 1958), and one which
has been penetratingly documented for the
Bimin-Kuskusmin by Poole (1982). Thereafter novices
are subject to the liminal constraints of "batch
living," in Goffman's (1961) felicitous phrase:
elders judge and support them as a cohort against
rigid rules, taboos, and stereotyped expectations
about behavioral performance. But what makes this
long period of ritual training so powerful compared
to the bureaucratized situations sociologists
bureaucratically study -- college fraternities, army
boot camp -- is that in Sambia initiation there
literally are no exits, no alternatives, no
provisions for dropouts (Schwartz and Merten 1974;
Tiger 1970). This is where the Western analogies
fail: the litmus-test of Highlands' initiation was
real (not potential or simulated) war and death and
survival.

In the Sambia model, conformity to custom is good, deviations are bad. The elders (who have, after all, survived everything) demand complete obedience to ritual directives, saying that they know best how to survive. And what eight-year-old child, in traumatic circumstances, would not succumb to such authority? It is essential to understand this context of ritual indoctrination, for it helps explain the moral force underlying all ritual customs, even the ones that make "good people do bad things" (Tuzin 1982). In the face of such authority it is impossible to separate the true from the false, the indispensable from the dispensable. One is -- and must be -- accountable to it all.

Many profound changes are involved in the ritual transition from *kwulai'u* to *kuwatni'u*. My aim is to survey the nature of first-stage initiation by examining the key premises it entails. These premises compel adjustment to the ritual cult in general, and teleologically, they direct a boy's social development along the lines of the moral standards encumbant upon the role and status of being a ritual initiate. I have tried to follow a chronological ordering of the actual events in initiation; however, it will become clear that some of these premises are "redundantly coded" (Bateson 1972) throughout different phases and context of initiation.

1. MATERNAL SEPARATION. Boys are taken from their mothers -- if necessary by force. This physical separation is essential to everything initiation must do: strip away "feminine" elements, instill "masculine" elements, train initiates to be independent and producers, while beginning the cultural transmission of ritual secrets. This separation has several objects. One is physical separation from mother as a protective, nurturant, attachment figure (Herdt 1982c). This detachment also represents a physical break with one's parents' home and hearth. By extension, avoidance taboos forbid any subsequent physical or social activity in

or around women's houses. Sexual separation also means that boys are separated from all other female siblings or uninitiated male siblings, and play with children is ruled out. In sum, these separations amount to boys' removal from the female domain, its cultural directives, interpersonal relationships and events.

The ritual directive here is verbally explicit and could not be behaviorally clearer: *Separate from females; be a separate person.*

2. PURGING ORDEALS.[9] The boy's body is purged of all materials believed inimical to his rapid, "masculine" growth (one of the processes I have referred to as masculinization [Herdt 1981]). The emphasis is upon physical removal or egestion of harmful materials on or inside of the body. The purgings include beatings and scrapings of the skin to remove skin flakes, which thereby "open" or stretch the skin so it grows quickly. Cane-swallowing, which has now been halted, was formerly used to induce vomiting. Nose-bleeding is still extremely important in removing contaminated blood and "bad words" associated with mother and femaleness. These materials are culturally defined as "feminine," and they are all believed harmful, even lethal, to male functioning. Purging ordeals are forced upon boys, often with violence. Yet, as I have shown elsewhere, the ritual premise is that once mature and strong, elders expect initiates to be self-accountable in secretly performing these rites upon themselves to preserve vital strength and health (Herdt 1982c). This ritual directive is also verbally explicit: *Get rid of female stuff in your body so you can be masculine and strong.*

3. TABOO (*ritual avoidance behaviors*). Alongside of egestion rites, boys learn of many ritual taboos required to be an initiate. These directives are of two types: things one is forbidden (*kumaaku*) to eat, drink, or otherwise take into one's body; and what things one must avoid (*kumaaku*) touching, seeing,

saying, or otherwise doing. Most food-taboos are
based on ideas (logical, analogical or metaphorical)
that the forbidden substances are "female" and can
harm one. Avoidance behaviors rule out, on pain of
punishment (and ultimately death), any and all
contacts with women, so that initiates literally
live for years without heterosexual interactions
(except of distant, indirect form, e.g., seeing
women from afar). But these avoidances also include
children and childish games, and the utterance of
one's childhood name or those of one's agemates.
The resulting directive: *Avoid ingesting or
contacting what harms you, which includes many
things female.*

4. INGESTIVE RITES. The other side of the coin is
the directive that one should constantly consume
materials necessary for rapid growth and strength.
Typically these items are defined as "masculine."
They include taro, special leaves and myriad forest
plants seen as ritually efficacious. In this
category semen, taken in through secret homosexual
fellatio contacts, is believed vital to
masculinization. Insemination may be seen as a
confirmation of one's ritual incorporation into the
secret cult; and it is important to understand that
previous ritual treatment (especially the purgings)
necessarily precedes it to facilitate the desired
effect. (However, since other ritual substances are
ingested, I separate this directive from that of
sexuality below.) The premise underlying ingestive
rites is simple: *Get male stuff in your body so you
can be masculine and strong.*

5. WARRIORHOOD. No part of Sambia initiation is
unconnected to warrior training. Boys are
constantly lectured that they could run free as
children *because* men and initiates were vigilant and
provided protection for the village. Now it is time
to take their place in the warriorhood; they must
carry their share of the burden. The image
presented of enemies in initiation is one of

horrible ghouls, or bloodthirsty and ruthless
enemies -- more like superpowerful ghosts than human
beings. They are told that the rough ordeals of
initiation are to make them tough and watchful at
all times, to prevent surprise attack. All their
training and hardship must be directed at learning
how to fight, journey on war raids, keep strong, and
be skilled in survival techniques. Staying healthy
and ritually pure by avoiding anything female are
essential to being a good warrior. They are
instructed to do whatever necessary to grow big and
strong quickly so that they can take part in war.
Even dreams must be watched for signs of impending
attack or sickness that their comrades should know
of. They also learn to watch their dreams, the
shamans, and their own (hallucinogenic) visions in
narangu cult ceremonies and everyday life for signs
of spirit familiars (*numelyu*) attracted to them
which offer protection and strength in war and
hunting (Herdt 1977). Initiates are thus held
accountable to various directives that can help them
be the best warriors. So the explicit message is:
Be a strong warrior.

6. ECONOMIC DUTIES. Among the many practical
aspects of socialization are those ceremonies and
teachings concerned with initiates' economic duties
and rights. Hunting is the most important activity.
Boys are lectured that they must learn to trap and
hunt with bow. It is considered a duty to help
other men, especially one's age-mates, in hunting to
secure meat prestations for their marriage
obligations. In general boys are constantly
instructed to be hospitable to visitors in the men's
house: they must make gardens, harvest, and fetch
consumables (sugar cane, tobacco, betel-nut, etc.)
for others. A range of directives involve the need
to be strong gardeners and providers -- climbing
trees, clearing garden tracts, setting up
supporting-poles for banana trees, etc., and
building fences. Eventually, their wives and
children will depend upon them for this economic

support. Their labor is said to be how they can "pay back" others who have for years supported them. The unambiguous directive here is: *Be a strong provider*.

7. SEXUALITY. The critical directive of initiate life is the absolute taboo forbidding any heterosexual activity. Boys are warned that any contacts with women may lead to sexual intercourse, and that such could pollute them and prematurely rob them of their soul-substance and masculine strength. Furthermore, adultery is punishable, ultimately by death. Therefore, only homosexual contacts are permissible; initiates must only function as fellators (recipients), not fellateds (donors). The secret directive of the cult is for boys to ingest as much semen as possible to grow strong and attain adult reproductive competence quickly. They are, as individuals, self-accountable to these directives for the remainder of childhood and adolescent development. The ritual premise is thus: *Be a semen recipient and grow strong and masculine*.

8. MATCHING WITH AGEMATES. Initiated as a cohort, agemates -- who are thought to be of like age, physical size and social capacity -- are directed to match their peers' accomplishments in every domain of masculine performance. (Bateson [1958] called these "symmetrical relationships.") In virtually all other respects, boys are taught to subordinate themselves to the directives or interpersonal arrangements of adults. But among their peers boys are urged to compete. Indeed, in initiation contexts, boys are verbally judged by the audience as being either "weak" or "strong," a "rubbish man" or a "war leader," according to their endurance, tendency to cry or be stiff lipped, ability to withstand pain, and their desire to actively undergo the rituals. Thus, some novices are held up as exemplary models of "good" novices, while others are shamed or punished for their "bad" failings. Boys also learn that they are held accountable as a

cohort when one of them commits a wrong, or fails to follow instructions; hence, the group is punished for the individuals' failings.   In time, after first-initiation, it emerges that boys are pitted against each other in a kind of "race" to see who grows the quickest and achieves more recognition for positive accomplishments in areas like hunting and fighting.   The premise here is: *Match your peers' achievements (and eventually outdo them)*.

9. RITUAL OBEDIENCE.   The final directive subsumes all the others: learn to obey ritual directives. (What Bateson [1972] called deutero-learning.)   Boys first learn to obey their elders' orders.   Elders are seen as being paramount authorities *in all areas* of initiate life.   By virtue of their age, ritual knowledge and experience, and their social achievements, elders are held up as models to emulate.   In this regard, the moral expectation is that initiates are to follow ritual ways, but otherwise "be seen and not heard."   Initiates begin with no "thought" -- without "good" selfhood -- based on ritual experience.   They have nothing to teach and everything to learn.

Eventually, the expectation to obey ritual elders, or the need to avoid physical punishment for their wrongs, is transferred to the directive that initiates obey ritual customs.   Particularly in the domain of ritual secrets, boys learn that they must do whatever necessary -- including being prepared to kill women or children -- in order to keep the ignorant afraid and ignorant.   Ritual ways must be obeyed and perpetuated at all costs.   Being accountable to this directive, of course, effects: an identification between a boy, his elders and ritual ways; makes the initiate an "insider" *vis-a-vis* noncult members; and also makes him a team-player, preparing to take his place in the ritual hierarchy of the following generation.   The open directive here is: *Obey ritual authorities (elders, customs, secret rules)*.   The covert premise is: *Be one of us (i.e., a cult team member)*.

What may we surmise about the general trends of these ritual directives? It is fundamental to the male ethos that men invariably attend to the concrete transactions between the body and environment in initiation. The body is treated as a vessel: the impact of childhood upon body development and masculine functioning is of great concern. Like a microcosmic stage Sambia initiation scoops up and encloses past experience, sheds past influences, and sets a course for future action. Like most Highlanders (Newman 1964) Sambia attend first to the practicalities of life, which here entails "positive" and "negative" aspects. The body, and housed within it one's thought (self) and soul, is reconstituted and defended against alien (i.e., female) contaminants and the death they bring. Yet these measures also mean affirmation: the body is stimulated to grow and is freed of its earlier shackles.

Initiation directives obviously dictate the moral limits of initiates. Behaviorally, boys must account to them in all social action. Various sanctions -- physical as well as psychological -- are used to reinforce conformity to these standards (Forge 1970:288). Ritual ordeals and such sanctions do create trauma, which, among other things, makes boys angry (even though they cannot directly express their anger), and afraid -- two emotions that are "bad." Yet they are told that these measures are taken to create "good" qualities in them; and the people who say this (father, elders) are known to be good people. Perhaps that awareness is equally as painful: even seemingly harmless words -- "be a good provider" -- can wound because those one loves join others in enforcing harsh and impersonal standards which supersede such love. Subjectively, then, initiates learn in time to explain their behavior by making accounts based on these involuntary directives. So the magical circle of reproducing personhood is completed: the ritual cult has drawn a cultural boundary around one's self through directives that are both internal and external --

enabling the person to take himself both as subject and object in social life.[10]

Take note that the chronological sequence of initiation first instills principles of *negation*. Before boys can be masculine they must separate from the female domain and be rid of female substances. Later they avoid the same. Only then can ritual-based personhood follow. All these advancements require a "rejection" of childhood attachments, social activities, desires. Compliance to principles of negation could be seen as the results of active coercion -- negative punishments (and countervailing rewards) that "brain-wash" one's primary childhood identity (Whiting et al. 1958). Then follows the chronologically later measures of identification: get male stuff in one's body, be a strong warrior and strong provider, etc. These latter directives define behaviors which make it seem: "I am being masculine . . ." (in such and such way). Such prescribed actions, both positive and negative, signify that initiates are becoming "contra-suggestible to the female ethos" (Bateson 1958). Yet the negations precede the affirmations; and I believe that this developmental sequelae in initiation lays down a behavioral pattern in subsequent ritual and social behavior. Thus, to assert that one is masculine, even in adulthood, one first negates contrary aspects of one's existence (i.e., "the feminine"). (Is this why warfare, hunting, ritual, and sex -- the key performative contexts of adult masculinity -- are preceded by purificatory measures that remove "feminine" elements from oneself?) "Brainwashing" is therefore too simple an analogy: Why does one need to keep removing what has been removed? The answer must be that such "rejections" or "negations" or "removals" are identity signs -- to oneself and to others -- that one is still accountably masculine. (When, in later life, negation is simultaneously affirmation, we could label such acts "protest masculinity.")

Ritual accountability has, apparently, three "tenses": past, present, and future. Although accountability to initiation directives can only be observed through communicative acts, its locus is subjective, for one must be able to account for the whole of one's self. For the present, accountability is *behavioral conformity* -- first to coercive rites, then to others' social expectations in customary settings. For the future, accountability is *anticipatory awareness* (e.g., internalization) that one's eventual course of actions must answer to ritual directives. For the past, accountability is the *retrospective awareness* (e.g., fantasy) that one's previous actions are open to scrutiny and must be defensible (*ex post facto*). These frames of accountability are, of course, influenced by many psycho-social attributes and contexts, including social status, ritual grade, age, sex, relationship to one's alter, nature of the encounter, as well as personality traits (self-esteem, paranoidness, etc.). In short, the signs of a particular individual's accountability are set by his social personhood at that moment in the developmental cycle; these signs define selfhood by limiting perception of choices, reinterpreting personal history and scripting in the present accounts of one's future.

Now it is true that every society makes use of such manipulations of time in safeguarding movements through rites of passage, and, thereby, in reconstructing the individual's personhood. Perhaps the timelessness one glimpses in the liminal ordeals of Sambia initiation may even be seen as a "stage of reflection" (Turner 1967:105) necessary to boys' resocialization. Nevertheless, of the negations and affirmations described above, more can be said. Those ritual directives -- the signs by which boys will be judged accountable -- point towards moral splits, institutionalized through initiation, that oppose the existence of initiates to earlier childhood experience.

What is the nature of these moral splits? The most fundamental concerns the negation of the women's world. Sambia boys are reared to be good

people by adults -- mother and father -- whom they
see as good people. What makes them good is the
love they felt for years and the fact that most of
this maternal behavior is defined in public,
especially by women themselves as good, not bad.
Whatever badness preinitiates feel or attribute
towards their mothers (whether it stems from their
own or their fathers' attributions), I believe that
it takes backseat to the positive expressions of
maternal love. Moreover, these public
understandings of what is good and bad do persist:
initiates, like all Sambia, should not steal or rape
or be lazy, *vis-a-vis* fellow villagers. What
initiation does substitute are images like the one
that women (i.e., mother) have bad stuff which must
be purged from one's body and avoided at all costs.
It is ironic that, in later life, men distinguish
between types of females (mother versus wife),
recognizing some as more dangerous than others,
fearing especially their wives; but by then such
distinctions (of which boys are more ignorant) seem
trivial compared to the stilted images long since
accounted to. Thus, although initiation succeeds in
a disconnection from mother and her profane world,
its success in eliminating her presence inside one's
self is more doubtful.

Ritual measures, especially secret ones, help
maintain the compromises inherent in that internal
moral split. Homosexual practices and
nose-bleeding, the most secret of ritual activities,
speak to this issue. They draw their excitement, in
part, from qualities like mystery, secrecy, and
fetishization, which polarize maleness and
femaleness in the world and in one's self, allowing
the hidden expression of the forbidden ("feminine")
part of self -- the compromised part which is never
successfully negated, ritual directives or not.
Here, for example, we see a dramatic split in the
moral norms of sexual behavior: on the one hand,
boys are lauded for being promiscuious parties in
homosexual practices for years; while on the other
hand all heterosexual activity for them is

condemned, and Sambia men are, by and large, prudish and suspicious regarding adultery and their erotic enjoyment of women.

The traumatic nature of Sambia initiation not only underscores the high stakes involved in making boys accountable to a Spartan cult, it also attests to the great moral dilemmas with which men are faced throughout later life. The rigidity paraded as ritual obedience acknowledges that the initiate's moral development is dangerously disjunctive; therefore, it must always be situationally controlled. It could not be otherwise where moral dictates are defined as much by negation as affirmation, despite the objective persistence of notions of bad and good which are basic to Sambia culture.

Being an accountable man is thus necessary and burdensome. An insult or an honor demands an equal show of strength (Herdt 1982b). Such are the accounts of men in public. However, if one sits around long enough and is vulnerable (the ethnographer's nihilism), some men -- in quiet moments removed from life's necessities -- look back nostalgically upon their childhood days as the happiest they have ever known. Can we not sense in such reflections a fairytale wish, not so alien from us, to be free from their accountability?

CONCLUSION

The subject of this essay -- "accountability" -- is actually a study in what Read (1955) called a "category of thought," or, more precisely, a "meta-anthropology" of that category in Sambia culture and experience. That Read pioneered such Highlands studies is one reason we honor him. That we are only now getting around to doing new studies of his old interest shows that Mick Read was ahead of his time.

Viewed in historical perspective the regimentation of accountability in face-to-face

relationships, among the small-scale societies of
Highlands New Guinea, must surely have emerged from
the material conditions of their behavioral
environment, especially warfare. Read (1954:4)
himself first noted that warfare was "the dominant
orientation of the Highland cultures." Boys were
seen as being trained for "physical aggression"
through initiation rites and the social esteem
accorded the warrior role. Even more:

> Physical aggression is not merely a
> corollary of intergroup hostility. It is
> a more fundamental trait, the obverse of a
> more far-reaching insecurity in
> interpersonal and group relations.
> Physical violence and antagonism are the
> warp of the cultural pattern . . . They
> receive innumerable forms of symbolic and
> institutionalized expression. (Read
> 1954:23).

Accountability may be seen as one of those symbolic
forms.

Langness (1967) elaborated a parallel view of
sexual antagonism some years later. Sexual polarity
and politics resulted from behavioral adaptation to
such a hostile environment. Survival of the
community required men's absolute allegiance to
their peers as comrades in village-based ritual
cults. Men had to deny their attachments to women.
Hence, moral cohesion was tied to the usurpation of
childhood bonds and the continous polarization of
spouses after marriage. This ecology of warfare and
sexual polarity thus interacted with systemic
effects upon psychosocial development to produce
initiation cults. These cults, in turn, facilitated
the social training of young warriors, the cultural
transmission of knowledge (Spindler 1974),
recruitment to cult hierarchy, and the reproduction
of the social order governed by men. These societal
continuities, however, were purchased at the expense
of perpetuating trauma in successive generations:
individual discontinuity between childhood and
adulthood.

Because everything that matters most -- village survival, perpetuation of the ritual cult -- depends upon initiation, no exceptions to its fundamental premises can be allowed. Such obedience to strict norms in the narrow quarters of a village is a psychological burden. The awareness that there are no exits is infused in Sambia conceptions of existence and moral action. This awareness *is* accountability; it bandages a loophole in Sambia life. As Nadel (1953:271) wrote:

> The adoption of specific mechanisms of control, therefore, apart from corresponding to the requirements of a less closely geared social system, also represent [that there is] a loophole in a social system too rigidly and permanently penalizing transgression.

The fact that there are no exits makes fierce initiations necessary; and we can understand better why secrecy is institutionalized on a widespread scale; why the self is "disguised . . . to submerge individual in group identity" (Strathern 1979:249); why physical threats, anger, and shaming are pervasive but often veiled (Strathern 1975a, 1975b); and why duplicity and lying are used to keep people in line. These denominators of Sambia accountability are harsh; yet we must not forget that in their view they added up to survival.

What kind of personhood emerges from such a pattern of socialization? Its adult form begins, as we saw, in conscious negation. What is repudiated and avoided is one's primary childhood experience, a sense of self set more in emotional bonds of primarily maternal attachment. What is substituted are new ideas, intellectual training and ideology instilled through ritual ordeals. This later sense of selfhood is equilibrated by ritual directives that demand compliance of the person. Thus, it ultimately is this imperative (to obey ritual authority) that operates as a metapsychological frame[11] for all other directives -- excluding and including certain messages, ordering premises and

contexts of self-presentation, and thereby
regulating communications -- according to a
perceptual gestalt finally matched against the image
of the paramount elder.

In time, what was at first consciously rejected
becomes unconsciously repressed. Freud's
(1963a:214) words on this subject are still
instructive:

> Negation is a way of taking account of
> what is repressed; indeed, it is actually
> a removal of the repression, though not,
> of course, an acceptance of what is
> repressed. It is to be seen how the
> intellectual function is here distinct
> from the affective process. Negation only
> assists in undoing *one* of the consequences
> of repression -- namely, the fact that the
> subject-matter of the image in question is
> unable to enter consciousness.[12]

When Sambia men account to the rule: "get rid of
female stuff in your body," they are consciously
avoiding "female contamination" to remain "purely
masculine." But what this negation signifies also
is an unconscious repression of that "feminine" part
of self they cannot accept and which is kept out of
consciousness. Bateson (1946) long ago referred to
an identical process among the Iatmul as "conversion
reaction."[13] Only in secret ritual and myth, and
then, of course, in a form different from everyday
waking consciousness, can men re-experience
emotional aspects of that earlier, repressed core of
self (Herdt 1981; Stoller and Herdt 1982).

In sum, the outcome of initiation is for boys
to see the women's world as bad and the men's world
as good. This transformation in the boys' ethos is
necessary because of the internal contradiction in
Sambia society that men rule public affairs, whereas
women rear children, and yet a boy's sentimental
bonds must be deflected away from the female world
to ensure solidarity with men. We may "read" into
this necessity a "hidden curriculum" (Precourt 1975)

in a double sense: on the one hand, boys are not
aware of ritual secrets at the start and they cannot
foresee the outcome of their resocialization; and on
the other hand, the men do not seem fully aware that
they are as responsible as women for boys' early
feminine contacts, lack of adult masculine sex-role
training, and the resulting psychosocial "deficits"
which initiation "corrects." The urgent and harsh
ordeals of initiation involving radical
resocialization are registered, I think, in the
relative early age at which boys are initiated among
Sambia (and in groups like the Bimin-Kuskusmin,
Marind-anim, Ilahita Arapesh, etc.) compared to
others, in whom we may infer that the internal
contradictions are not as severe or in need of so
much discontinuity (Herdt 1981, 1982a). Are the men
guilty over their aloofness towards boys? Perhaps.
And perhaps we can see in the harshness and
emotional involvement in initiation rites men's
over-compensation for their lack of childhood
discipline of boys, their ambivalence towards women
and the female world, and their own knowledge that
they, too, were not accountable as children. Not
masculine as their own fathers were not -- an image
which they project onto boys, whose "nots" of
awareness they try to erase and supplant. It is
true that in childhood boys are headed in the
direction of adult gender roles; we can see gender
differentiation already at work then. But the fact
that New Guinea initiation rites occur within secret
societies, contra Precourt (1975), and the boys'
moral images and directives are inverted, means also
that the "messages" initiation transmits to boys are
opposed to those of their childhood training (Barry
and Schlegel 1980:143-144). Being accountable to
initiation directives is eventually secreted in
private rites like nosebleeding (Herdt 1982c), when
one conforms when alone. That final internalization
is most properly called *self*-accountability. It
signals, of course, that one is so well wedded to
masculine norms that he can be depended upon to be a
responsible socializer of boys in new initiations.

Secrecy remains a key puzzle in understanding a complex phenomenon like accountability. If we could describe the origins and dynamics of secrecy in individual development we could then explain the equally perplexing process of switching frames between public, private, and secret contexts of self-presentation. Sociologically, there is no mystery about why secrecy is so important to personhood, for it is institutionalized in many Highlands cultures. Psychologically, though, it is the individual who must be able to manage those constant shifts between secret and public without detection. The fear of shame adds weight to this burden. For, as Oosterwal (1961:121) wrote of the Tor, "In this community, the severest punishment of all is to be made to look ridiculous in the eyes of one's own fellow-villagers." Secrecy also creates the truth value of information (Barth 1975:186), so it becomes a powerful public force (Langness 1974). And what does that do to individual privacy? As Shils (1956:201) wrote in another context: "In order for secrets to be safeguarded, privacy must be invaded." (Simmel [1950] went so far as to describe ritual cult secrecy as a "de-individuation" of the self.) The point is that a society that sanctifies secrecy simply distrusts individual privacy. That is why personal accountability is pegged to initiation instead of being left open to choice.

In the final analysis the success of a society should be judged not only by its survival but by its ability to release human potential (Read 1955), and the latter depends upon its vision of socialization, of its utilization of both childhood and adult experience. As Devereux (1967:36) put it: "Culture both exploits and implements man's capacity for including within his self-boundaries something outside himself." The emergence of the category "childhood" (and concomitant formal education) in Western culture is a far-reaching illustration of how changes in ideas of socialization implicate real consequences for human development (Aries 1962). The "cultural amnesia" of Western childhood belongs to a similar realm as that of Sambia resocialization, though the consequences for human potential seem less clear. Yet perhaps our discontinuities effect moral development more than we suspect: we welcome and value the other only tentatively, as we favor more than all "the freedom of the self to pursue its self-chosen ends" (Van Baal 1981:313), whether or not this results in partnership.

The success of ritual resocialization in Highlands cultures must be measured against the outcomes they impose upon self and social development. Communities survived by idealizing the image of the warrior. Yet this model called for the harshest initiation -- which turned the world upside down -- and still its standards were so exacting that absolute directives were needed to keep people in line the rest of their lives. It is a monumental task to make boys negate their past and repress a part of self. Indeed, the task is so great that long cycles of initiation removed boys, literally for years, from "normal" domestic interactions in the public (i.e., heterosexual) domain. Otherwise, though, Highlands cults like that of Sambia would probably never have been able to regulate boys' sexual behavior or manipulate women (Herdt 1982c). For such Highlands groups, then, van Gennep's old tripartite schema of transition rites, involving temporary seclusion and liminality, followed by reaggregation into society, no longer makes much sense (Turner 1967). For what is "liminal," and what is "normal," in a society that requires a third (or more) of one's life to be removed from public domestic interaction? Where "liminality" extends so long, involving avoidance and hostility to one-half of the world's population, and where rules of accountability brace adulthood, the success of ritual resocialization is tenuous, at best. Better to think that there are two modes of existence -- the domestic, from which one is separated, and the ritual mode, into which one is initiated -- different worlds that are never quite reconciled.

Ritual directives will always be needed, under such a disjunctive developmental regime, to keep men from slipping back into the preaccountable awareness of childhood freedom.

FOOTNOTES

1. Field research (1974-1976, 1979, 1981) among the Sambia in Papua New Guinea has been supported by the following agencies: the Australian-American Education Foundation, the Research School of Pacific Studies at the Australian National University, the National Institute of Mental Health, and the Department of Psychiatry within U.C.L.A.'s Neuro-psychiatric Institute, the Wenner-Gren Foundation for Anthropological Research, and Stanford University. I gratefully acknowledge with thanks the support of each.

2. Except perhaps in the situation of rapidly changing societies, a problem generally ignored in the anthropological literature, but not by Read (1965). Sambia are undergoing dramatic social changes now, but, in this essay, I shall rely upon that convenient fiction "the ethnographic present" (of the period 1974-1976), as the baseline period of my description.

3. LeVine (1963:379), in reviewing cross-cultural studies on primacy effects, has written of "the assumption that behavior patterns acquired early in life are more enduring than and dominant over tendencies learned in adulthood. In cross-cultural studies of personality development like that of Whiting and Child, this consideration does not usually become explicit because the societies are assumed to have a sufficient degree of cultural stability and functional integration so that the patterns learned at different points in the life span are not violently at odds with one another." LeVine notes that Whiting et al. (1958) is an exception to the rule.

4. The question of personhood can be answered in
    normative terms without much attention to
    personality variation. Selfhood explicitly
    raises problems of experiential and personality
    variation that are too complex to examine here.

5. Males and females are initiated separately at
    different points in the lifecycle. However,
    males are initiated years before females; the
    experience is far more violent and lengthy than
    that of females; thus, I believe that it is
    more traumatic and creates greater
    developmental discontinuities. Ritual social
    controls are a relative measure of the social
    and intrapsychic conflicts created by these
    discontinuities among males, which make them
    more accountable to demonstrate masculine
    personhood in more social situations than
    females, an argument taken up elsewhere.

6. I am thinking of the rich discourses on
    individualism and the social contract by
    William James, Freud and Jung; of Weber and
    Durkheim on meaningful social action and
    personal morality; of the philosophers Husserl,
    Wittgenstein, Piaget, Ryle, and Sartre; and,
    more directly, the works of social theorists
    like George Herbert Mead, Ruth Benedict,
    Geertz, Goffman, Habermas, Levi-Strauss, Victor
    Turner and others (reviewed in Giddens [1976],
    Goffman [1974:1-14], and Skorupski [1976]).
    For a pertinent review of Durkheim's theory of
    moral authority that touches upon
    accountability, see Giddens (1976:40); cf.
    Garfinkle (1967).

7. 'Selfhood' here would be isomorphic with the
    whole set of one's identities irrespective of
    discontinuities in socialization (childhood
    versus ritual initiatehood), secrecy
    (experiences in secret rituals versus domestic
    interaction), and role segregation between the

sexes in adulthood. Thus, it includes: one's earliest sense of awareness of existence and identifications with loved objects (including unconscious fantasies of "inserts": Leites [1970:82-83]; life goals -- in *childhood* -- that may be repressed or consciously secreted in adults; as well as private beliefs, daydreams, and subjective orientations about social matters that one shares with no one else and keeps private in *adulthood* (see Stoller [1979] on erotic fantasies and Freud [1963b:19] on the "solitary" character of obsessive acts and religious practices).

8.   Koontu may be used as a reflexive nominalized verb ("I *think* that . . . ") or as a noun ("I had the *thought* that . . . ").

9.   See Herdt (1981:221 ff.) for a more extended description of types of ritual treatment.

10. Here is, at least in outline, an ethnographic model that responds to George Herbert Mead's old hermeneutic question: "How can an individual get outside of himself (experientially) in such a way as to become an object to himself?" (1934:138)

11. See Bateson (1972:177-193) for a fuller discussion of this metapsychology.

12. Freud (1963a: 214-215) could have been speaking of Sambia when he wrote: "The function of judgment is concerned ultimately with two sorts of decision. It may assert or deny that a thing has a particular property; or it may affirm or dispute that a particular image [*Vorstellung*] exists in reality. Originally the property to be decided about might be either "good" or "bad," "useful" or "harmful." Expressed in the language of the oldest, that is, of the oral, instinctual impulses, the

alternative runs thus: "I should thus like to eat that, or I should like to spit it out;" or, carried a stage further: "I should like to take this into me and keep that out of me." That is to say: it is to be either *inside* me or *outside* me . . . From its point of view what is bad, what is alien to the ego, and what is external are, to begin with, identical."

13. "The Middle Sepik is an area in which male potency is very highly valued. The adult male character is built upon strong prohibitions of passivity and is indeed an over-developed compensatory reaction to latent passivity induced by early female identification." (Bateson 1946:122)

REFERENCES

ARIES, PHILLIPE. 1962. *Centuries of Childhood* (R. Baldick, trans.). New York: Vintage Books.

BARRY, HERBERT III and ALICE SCHLEGEL. 1980. Early Childhood Precursors of Adolescent Initiations Ceremonies. *Ethos* 8:132-145.

BARTH, FREDERIK. 1975. *Ritual and Knowledge among the Baktaman of New Guinea*. New Haven: Yale University Press.

BATESON, G. 1946. Arts of the South Seas. *Art Bull* 28:119-123.

BATESON, G. 1958. *Naven*. 2nd edition. Stanford: Stanford University Press.

BATESON, G. 1972. *Steps to an Ecology of Mind*. San Francisco: Chandler Publishing Company.

BENEDICT, R. 1938. Continuities and Discontinuities in Cultural Conditioning. *Psychiatry* 1:161-167.

DEVEREUX, GEORGE. 1967. *From Anxiety to Method in the Behavioral Sciences*. Paris: Mouton & Co.

FORGE, ANTHONY. 1970. Learning to See in New Guinea. *Socialization: The Approach from Social Anthropology* (P. Mayer, ed.), pp. 269-291. A.S.A. Monograph 8. London: Tavistock.

FREUD, SIGMUND. 1963a. Negation. *General Psychological Theory, Papers on Metapsychology by Sigmund Freud*. (P. Rieff, ed.), pp. 213-217. New York: Collier Books.

FREUD, S. 1963b. Obsessive Acts and Religious Practices. *Character and Culture, The Collected Papers of Sigmund Freud*. (P. Rieff, ed.), pp. 17-26. New York: Collier Books.

GARFINKEL, HAROLD. 1967. *Studies in Ethnomethodology*. Englewood Cliffs, N.J.: Prentice-Hall, Inc.

GEERTZ, C. 1973. *The Interpretation of Cultures*. New York: Basic Books.

GIDDENS, ANTHONY. 1976. *New Rules of Sociological Methods: A Positive Critique of Interpretive Sociologies*. New York: Basic Books.

GOFFMAN, ERVING. 1961. *Asylums*. Garden City, New York: Anchor Books.

GOFFMAN, ERVING. 1974. *Frame Analysis*. New York: Harper and Row.

HERDT, G. H. 1977. The Shaman's 'Calling' among the Sambia of New Guinea. *Journal of the Society of Oceanistes* 56-57:153-167.

HERDT, G. H. 1981. *Guardians of the Flutes: Idioms of Masculinity*. New York: McGraw-Hill.

HERDT, G. H. 1982a. Fetish and Fantasy in Sambia Initiation. *Rituals of Manhood: Male Initiation in New Guinea* (G. Herdt, ed.), pp. 44-98. Berkeley: University of California Press (In Press).

HERDT, G. H. 1982b. Uses and Abuses of Alcohol and the Urban Adjustment of Sambia Masculine Identity. *Through a Glass Darkly: Beer and Modernization in Papua, New Guinea* (M. Marshall, ed.), pp. 227-244. Port Moresby: Institute of Applied Social and Economic Research.

HERDT, G. H. 1982c. Sambia Nosebleeding Rites and Male Proximity to Women. *Ethos* 10:189-231.

KELMAN, H. C. 1958. Compliance, Identification and Internalization: Three Processes of Opinion Change. *Journal of Conflict Research* 2:51-60.

LANGNESS, L. L. 1967. Sexual Antagonism in the New Guinea Highlands: A Bena Bena Example. *Oceania* 37:161-177.

LANGNESS, L. L. 1974. Ritual Power and Male Domination in the New Guinea Highlands. *Ethos* 2:189-212.

LANGNESS, L. L. 1981. Child Abuse and Cultural Values: The Case of New Guinea. *Child Abuse and Neglect: Cross-Cultural Perspectives* (Jill E. Korbin, ed.), pp. 13-34. Berkeley: University of California Press.

LeVINE, ROBERT A. 1963. Behaviorism in Psychological Anthropology. *Concepts of Personality* (R. W. Heine, ed.), pp. 361-384. Chicago: Aldine Publishing Company.

LEITES, N. 1970. *The New Ego*. New York: Science House.

MEAD, G. H. 1934. *Mind, Self, and Society*. Chicago: University of Chicago Press.

MEAD, MARGARET. 1930 (1968). *Growing Up in New Guinea*. New York: Dell Publishing Company.

MEGGITT, MERVYN. 1964. Male-Female Relationships in the Highlands of Australian New Guinea. *New Guinea: The Central Highlands* (J. B. Watson, ed.), pp. 204-224. Volume 66, Part 2, *American Anthropologist*.

NADEL, S. F. 1953. Social Control and Self-Regulation. *Social Forces* 31:265-273.

NEWMAN, PHILLIP. 1964. Religious Belief and Ritual in a New Guinea Society. *New Guinea: the Central Highlands* (J. B. Watson, ed.), pp. 257-272. Volume 2, Part 2, *American Anthropologist*.

OOSTERWAL, G. 1961. *People of the Tor*. Assen: Royal Van Gorcum Ltd.

POOLE, F. J. P. 1982. The Ritual Forging of Identity: Aspects of Person and Self in Bimin-Kuskusmin Male Initiation. *Rituals of Manhood: Male Initiation in Papua New Guinea* (G. H. Herdt, ed.), pp. 99-154. Berkeley: University of California Press.

POWERS, WILLIAM T. 1973. *Behavior: The Control of Perception*. Chicago: Aldine Publishing Company.

PRECOURT, WALTER E. 1975. Initiation Ceremonies and Secret Societies as Education Institutions. *Cross-Cultural Perspectives on Learning* (R. W. Brislin et al., eds.), pp. 231-250. New York: Wiley.

READ, KENNETH E. 1952. Nama Cult of the Central Highlands, New Guinea. *Oceania* 23:1-25.

READ, KENNETH E. 1954. Cultures of the Central Highlands. *Southwestern Journal of Anthropology* 10:1-43.

READ, KENNETH E. 1955. Morality and the Concept of the Person Among the Gahuku-Gama. *Oceania* 25:233-282.

SAPIR, E. 1938. Why Cultural Anthropology Needs the Psychiatrist. *Psychiatry* 1:7-12.

SCHWARTZ, GARY AND DON MERTEN. 1974. Social Identity and Expressive Symbols: The Meaning of an Initiation Ritual. *Education and Cultural Process* (G. D. Spindler, ed.), pp. 154-175. New York: Holt, Rinehart and Winston.

SHILS, E. 1956. *The Torment of Secrecy*. Glencoe, Illinois: The Free Press.

SIMMEL, GEORGE. 1950. *The Sociology of George Simmel* (K. H. Wolff, ed. and trans.). Glencoe, Illinois: The Free Press.

SKORUPSKI, J. 1976. *Symbol and Theory*. Cambridge: Cambridge University Press.

SPINDLER, G. 1974. The Transmission of Culture. *Education and Cultural Process* (C. D. Spindler, ed.), pp. 279-310. New York: Holt, Rinehart and Winston.

SPINDLER, G. AND L. SPINDLER. 1982. Do Anthropologists Need Learning Theory? *Anthropology and Education Quarterly* 8:109-124.

STOLLER, ROBERT J. 1979. *Sexual Excitement: Dynamics of Erotic Life*. New York: Pantheon.

STOLLER, R. J. and G. H. HERDT. 1982. The Development of Masculinity: A Cross-Cultural Contribution. *Journal of the American Psychoanalytic Association* 30:29-59.

STRATHERN, A. J. 1975a. Veiled Speech in Mount Hagen. *Political Language and Oratory in Traditional Society*. (M. Bloch, ed.), pp. 185-203. N.Y.: Academic Press.

STRATHERN, A. J. 1975b. Why is Shame on the Skin? *Ethnology* 14:347-356.

STRATHERN, M. 1979. The Self in Self-Decoration. *Oceania* XLIX:241-257.

TIGER, L. 1970. *Men in Groups*. New York: Vintage Books.

TURNER, V. W. 1967. *The Forest of Symbols*. Ithaca: Cornell University Press.

TURNER, V. W. 1968. Mukanda: The Politics of a Non-Political Ritual. *Local-Level Politics*. (M. Schwartz et. al., eds.). Chicago: Aldine Publishing Company.

TUZIN, D. F. 1982. Ritual Violence among the Ilahita Arapesh: the Dynamics of Moral and Religious Uncertainty. *Rituals of Manhood: Male Initiation in Papua New Guinea*. (G. H. Herdt, ed.), pp. 321-355. Berkeley: University of California Press.

VAN BAAL, J. 1966. *Dema*. The Hague: Martinus Nijhoff.

VAN BAAL, J. 1981. *Man's Quest for Partnership*. Assen.: Van Gorcum.

WHITING, J. W. M. et al. 1958. The Function of Male Initiation Ceremonies at Puberty. *Readings in Social Psychology* (E. E. Maccoby et al., eds.), pp. 359-370. New York: Holt.

YOUNG, FRANK W. 1965. *Initiation Ceremonies: A Cross-Cultural Study of Status Dramatization*. Indianapolis: The Bobbs-Merrill Co., Inc.

Morality, Personhood, Tricksters, and Youths: Some Narrative Images of Ethics among Bimin-Kuskusmin

Fitz John Porter Poole

> To the Gahuku-Gama . . . man is primarily a social
> individual . . . [and] Moral responsibilities
> devolve on him as such . . . .
> Kenneth E. Read (1955:280)

INTRODUCTION

In his remarkable exploration of "Morality and the Concept of the Person Among the Gahuku-Gama," Kenneth E. Read (1955:234) admirably focuses on the lineaments of the "conceptual framework of . . . moral life," rather than on the articulation of and the adherence to moral rules *per se*. Arguing that "moral diversity is not proof of ethical relativity" (1955:279), he emphasizes that he is concerned with a study in "comparative ethics" (1955:233), by which he means theories of value and concepts of human nature and relationships that underlie and inform moral principles and that allow for comparative analysis. Thus, "the ethical contrast centres on a differing concept of man, of moral obligation and responsibility" (1955:280). In this respect, Read elaborates significantly upon Ginsberg's (1968:240) suggestion that a central feature of the comparative

study of ethics must be an analysis of "the range of
persons to whom moral rules are held to be
applicable."

In contrast with certain fundamental ideas in
Western ethical systems, Read (1955:255) notes that
the Gahuku-Gama conception of ethics "does not allow
for any clearly recognized distinction between the
individual and the status which he occupies." The
"moral agent is the individual in his various social
capacities" (1955:280), and the Gahuku-Gama do not
"grant him an intrinsic moral value apart from that
which attaches to him as the occupant of a
particular status" (1955:257). Thus, they
acknowledge "no common measure of ethical content
which would serve as a guide for the moral agent in
√ whatever situation he finds himself" (1955:260).
They do not conceive people "to be equals in a moral
sense: their value does not reside in themselves as
individuals or persons; it is dependent on the
position they occupy within a system of
inter-personal and inter-group relationship."
(1955:250). Despite a recognition of "a certain
√ minimum of behavior which is considered appropriate
to human beings," the fact of being human "does not
necessarily establish a moral bond between
individuals, nor does it provide an abstract
standard against which all action can be judged"
(1955:261). Rather, "it is the social context
itself which . . . determines the moral character of
a particular action" (1955:260). Neither common
humanity nor individual variability are central
features of the ethical system of the Gahuku-Gama of
Papua New Guinea.

Read's sensitive study of this ethical system
remains a highly significant and original
contribution to the anthropological investigation of
personhood, morality, and ethics, both in general
and in the ethnography of New Guinea.[1] He creates a
lens and a framework for analysis that are
exceptionally valuable. Indeed, Read's analytic
perspective provides a splendid example of the
importance of Langness' (1976:97) insistence that

"fundamental historical, philosophical, and religious convictions about the nature of the life process itself" must become a prominent focus of ethnographic concern in the anthropology of New Guinea (Poole 1981b, 1982a, 1982b).

In this essay, I am deeply indebted to Read's provocative insights concerning the relationship between personhood and ethics, but I select a somewhat more restricted and different focus for my analysis, which is only implicitly comparative.   I explore some of the ways in which a special category of "trickster tales" (*utuum-khriin sang*) -- a genre of the broader class of "wisdom narratives" (*agetnaam sang*) -- subtly pose or reveal moral dilemmas or uncertainties and often facilitate at least partial resolutions of ethical problems that are part of the fabric of epistemological concern and everyday life among the Bimin-Kuskusmin, of the West Sepik hinterland of Papua New Guinea.[2]   These stories portray the exploits of *gabruurian* ("wily boy-man being") and *kamdaak waneng* ("wandering woman being") in and beyond the socio-moral order of the human community, and these figures are prominent in narrative images of the "moral imagination" of the Bimin-Kuskusmin (Beidelman 1980).[3]   Although their characteristics are often bizarre, these male and female "tricksters" confront recognizable dilemmas, uncertainties, and problems that frequently arise in regard to the more disorderly, ambiguous, or even contradictory aspects of particular social and personal situations; and the narrative illumination of these difficulties leads to an exploration of matters of choice, judgement, and value that are embedded in fundamental concepts of personhood and of morality and ethics.

Particular selections from this genre of folktale form a mandatory part of the special "moral instruction" (*weeng keeman*) that is given to youths of approximately *kaataarangiinok* age (about nine to twelve years) in their hamlet communities between the first and second stages of the male initiation cycle (Poole 1982b).[4]   These selected stories are

said to contain a "man's path" (*daib kunum*), which
is a theme that is believed to be of special
significance to the development of masculinity and
manhood.[5] Narrated by the ritual elders who oversee
the course of initiation and told at night in the
firelight of the men's houses before an audience of
only newly initiated boys and fully initiated men,
the tales are said to enlighten the youths in
important ways concerning their new identities,
capacities, and responsibilities as "becoming new
men" (*kikiisarokhaimin kunum kikiis*) and, thus, to
prepare them for their new roles in community life
and for the impending second stage of their
ten-stage, decade-long initiation experience.[6]
Indeed, there is a special affinity between this
particular category of "trickster tales" and the
intense experience of initiation -- a relationship
that has not been examined in the literature on
either subject. In the bounded, marked contexts of
these narrations, the boys are encouraged and
provoked to consider how initiation experiences and
community life are interconnected, to explore their
images of themselves in an imaginative manner
released from and yet articulated with the everyday
constraints of the community, and to reflect upon
the dilemmas posed by the constitution of the
individual-in-society.

As Bettelheim (1978) notes, such tales may
provide a boy with a vicarious means of confronting,
exploring, and even partially resolving problems of
growing up, of discovering his identity. Indeed,
the narrative presentation "is suggestive; its
messages may imply solutions, but it never spells
them out . . . tales leave to the child's
fantasizing whether and how to apply to himself what
the story reveals about life and human nature"
(Bettelheim 1978). Yet, the ritual elders and older
men provide certain exegesis on the skillfully
constructed narratives that brings some of their
themes into relationship with the personal, ritual,
and social experiences of the boys. Thus, as
Burridge (1969:410) observes,

. . . narratives run a course in
experience, pose problems and suggest
solutions. And though both problems and
solutions tend to be oracular, forcing men
in community to formulate and make the
moral decisions for themselves, the
process of narration marshals experience,
conjures an awareness of what is involved,
and so generates further comprehensions.

The subtle bracketing and shaping of experience in
this class of "trickster" narratives, however, is
intended to reveal only certain problems of male
development and personhood, and to obscure other
(and often related) themes that can be explored and
understood only in other genres of tales and only
after the ritual experience of subsequent stages of
male initiation.[7]

TALES AND "TRICKSTERS"

Among the numerous categories of
Bimin-Kuskusmin narrative tradition, "trickster
stories" that follow a "man's path" stand apart as
critical lenses for certain facets of moral
discernment. Indeed, they also stand apart from the
larger class of other "trickster" narratives that
are told in different contexts. With respect to
newly initiated boys, these special narratives are
intended to bring into question earlier beliefs and
values which have been largely taken for granted and
rarely brought into discussion, and to transfigure[8]
the social landscape of boyhood before initiation.
In introducing the youths to problems of cultural
understanding and social action in the realm of men,
the tales are concerned with not only commonly
expressed precepts, but also ambiguities and
contradictions that are inherent in their cultural
interpretation and social implementation. The moral
points to be made in these narratives are almost
never made without equivocation; they do not offer
ready answers to simple and naive questions. Youths

are not expected to be able to reflect articulately
upon moral codes and propositions and ethical
principles, but they are believed to have the
capacity to recognize many significant distinctions
and principles that, under the guidance of the
elders, must enter into their imaginative
interpretations. In such stories, every idea,
action, or reference is set against a background
which embodies myriad images, themes, associations,
reinforcements, negations, ambiguities, and
possibilities that are latent or manifest at
different moments in the narrative, and features of
this background are more or less recognizable to the
boys. Other, less apparent features and
implications are provided in the commentary offered
by their elders, who do not explain the tales,
however, in an unambiguous manner. Indeed, these
stories serve most forcefully both as a means of
moral instruction and as an exploration of the
ethical premises of a moral order by subtly
interweaving the known and the unknown, the
apparently given and the unexpectedly doubtful, the
consistent and the contradictory, in a manner that
is both continuous and discontinuous with the boys'
prior experience in the community.

The narratives often establish an initial scene
or situation and a protagonist which are ambiguous.
The expected boundaries which define common, but
important social distinctions, categories, statuses,
groups, and symbolic constructions are temporarily
blurred in a manner that is believed to lay the
groundwork of ethical dissonance by promoting
uncertainty, doubt, ambivalence, and anxiety. Thus,
Bimin-Kuskusmin "trickster tales" characteristically
constitute moral dilemmas by portraying both subtle
and outrageous violations of cultural categories,
social experience, and moral order. Both
affectively and cognitively, by negating,
confounding, or holding in abeyance certain
conventional meanings, they encourage active
engagement and imaginative participation in their
focal themes as the boys struggle to reflect

critically upon traditional customs and values that, for them, have remained poorly understood but largely untested and unchallenged. By realizing and interpreting these customs and values in narrative images, the stories can explore the interplay between what is socially given and what is imaginatively possible in a manner that is both recognizable and yet not firmly constrained by conventional formulation. The plots and the characters both resemble and differ from normative experience of social reality in that they are simplified, focused, and stereotyped as extreme and limiting cases. Many common understandings of the everyday socio-moral order are dramatically and metaphorically restructured to illuminate particular ambiguities and contradictions within them.

In a highly significant fashion, Bimin-Kuskusmin "trickster stories" are markedly different from Beidelman's (1980:33) characterization of certain, apparently similar Kaguru narratives in which,

No more than one or two principles or problems are explored within a limited social framework, and in terms of accentuated moral facets and short-lived situations . . . *stories avoid the complexities of possibilities in these daily problems,* [but] they do point out implications and difficulties . . . *Their very simplicity gives stories their attraction* . . . These stories are odd, not in the sense that they do not represent recognized characteristics, feelings, motives and roles, but in the sense that, whereas in real life these cannot all be properly judged and met by the same person or in one situation, *here they are clearly defined and resolved. Indisputable, unambiguous moral judgments and permanent resolutions must remain imaginary* . . . [emphasis added]

In contrast, although Bimin-Kuskusmin "trickster" narratives also portray limited themes, much of their appeal and significant function in the realm of "moral instruction" is to be found in their complexity as they are articulated with ritual and non-ritual experience. The narratives open up the possibilities of imaginative exploration of ambiguities and contradictions in community life that the social codes and sanctions of community life itself stifle, repress, and rigidify. The stories do *not*, however, resolve these problems in any unambiguous fashion. Indeed, the stories are intended to reveal something of both the illusions and the triumphs of moral order in a social community -- an inherently fragile order that is founded upon a recognition of the problematic relationship between the person and the individual-in-society which only narratives can display without significant social consequences in community life.

Bimin-Kuskusmin "trickster tales" often explore the proposition that an accepted, traditional pattern of social behavior or a moral tenet has no necessity or certainty beyond the authority of convention (Tuzin 1980, 1982). In so doing, the narratives seem to emphasize that immersion in the established values and conventions of the socio-moral order must be offset occasionally by detachment and experimentation, by a kind of liminal perspective that permits scrutiny of the premises of that order. Thus, such tales present possibilities of the denial, negation, distortion, or inversion of manifest cultural patterns or values, and probe the consequences of these imaginative constructions. The idioms of this narrative exploration are often cast in a form which suggests an indeterminate and problematic relationship between social position and individual disposition, which entails an examination of fundamental Bimin-Kuskusmin concepts of personhood and of the individual-in-society. The images cast in this form play with possible contrasts and contradictions between cleverness and wisdom, propriety and moral worth, strength and fortitude, gluttony and abstinence, selfishness and sharing, ritual secrecy and ordinary deceit, social position and moral character, and the like. Most narrative constructions set these contrasts and contradictions within the contexts of relations between man and woman, elder and younger, ritual adept and novice, and kin and stranger (Beidelman 1980:28-31); of sharing, reciprocity, commensality, and food (Richards 1969:30); and of community and forest (Meggitt 1976:68).

The narratives themselves are complex constructions marked by dramatic irony, in which one character knows something of which another is ignorant or the audience learns something which the characters do not discover. Both subtle allusions and fantastic illusions abound. Metaphors and other forms of trope build upon the possibilities of linguistic expression, but allegory tears at the fabric of expectation about language and meaning (Nadel 1964). Dramatic punctuation takes the form of entrances, exits, drums, chants, silences, and animal noises, and marks the boundaries of critical episodes, emphasizing points of impasse, crisis, and change. Although there is often a progressive movement toward the resolution of moral problems in these stories, the ambiguity of the beginning re-emerges at the end; for the abrupt narrative conclusions rarely exhibit thematic closure. Thus, the newly initiated boys constantly have a sense of participating actively in the narrative presentation by constructing, unraveling, and also interpreting images of their socio-moral milieu, by recognizing themselves and their experiences within those images, and by providing what tentative diagnosis (but *not* closure) they can in comprehending the moral dilemmas of the narratives. This interpretive process is considered to be of special importance to the proper social development of these boys, for, as Burridge (1969:241) has noted in Tangu tales, "Again and again the narratives take up the theme of how boys may be made into responsible men, moral beings

in the fullest sense." Yet, by exploring this theme
in "trickster tales" with a "man's path," the
Bimin-Kuskusmin narratives provide no clear answers.
Indeed, the figures of *gabruurian* and *kamdaak waneng*
are a poor narrative vehicle for bearing the weight
of unambiguous prescriptions of morality or
standards of responsibility. They elegantly serve,
however, to illuminate why moral precepts and social
order rest upon problematic and recognizably human
foundations, and how the boys themselves must
reflectively struggle to glimpse and to sense some
of the ways in which masculine moral responsibility
may be realistically achieved in community life.

Many of the general features of these stories
are well suited to the characteristics attributed to
gabruurian and *kamdaak waneng*, the so-called male
and female "tricksters." I have placed "trickster"
in quotations because I share with Beidelman (1980)
some unease about the generality and utility of the
term as a comparative category or as an analytic
concept, but I have no doubt that the most general
class of the Bimin-Kuskusmin "tricksters"
(*utuum-khriin min*) does possess certain traits that
are not only clearly patterned, but also
significantly overlapping with some central
attributes of the putative general comparative or
analytic category of "trickster" (Babcock-Abrahams
1975; Pelton 1980). In general, the Bimin-Kuskusmin
tricksters, usually paired in stories, are complexly
ambiguous and paradoxical, commonly challenging
order and threatening chaos. As narrative
personae, they are fictional beings who often appear
in at least partially animal form, but they convey
impressions and insights that are derived and
understood from observations of people; and the
animals that they represent are often creatures
endowed with at least some attributes of
Bimin-Kuskusmin personhood. Yet, they are not
firmly constrained by the mores of community life
and allow certain normally repressed desires and
ambivalent attitudes to be brought into focus,
although the consequences of their actions are not

immune from normative moral evaluation and sanction. They frequently possess many liminal traits in being simultaneously creative and destructive, comic and tragic, and social, asocial, and antisocial. Each figure may be both fool and sage, victim and hero. Each character may play the role(s) of male and female, old and young, kin and stranger, or ritual elder and novice. Although *gabruurian* and *kamdaak waneng* are usually male and female, respectively, they are sometimes depicted as hermaphroditic; and their sexual ambiguity may also take the form of exaggerated libido without clear procreative function. Their ambiguous sexuality is bound up with the cultural image of them as cannibals *par excellence* (Poole 1983).

The Bimin-Kuskusmin tricksters are often depicted as deformed or disabled, both physically and morally, and they habitually interfere with and transgress the normative socio-moral order. They frequently violate boundaries, confound distinctions, breach etiquette, break taboos, and overturn conventions in dissolving but never quite resolving the narrative events in which they participate. They play with discrepancies between personal dispositions and status expectations. They are marginal figures in that they are both in and out of the community and often at its edges, both morally and as nocturnal adventurers beyond the periphery of the hamlets. Their solitary endeavors both depart from and return to the constraints of communal life, but their exploits often take them into the remote, dense, towering forest where there is an absence of human community -- thus forcing the tricksters upon their own resources and moral standards. Through clumsiness and shortsightedness, they may appear doomed to failure, but may retrieve some temporary and limited success. Through agility and insight, they may grasp success only to lose it for the moment. By proving themselves to be morally deficient, they may forfeit rights in the community temporarily. By demonstrating virtue, they may claim such rights in a qualified manner. But the narratives show that fundamental aspects of their personhood are almost invariably flawed or at least underdeveloped, and they generally remain morally ambiguous, neither ignorant, nor knowledgeable, nor detached, nor steadfast, nor incorrigible with respect to moral understandings. As their characters and problems develop throughout the course of a story, they illuminate some of the complications of community life and of growing up in a community to the newly initiated boys.

Although many of these characterizations of *gabruurian* and *kamdaak waneng* will be more or less apparent in the tales to be presented and interpreted, there will be some unexpected differences; for these general attributes of *gabruurian* and *kamdaak waneng* are most clearly constructed in narrations of the general category of "trickster tales" (*utuum-khriin sang*), in which these characters are generically classified as "tricksters" (*utuum-khriin min*). Indeed, in the present context, the narrators presume that the newly initiated youths are familiar with these popular stories and the common characterizations of tricksters embedded within them. In fact, the elders depend upon this background familiarity and assume that the boys will expect to encounter ordinary tricksters which, unconstrained by the social forces of the community, challenge and subvert the moral order in their predictable ways. Against these expectations, however, the elders portray images of *gabruurian* and *kamdaak waneng* that are significantly different. In those tales that follow the "man's path" and are a part of the "moral instruction" of manhood, these figures become "trickster spirits" (*utuuum-khriin finiik*), which constitute a special sub-class of the generic category of tricksters that appears only in these particular stories.

As trickster spirits, *gabruurian* and *kamdaak waneng*, or at least one of them in any given story, are presented as immoral personae who ultimately accommodate to or are banished from living in accordance with the moral values of the community. One of these trickster spirits is often contrasted with the other as a representation of the triumph of community standards over the threat of moral disruption, inversion, and chaos. The expected fascination with marginality is transformed into fear and anxiety, but important vestiges of the more familiar ambiguity of tricksters remain as a puzzle.

Although the tricksters and trickster spirits are not rendered anonymous and are deployed narratively to reveal important aspects of Bimin-Kuskusmin personhood, they are not depicted as persons in any usual sense. Rather, they remain morally ambiguous narrative figures that tend to focus audience attention on dimensions or refractions of the meanings of personhood in particular ways and under particular circumstances (Burridge 1969:250). Through this selective attention, these trickster narratives bring into relief significant features of Bimin-Kuskusmin personhood and address puzzling existential problems of the person in a socio-moral order that are considered to be of paramount importance to the newly initiated boys, who must begin to participate in the community as "becoming new men" for the first time and to consider the social and moral consequences of their developing masculinity and manhood in community life. The narrative explorations of these problems, through the interweaving of plots and characters in the trickster tales, not only implicate key facets of personhood, but also entail matters of choice, judgement, and values that reveal critical aspects of the relationship between concepts of the person and the ethical foundations of Bimin-Kuskusmin moral discourse.

ETHICS AND PERSONHOOD

In a virtuoso examination of philosophical approaches to the foundations of ethics, Novick

1981:401) has suggested that,

> The tasks of ethical theory are to
> demarcate both the moral pull and the
> moral push. Ethical theory must show and
> explain why and how the value of a person
> gives rise to determinate conditions, to
> moral constraints upon the behavior of
> others; ethical theory must also show and
> explain why and how a person whose life
> befits his own value will (thereby) be led
> to behave toward others in specified ways,
> why and how a person is better off
> behaving morally toward others -- in
> accordance with their moral pull.

Although Novick is ultimately concerned with
possibilities of objective values and truths in a
universal conception of ethics, this proposal may
also be consistent with a person-centered
comparative ethics of the kind suggested by Ginsberg
(1968) and Read (1955) and explored in this essay.
By focusing comparison upon an analytic concept of
personhood with respect to culturally variable
concepts of the person *and* individual-in-society
(Shweder and Bourne 1982), such an approach may
avoid certain dilemmas inherent in an *a priori*[10]
adherence to some tenets of ethical relativism,[11]
ethical individualism,[11] and social ethics[12] that
have thwarted anthropological efforts toward
constructing an analytic framework for a comparative
ethics (Little and Twiss 1978). Such an approach
may explore the balance between moral pull and push
in terms of comparisons of culturally constituted
notions of the person and of the
individual-in-society as the foundations of ethical
systems that vary more markedly in the content of
moral precepts (Brandt 1959:92-103). Particular
variations in cultural ideas about the person and
the individual-in-society may correspond to
particular differences in the relative balance
between moral pull and push.

This perspective on a comparative ethics must
attend to the foundations of moral obligations,

rights, and constraints with respect to persons and individuals. Is virtue (or vice) intrinsic or extrinsic to the person or individual? What are the features or contexts by which it is recognized? What are its motivations, modes of justification, and "situations of accountability," if any (Much and Shweder 1978)? Is it objective, subjective, or social in its cultural constructions and social recognitions? Is it mandatory either objectively, subjectively, or socially? What are the cultural analogs of Kant's (1959) "categorical imperative," Freud's (1962) "superego," or Durkheim's (1974) "collective conscience," if any? Under what circumstances, if any, may legitimate interference constrain the person or individual in the name of morality? What forms may such interference take? What is the nature of the relationship between the jural and the moral with respect to persons and to individuals? What constitutes moral injury? How does it extend to the person or individual? How is protection from moral harm conceived and implemented? What is included within the sphere of the person or individual that is vulnerable to harm and worthy of protection? What are the relevant similarities and differences among persons or individuals that are linked to equal or unequal moral status and treatment? These and related questions concerning moral obligation, right, and constraint must be embedded in considerations of the morally relevant attributes and capacities of the person or individual -- that is, the boundaries, extensions, "natural" endowments, gender, maturity, social identity, ethnicity, social encompassment, autonomy, agency, rationality, judgement, responsibility, intentionality, and so on, of the person or individual.

The conception of personhood refers to those critical, culturally constructed attributes, capacities, and signs of "proper" social persons that mark a moral career (and[13] its jural entitlements) in a particular society. Personhood involves some attribution of culturally delimited

powers to the person that are linked to notions of
control and intentional agency in a socio-moral
order and to related ideas of responsibility for
judgement, choice, and action.[14] Although such
powers may also be linked to notions of bodily
structures, states, processes, and
interrelationships, which may provide some
foundations, limitations, and idioms for their
expression, corporeal limits neither encompass nor
define the person.[15] Indeed, persons tend to be
essentially social beings that develop gradually and
to different extents in a "culturally constituted
behavioral environment" (in Hallowell's phrase). It
is important to note, however, that the attributes,
capacities, and signs of personhood may be imposed
upon (or denied to), in whole or in part, not only
particular human actors,[16] but also categories or
collectivites of human actors, or nonhuman
entities.[17] But personhood typically does not
encompass at least some beings that are recognized
to be human in some manner.

Various endowments of power, control, agency,
and responsibility associated with personhood are
frequently predicated upon a notion of an
experiential self that is the foundation of
judgemental capacity and that is shaped by some
combination of innate, inherited, experienced,
acquired, and reflexively considered and appraised
traits of the person. This more or less conscious,
reflexive self, on the one hand, and the particular
social statuses and identities in which personhood
is demonstrated, on the other, are implied in
Fortes' (1973:311) claim that, for the actor, "it is
surely only by appropriating to himself his socially
given personhood that he can exercise the qualities,
the rights, the duties and the capacities that are
distinctive of it."

Constructions of personhood are variously
posited in different kinds of socio-cultural
systems, but each cultural construct implicates in
some way problems of identifying and locating the
individual-in-society (Shweder and Bourne 1982).

Thus, Geertz (1976:225) is concerned to explore,

> . . . the Western conception of the
> person as a bounded, unique, more or less
> integrated motivational and cognitive
> universe, a dynamic center of awareness,
> emotion, judgment, and action organized
> into a distinctive whole and set
> contrastively both against other such
> wholes and against its social and natural
> background . . . .

The Western person qua individual is considered to
be of interest, consequence, and intrinsic worth,
ontologically prior to society and incorporating all
significant attributes of humanity (Dumont 1965),
and his "moral responsibilities both to himself and
others, transcend the given social context" (Read
1955:280). Although the Western idea of the person
qua individual is historically complex (Macfarlane
1979), it has remained a critical premise of
philosophical concern with problems of ethical
individualism in several forms (Lukes 1973:99-106;
Norton 1976). In contrast, the Bimin-Kuskusmin
notion of the "person" (*kunum*) is most elaborately
and forcefully a social concept, entailing a moral
community of persons, living and dead and bound
together by shared and revered tradition, who
recognize and acknowledge one another's positions in
the realm of social relations as reasons for
actions. Within the Bimin-Kuskusmin community,
ethical considerations attend to differences of
gender, maturity, genealogy, marital and parental
status, residence, ritual authority, and other
social discriminations in a "distributive" form of
morality (Read 1955:257). Beyond the pale of that
community, moral sensibilities do extend, but with
decreasing scope and force, to some other "human
beings" (*fiitep*), but reckonings of a less densely
woven fabric of social relations generally governs
that extension. Most moral concern diminishes and
then largely dissolves long before one reaches the
outer spheres of beings known to inhabit the region
(Poole 1983). Personhood is also distributed into

the "natural" world, marking certain crystals,
cassowaries, taro, pandanus trees, and other
entities, as worthy of moral considerations. Moral
propriety, however, is primarily a matter of
accommodating oneself to a given socio-moral order
that presents a sense of identity and of right and
wrong. Self-sufficiency or moral obligation beyond
the widest extensions of that order are deemed
absurd except in particular moments and under
particular circumstances.

Of course, the very idea of *accommodation* to a
socio-moral order implies some slippage and
ambiguity in the Bimin-Kuskusmin concept of the
social person. Indeed, even Mauss (1968)
acknowledged that the *"personne morale"* invariably
leaves some sanctuary for the *"moi."* Thus,
Bimin-Kuskusmin are often concerned with
discrepancies and contradictions between the person
and the individual-in-society. They recognize that
attempts to monitor and to control vital processes
of "natural" development, socialization, and
enculturation cannot insure conformity to
socio-moral ideals (Poole 1982a, 1982b). They admit
that matters of individual temperament, capacity,
and history do and should enter into moral
evaluations of actions under some circumstances;
that self-interest is not always consistent with the
interests of others, but failures of mutuality need
not be exaggerated, antisocial, or immoral in all
such instances; and that assumptions of determinate
relationship between social position and moral
character often give rise to serious contradictions.
They maintain that the ideal fidelity between
intention and action is frequently uncertain in the
course of events and is sometimes obviously lacking.
Largely individualistic impulses should be mastered,
especially when they disrupt expectations of the
person and moral behavior, but they can never be
either obliterated or ignored in action, or its
evaluation. Individual variability is subtly
entered into moral accounts, and it is implicitly
and, more rarely, explicitly recognized in

Bimin-Kuskusmin considerations of the ethical premises of their socio-moral order. It is in narrative and ritual contexts that such recognitions are most explicit.

ETHNOGRAPHIC PRELUDE

About one thousand Bimin-Kuskusmin live in the rugged high valleys of the southeastern Telefomin District of the West Sepik Province, Papua New Guinea. Speaking a Mountain-Ok language, they note with pride the boundedness, distinctiveness, and enduring vitality of their cultural traditions and emphasize the splendor of their legacy of myth and ritual. Although significant social relations of many kinds bring them into regular contact with other groups of the Mountain-Ok region and beyond, they do not consider people beyond the pale of their own community to be "true persons" (*kunum fen*). They have known something of Europeans at least since the Kaiserin-Augusta-Fluss expedition (1912-1914) arrived at the Telefomin plateau to the west, but on the eve of fieldwork (1971) they still held most moral precepts of government and mission to be strange and without ethical foundation in their world. Indeed, with first direct contact in 1957, the realm of Europeans was still largely unknown and much feared in most respects.

Bimin-Kuskusmin social structure is marked by complex arrangements of kindreds, lineages, clans, ritual moieties, and initiation age groups, and the idioms of agnatic descent reveal cognatic complications. Indeed, these idioms, which are cast in the form of bodily substances laid down in procreation and reinforced in ritual, food sharing, and social participation, are central to constructions of personhood. The hamlet and parish settlements are ideologically associated with particular lineages and clans, respectively, and these communities exhibit an elaborate segregation

of men and women in residence, political affairs,
economic pursuits, and a variety of social
activities and spaces that is carried over into
sexual divisions of labor in subsistence and ritual
activities beyond the settlements. Gender
difference is highly elaborated in myriad ways and
is a central feature of the reckoning of personhood
(Poole 1981b, 1982b). Although ceremonial exchange
is impoverished by Highlands standards, complex male
ritual endeavors punctuate the social calendar and
are one of the primary contexts for the most
abstract, formal exegesis on matters of personhood
(Poole 1982b). In nonritual contexts, however,
certain narrative genres become significant in
explications of the features and contours of the
person and of the individual-in-society. Trickster
tales that follow the "man's path" and that are a
central part of the moral instruction of newly
initiated boys are prominent among these narrative
forms.

In both narrative and ritual contexts,
Bimin-Kuskusmin constructions of personhood are
bound up, implicitly and explicitly, with the
polysemic notions of *finiik* and *khaapkhabuurien*,
which are both complementary and antithetical
aspects of a life-force or "spirit" (*kusem*) that
marks all beings endowed with personhood. The
finiik is a male procreative contribution that
originates in an ancestral corpus of agnatic spirit,
is transmitted through semen at conception, forms a
particular ancestor spirit at death, and is the
idiom of linkage between a person and his clan,
ritual moiety, and initiation age group. During
life, it develops gradually, gaining solidity,
strength, shape, and force from male foods, rituals,
and social nurturance, and from being concentrated
in the male organ of the heart, in which it is
invigorated by its interaction with semen and male
blood.[18] In general, the *finiik* represents the most
significant social dimensions of the person that are
recognized by Bimin-Kuskusmin -- the ordered,
controlled, careful, thoughtful, stable, judicious,

moral, socially proper aspects of personhood. It is the foundation of learning, stores socially significant knowledge and experience, and becomes the Durkheimian *conscience* and valued intellect of the person. It encompasses feelings and thoughts that have a distinctively social character. It merges desire, will, and propriety, informs judgement, and guides action in a manner that focuses upon abstract qualities of the person embedded in social relations and a moral career.

In contrast, the *khaapkhabuurien* -- a less elaborated concept -- is created *de novo* at birth and is extinguished soon after death. It is shaped entirely by the idiosyncratic life experiences of the individual and, therefore, is indelibly marked by those peculiar traits of character by which the person is recognized as an individual actor. Thus, implying an individual with a personal biography who stands out against a social background in blurred relief, the *khaapkhabuurien* represents individual temperament or disposition and the more unmodulated, idiosyncratic aspects of personhood. The shifting contrasts and balances between *finiik* and *khaapkhabuurien* become a common theme for exploring relationships between the person and the individual-in-society, and this theme, focused on matters of ethics and morality, is developed in most Bimin-Kuskusmin trickster tales that are marked by a "man's path."

INTERPRETING TRICKSTER TALES, MORALITY, AND ETHICS

In the interval between the first and second stages of a particular male initiation cycle (Poole 1982b), I collected, translated, and annotated a corpus of thirty-one texts of trickster tales with a "man's path" that were narrated in formal contexts of moral instruction for newly initiated boys in the men's houses of seven hamlets. I also recorded the accompanying exegeses offered by ritual elders and

fully initiated men, the various interpretations
presented by the youths, and the discussions between
adepts and novices about the particular tales and
their moral and ethical implications. From this
collection of stories, I have selected four examples
that represent well some particularly prevalent
themes that are more or less characteristic of the
entire set of recorded texts from this narrative
genre. Because most of these texts are quite long
and elaborate, I present only brief synopses of them
that highlight the focal developments of scene,
plot, and character and that are focused on the
central "man's path," which is considered to be the
"moral kernel" (*dop keeman*) of these trickster
tales.[19] The synopses take the form of carefully
edited, chronologically ordered selections from the
narrative sequence of each text. After presenting
these condensed stories, I trace the general
contours and particular emphases of both the adult
men's commentaries and the youths' interpretations
in order to explore the constructions and
understandings that are embedded in the tales. In
this exploration, I note not only explicit features
of narrative presentation and commentary, but also
tacit understandings shared by narrator and audience
that enter significantly into interpretation.

The skillful narration of trickster tales
involves a complex interaction of form, content, and
performance. However, I shall not deal with the
intricacies of linguistic expression, narrative
imagery, and performative style in this essay.[20]
Rather, I shall emphasize the "strong words" (*weeng
kitiir*), which are said to be the thematic foci of
the stories, and I shall provide the necessary
narrative context for their most common
interpretations. These "strong words" concentrate
attention upon the themes of personhood and of
ethical and moral problems in contexts of relations
between man and woman, kin and stranger, elder and
younger, and ritual adept and novice.

Man And Woman: "Forest Drum, Stream Song"

In the flickering shadows of a moonlit forest clearing, the old *gabruurian* sat on the wet moss beneath a *kuutok* tree. The moonlight made his skin glisten . . . The moonlight showed large sores on his skin . . . It happened not long ago . . . Old *gabruurian* of the blackened face saw a *tiinba* leaf floating in the nearby stream; he wrapped it around his penis. Then he laughed and danced . . . . His laughter echoed in the great cave nearby. He heard nothing but the echo of his wail. A large bat awakened in the cave and took wing . . . The *dapsaan* marsupial looked down from the trees above and shrieked "eee-ah, eee-ah" . . . .

Foraging for frogs and tadpoles, *kamdaak waneng* climbed along the mountain stream high into the misty karst . . . Soon she heard a drum and was afraid . . . She saw a fire in a clearing and hurried on. Suddenly, she came upon *gabruurian* of the leaf phallocrypt . . . He raged at her, shouting that she must go back . . . But she fell against the karst and began to bleed into the stream. Below, the *dapsaan* marsupial came to drink. Night birds stirred in the branches above . . .

Strong *kamdaak waneng* returned warily to the edge of the clearing. While old *gabruurian* raged and spat, she offered him taro in a *kiiran* leaf. He refused and ate the wet moss on which he sat. Then he began to make a drum from the *kuutok* tree. The work was hard. He sweated. He cut the great tree with a sharp piece of chert. Again, *kamdaak waneng* offered him the great, white taro. Again, he refused and then asked her for frogs and tadpoles.

He wailed his hunger and stamped angrily
on the ground . . . When he had grabbed
and eaten them, he laughed and danced and
put his hand on her smooth belly . . . He
sweated. His giant penis moved beneath
her skirt. She cried "I am your *naa-kunum*
("same person", implying a relationship of
friendship, kinship, or common ethnicity)"
and fled into the dark forest . . . .

Old *gabruurian* made a fine drum,
large and strong and black. He looked
about for a skin. Then he saw the *dapsaan*
marsupial in the forest nearby. He killed
the *dapsaan* with sparkling stones from the
great cave and put the belly-skin on the
new drum. The drum began to whistle
loudly and to hum softly. Hiding in the
forest, *kamdaak waneng* watched fearfully
and angrily . . . Old *gabruurian* beat the
drum, and it was weak and unsteady.
Again, strong *kamdaak waneng* came into the
clearing, and *gabruurian* raged. Again,
she offered him the long-grown taro;
again, he refused . . . In a sudden rush,
she took the drum and ran into the forest.
Old *gabruurian* raged and ran after her . .
. He looked and looked for many nights . .
. He heard the drum in the distance. He
heard thunder in the distance. He saw the
flickering shadows of the giant cassowary
beneath the pandanus trees . . . .

Being very weak and hungry, old
gabruurian returned to the clearing to eat
frogs and tadpoles. There were no frogs
and tadpoles in her netbag, but *kamdaak
waneng* had left the taro in the great cave
. . . As he ate, the great bat watched . .
. Then he saw a *dapsaan* in the high
branches and killed it with a shining
stone . . . He saw that the *dapsaan* was
pregnant, and he laughed and danced . . .
His mournful wailing filled the forest and

echoed in the cave . . . The *tiinba* leaf
fell from his long, bloated penis and
floated in the stream . . . The stream
gurgled loudly, and the sores on his skin
oozed pus . . . He called for *kamdaak
waneng*; he wailed and wailed . . . She had
gone to her hamlet far below . . . A great
earthquake shook the karst . . . Great
boulders crashed into a large hole in the
karst and filled it . . . In the morning
light, *gabruurian* began to sing of death
from the high branches . . . He was now
only a bird of the morning and soon flew
into the deep forest . . . .

The trickster narrative portrays a setting that
is ambiguous in several ways. All events take place
in and around an ominous clearing in the high
mountain forest, which is the realm of animals,
spirits, mysterious forces, unseen dangers, and
sacred phenomena. As "people of women's houses"
before initiation, the boys have been forbidden to
venture there and have been threatened with its
bogeymen, but, as they now know well, the secluded
performances of most stages of the male initiation
cycle take place in the high forest. At such times,
it is under the benevolent protection of a panoply
of ancestral spirits and is a place where the male
community displays its power and solidarity and
where the ritual "work" of transforming boys into
men occurs. Yet, it is generally a place of danger
and insecurity, for it is beyond the everyday
protection of the community. The youths are
familiar with other tales that tell of lonely,
desperate hunters and travellers in the high forest
becoming lost, hungry, and fearful of its mysteries
and isolation. Sometimes these wayfarers have never
returned to their hamlet communities far below, and
fragments of skeletons have been found occasionally
in the dense, treacherous undergrowth, indicating an
unknown fate. Legendary wanderers and known madmen,
unable to cope with the daily demands of community

life, have chosen to become hermits in its vastness,
and its seclusion is often sought by forlorn men
intent upon suicide by hanging. One finds the
remains of long decayed burial platforms there, and
the occasional newly built platform displays the
grisly decomposition of a human corpse. The boys
know too that the high forest is not only the abode
of malevolent forest spirits, angry souls of
warriors whose deaths are unavenged, and vengeful
khaapkhabuurien spirits lurking near the burial
platforms, but also the haunt of the capricious
gabruurian and *kamdaak waneng*.

The men's accompanying commentary focuses
attention upon the special significance of
particular features of this mysterious landscape.
The swirling mist, soggy moss, and jagged karst
suggest that this remote canopy of forest
encompasses the "spirit path holes" (*daib kusem
tem*), through which the *finiik* spirits of the
recently dead pass to the ancestral underworld. It
is the realm of the female *dapsaan* marsupial and the
male *fifiir* eagle, who guard these sacred passages
through the karst. It is the domain of the
androgynous, enigmatic cassowary and echidna, who
are associated, respectively, with the great
primordial ancestors Afek and Yomnok. In this
spirit-ridden, mist-enshrouded place, an unexpected
clearing -- far above the altitude of settlements
and gardens and ordinary human pursuits -- should
produce wariness in the lone traveller. It may
simply be a place where special trees have been cut
for a variety of purposes or where a ritual pandanus
grove is being cleared. It may also be the location
of a male initiation site or a sacred shrine, where
trespass by all but ritual elders is forbidden.
More ominously, however, it may be the secret lair
of some dangerous or unpredictable creature, spirit,
witch, or semihuman being, such as *gabruurian* or
kamdaak waneng. No proper human being would remain
long without special ritual protection in the high
forest.

The men note that this particular clearing is
characterized by its proximity to a cave, a stream,
and stands of pandanus trees. The cave may be an
ossuary, but this identification is left uncertain.
This allusion to death, however, enhances the vague
imagery of death that follows *gabruurian's* exploits.
The cave is clearly the source of sacred crystals,
which are represented by sparkling, shining stones,
and is the haunt of the great bat, which is a common
symbol of the founding ancestor Yomnok. It is also
the source of mysterious echoes that transform
gabruurian's laughter into mournful or plaintive
wailing. The ritual taro of *kamdaak waneng* is
placed inside the cavern. The men maintain that the
cave is "sacred" (*aiyem*), but they allow this
designation to remain highly ambiguous. The stream
is presented as both a boundary and a path, as well
as a medium through which mysterious objects and
moral values are brought into the clearing. As a
common ritual barrier, the stream separates the
clearing from both the normal high forest which
surrounds it and the communities and gardens below.
In the inverted world of tricksters, however, this
steam flows upward, carrying the *tiinba* leaf
phallocrypt, guiding *kamdaak waneng*, conveying her
blood, providing frogs and tadpoles, and attracting
the *dapsaan* marsupial. It also connects the
isolated clearing to the socio-moral order of the
distant settlements, bringing moral propriety
ambiguously in the form of *kamdaak waneng* and her
ritual taro. As a high mountain stream, it is
itself a spirit, reacting to the passing scene
through its movements and gurgles. Bearing the
floating *tiinba* leaf and *kamdaak waneng's* blood, it
resembles a diviner's pool of water, blood, and
floating objects, reflecting the exploits of
gabruurian and calling for judgements upon them.
The towering pandanus trees may be either wild or
ritually cultivated, and this matter is never
resolved. The pandanus trees produce clusters of
nuts which, like taro, are among the primary male

foods of ritual significance and which also nurture male substance and *finiik*.

The pandanus is associated with both the cassowary, which is a major symbol of Afek and the founding of the Bimin-Kuskusmin community, and the cannibalistic "great pandanus rite" (Poole 1983), which implicates the cannibalistic *gabruurian* in this narrative context. Yet, in this story, *gabruurian's* cannibalism, which is represented by the implication of his eating the pregnant *dapsaan* marsupial identified with *kamdaak waneng*, is motivated only by personal hunger and not by ritual concerns. Furthermore, *gabruurian* ignores the readily available, ritually important pandanus, just as he rejects *kamdaak waneng's* ritual taro until the end of the tale when his fate is set beyond repair.

The men emphasize the several key indices of moral character that are revealed and developed in the trickster figures. The narrative portrayal of *kamdaak waneng* repeatedly suggests that she is strong, both physically and morally. She has made the arduous ascent into the high forest alone, demonstrating stamina, perseverance, and bravery. She is properly fearful of what she witnesses in the clearing, but she displays courage, magnanimity, and altruism in returning to the clearing, in attempting to rescue *gabruurian* from his apparent fate, and in ultimately sacrificing herself in her efforts. With a smooth belly unmarked by the characteristic scars of female initiation, she is a young virgin. Her smooth belly also suggests that she is not disfigured, which would be a sign of flawed moral character. As a normal premenstruous maiden, her blood from any source is considered to be highly polluting because of the menstrual residues that have accumulated in her body without release, and she is associated with the menstruous *dapsaan* marsupial in this regard. More mysteriously, she is also associated with the female or androgynous *dapsaan* marsupial as a guardian of the fate of *gabruurian's finiik* spirit in the high forest near the "spirit path holes" to the ancestral underworld.

The virtuous *kamdaak waneng* fulfills her expected role in foraging for female food in the form of frogs and tadpoles, in attempting to offer appropriate male food to *gabruurian*, and in trying to avoid his sexual advance. Yet, she also possesses sacred attributes. She bears ritual taro, as suggested by the large, white tubers wrapped in *kiiran* leaves. She is vaguely identified with the shadowy cassowary beneath the pandanus trees, which is a prominent narrative image of the great ancestor Afek. In some manner, she is killed as *dapsaan*, lives on as the giant cassowary, and returns to "her hamlet far below" either in the valley settlements of the human community or in the ancestral underworld where Afek reigns. As the menstruous *dapsaan* and the bleeding or sexually violated virgin, she can be understood as the figure of a polluting woman. As the forager in the forest and stream and the bearer of food, she appears as an ordinary woman pursuing her everyday labors. As Afek the giant cassowary, she is associated with ritual power and androgyny, and the ambiguity of her sexuality is enhanced by her initial virginity, her sexual encounter with wily *gabruurian*, and her apparent pregnancy as *dapsaan*. The men stress, however, the ambiguity of her character as a cautious and wise female who attempts to uphold essentially male moral understandings in opposition to an unruly man who is morally flawed.

In contrast, although *gabruurian* is described as old and is explicitly associated with the adult male ritual activity of drum-making, he is portrayed in many ways as young and immature. He appears naked and only later playfully covers his penis with a leaf. Without proper implements of the hunt, he kills his prey with stones. When he is hungry, he stamps and rages in a childlike manner; and he pleads and grabs for female foods. When he finally partakes of male foods that are then too powerful ritually, it is only after rummaging in a woman's netbag for female foods; and the male foods that he devours are brought to him by a woman. He ignores

the implicit admonitions of *kamdaak waneng* with
respect to the propriety of his ritual endeavors,
his requests for food, and his failures to
acknowledge the *naa-kunum* relationship. He respects
neither her polluting qualities nor her virginal
sexuality. He becomes dominated by his libidinal
urges, and he confounds the sweat of ritual "work"
with that of physical labor and of sexual
intercourse. With blackened face, oozing sores, and
exaggerated penis, he is severely flawed in moral
character. He remains utterly oblivious to the
significance of the *kuutok* and pandanus trees,
tiinba and *kiiran* leaves, ritual taro and frogs or
tadpoles ui muss, laughter and its mournful echoes,
whistling and humming, thunder and drumming, bats
and cassowaries, night birds and birds of the
morning, *dapsaan* and *kamdaak waneng*, smooth belly
and disfigured skin, chert and shining stones,
earthquakes and landslides, forest and settlement,
clearing and stream, cave and karst, moonlight and
fire, and other omens embedded in the narrative.
Both his ritual drum and his *finiik* spirit, flawed
at the outset, have become weakened by his many
inappropriate actions. In the end, denied all
access to the ritual power of the ancestral
underworld as a consequence of his demonstration of
moral insensitivity, the failure and loss of his
drum, and the blocking of the "spirit path hole," he
is suddenly transformed into a bird of the morning.
This class of birds is a recognized symbol of not
only the wandering, fragile *finiik* and forceful
khaapkhabuurien spirits of the young and morally
uncertain, but also the incomplete manhood of boys
at the beginning of the male initiation cycle.

  After the commentaries on details of scene and
character, the men and boys begin to unravel the
"man's path" of the plot and to construct an
interpretation of the story together. Although the
youths are encouraged to offer opinions on the
meanings of the tale, the men direct the course of
discussion and shape the focus of proper
interpretation in a manner that accords with their

didactic purposes in the context of "moral instruction" (*weeng keeman*). I shall note only the key emphases of this unfolding interpretation and its general conclusion.

The trickster *gabruurian* is found utterly alone in a mysterious forest clearing. He is said to be old, and the very name of the story suggests that he may be a ritual elder engaged in secret and sacred ritual undertakings. Yet, his identity is rendered ambiguous almost immediately, and the opening scene is laden with ominous signs. The scene is set at night, which is a time when witches and dangerous spirits prowl in the forest and when *finiik* spirits are loosened from their bodily moorings to wander abroad. Moonlight, which is associated with menstruation and women in various ways, enlivens the unruly *khaapkhabuurien* spirit and clouds the ability to "see," that is, to understand. The high forest setting detaches the clearing from the human communities below, and night and moonlight mark activities that occur when the communities are quiescent. Some proper ritual performances, however, do occur at night under the protection of watchful ancestral spirits, for night is the time of greatest activity in the ancestral underworld. Surrounded by a stream, near a cave and karst "spirit path holes," and adjacent to stands of pandanus trees, the clearing seems to be linked to the ritual powers of the ancestral abode. Indeed, the "flickering shadows" of Afek the cassowary, later to be seen under the pandanus trees, suggest that the great ancestor has been attracted to ritual endeavors occurring in the clearing. But there are inauspicious omens as well. Yomnok the bat flies away, and the *dapsaan* marsupial gives its death scream.

Old *gabruurian* is not what he at first appears to be. He sits on wet moss in the manner of women who are menstruating, and, at such times, the *finiik* spirits of women are severely weakened. He crouches under a *kuutok* tree, which suggests that he is ill and seeks its curative powers, but the *kuutok* tree

is sought only in cases of female illnesses
associated with menstrual contamination. He has a
blackened face, which indicates either that he is
inappropriately dirty and unkempt at the outset of a
ritual undertaking or that he has adorned himself
with a pigment associated with sorcery, pollution,
and death in an "apparently" ritual context focused
on highly individualistic, asocial ends. The
moonlight reveals his glistening skin to be covered
with large sores, which are of a kind associated
with menstrual pollution and witchcraft attacks and
which later produce pus. Like Gahuku-Gama (Read
1955:266), the Bimin-Kuskusmin use "skin" (*kaar*) as
an idiom for various aspects of personhood and "in a
wide variety of contexts to convey information and
to express ideas about others . . . referring to . .
. moral character." A glistening skin, anointed
with boar fat and covered with the sweat of ritual
"work," is a sign of a strong *finiik* spirit and
proper manhood, but a dull, dirty, disfigured skin,
which shines as a consequence of the sweat of
ordinary labor and sexual activity, suggests a weak
finiik and a weak moral disposition. When large
sores exude pus, which is produced by semen and,
like semen, strengthens the *finiik*, there is a
general weakening of the person in all respects; and
the more or less capricious *khaapkhabuurien* becomes
dominant in thought, feeling, and action. In his
wretched state, *gabruurian* can no longer be seen as
a ritual elder.

Yet, in his nakedness, "old" *gabruurian* is not
only defective as a male person, but also immature
and, consequently, incomplete in his developing
personhood. His youthful lack of caution and
impaired judgement lead him to pluck a *tiinba* leaf
from the stream and to fashion it into a
phallocrypt. In so doing, he has offended the
spirits of both the stream and the leaf. He has
disrupted a divinatory omen that might have foretold
his impending fate. He has adorned his penis with a
highly sacred ritual leaf that is used to prepare
drumskins. Contact with the *tiinba* leaf is too

potent for his unstable, immature state.
Eventually, it will cause his penis to swell. Now,
it produces mist amidst the karst, obscuring the
ancestral ritual knowledge that emanates from the
"spirit path holes." The failure of his ritual drum
is certain, and his behavior will be judged in terms
of male standards of the communities below, which
are represented by the *tiinba* leaf floating up into
the high forest. The doomed *gabruurian* does not
understand, however, what he has already done by
blindly and foolishly overreaching his boyish
capacities. He merely laughs and dances, and he
does not comprehend why the cave echoes a wailing
sound of misfortune. He is caught up in the
immediacies of his acts and not their consequences.
Soon, as his penis becomes long, he will be overcome
by sexual urges produced by the angry spirit of the
tiinba leaf, urges that should be denied in male
ritual contexts.

Like the floating *tiinba* leaf, *kamdaak waneng*
comes from the distant settlements, a woman in
search of female foods. She hears a drum not yet
made and properly fears what will happen. By the
light of a fire unseen by *gabruurian*, she can
understand what he cannot comprehend in the mist and
moonlight. Perceiving only a woman who intrudes
upon male ritual events, *gabruurian* warns her to
retreat but frightens her so that she falls against
the sacred karst and bleeds into the stream. Her
polluting blood is consumed by the *dapsaan*
marsupial, with which she comes to be identified,
before it can contaminate the ritual clearing. The
anonymous night birds, forest spirits who see
everything about them at night, rustle in
recognition of the care with which *kamdaak waneng*
guards her polluting capacity.

Despite her injury and fear and his continuing
rage, *kamdaak waneng* returns to offer *gabruurian*
ritual taro to strengthen his *finiik* spirit against
the pollution that he is bringing upon himself.
Although the large, white taro is as ritually
powerful as the *tiinba* leaf, she has carefully

wrapped it in a protective *kiiran* leaf so that it
may help and not injure him. Indeed, *kiiran* leaves
are used in a variety of circumstances to shield the
young from harm when they must be brought into more
or less therapeutic contact with ritually powerful
substances because they are weak or ill. Refusing
the offer of taro and its implied moral relationship
of food sharing, however, *gabruurian* spits to make
himself "ritually hot" (*kaarkaar*) in anticipation of
his ritual undertakings, but his infantile, mindless
rage nullifies the intended ritual efficacy of
spitting. Then, he eats the polluting wet moss,
which will surely make him cold and contaminated and
unable to perform male ritual acts successfully.
After these unfortunate preparations, he decides to
carve his drum from the wood of the *kuutok* tree,
which is associated with female illnesses due to
menstrual or related forms of female contamination
of both men and women. The curative powers of the
kuutok tree are attributed, in part, to its
mysterious ability to absorb pollution into itself.
Releasing that pollution into the clearing,
gabruurian cuts the tree with a piece of chert,
which is often used to excise growths and to release
polluting substances from the body. Recognizing the
danger, *kamdaak waneng* again offers him ritual taro,
but he refuses and childishly pleads for female
foods, which he finally seizes from her and eats.
Laughing, dancing, and sweating with lust, he
attempts to seduce her, not recognizing the
significance of her smooth belly or understanding
the moral horror of sexual intercourse with a virgin
not yet initiated. Finally, denying the bond of the
naa-kunum relationship, he rapes her with his
exaggerated penis, and she flees. Through both food
and sex, he has ignored her claim to an ethically
significant relationship of kinship, friendship, or
ethnicity.

Imagining that he has made a proper drum,
gabruurian kills a *dapsaan* marsupial with shining
stones from the cave and fastens its belly-skin to

his creation. He does not comprehend that the menstruous *dapsaan* is highly polluting, nor does he know that in legendary salt-making rites the skin of the belly of a newborn male child is required to complete the ritual drum. He cannot understand that the shining stones he hurls so violently are sacred crystals which are infused with the ritual knowledge he violates at every turn (Poole 1982b). Thus, unlike a proper ritual drum that hums loudly when its nascent spirit is activated, *gabruurian's* drum whistles like a witch or malevolent forest spirit and hums only softly. Realizing the great abomination of the drum covered with the skin of her unborn *dapsaan* child, *kamdaak waneng* takes the drum and runs into the forest. During his long pursuit, *gabruurian* mistakes the thunder of Afek's anger for the sound of the lost drum. He attaches no significance to the shadowy presence of Afek as a cassowary beneath the pandanus trees. In a childlike manner, *gabruurian* succumbs to his hunger and searches *kamdaak waneng's* netbag for female foods. Finding none, he enters the cave and eats the ritual taro, which is no longer protected by *kiiran* leaves. With sacred crystals, he kills a pregnant *dapsaan* to eat, and there is the implication that he cannibalistically devours *kamdaak waneng*, who is his *naa-kunum* and the *dapsaan*. His laughter becomes the wailing cry of mourning. The *tiinba* leaf falls to expose his disfigured penis (or masculinity?), and his sores ooze pus. The spirit of the stream gurgles the anger of its divinatory judgement. His entreaties to *kamdaak waneng* go unheeded, for she has mysteriously returned to her human or ancestral "hamlet." Perhaps she is also Afek the cassowary, for an earthquake of Afek's rage causes a rockslide, sealing the "spirit path hole" in the karst and denying *gabruurian* access to the ancestral underworld and its ritual secrets. In the dawn light, *gabruurian* becomes a bird of the morning, sings of death, and disappears as a bird-spirit into the high mountain forest.

The "man's path" of this intricate narrative
explores certain aspects of the opposition and
complementarity between men and women and some
implications of the ambivalence of men's attitudes
toward women (Poole 1981a, 1981b). This exploration
is set, however, in the context of male problems of
growing up and premature youthful aspirations to
ritual prowess as a mark of full manhood. Among
Bimin-Kuskusmin, full personhood in its most
elaborated form -- expressed in the idiom of a
powerful *finiik* spirit -- is reserved for senior
male ritual elders, who are expected to understand,
represent, and uphold the ideal values of the
socio-moral order. If they are found to be
seriously wanting in moral qualities, they should
and sometimes do commit suicide. Yet, male ritual
power, which is most fundamentally associated with
the hermaphroditic ancestors Afek and Yomnok, is
linked to the mysteries of androgyny and to
elaborate male pseudo-procreative rites. Indeed,
men recognize that they are politically and ritually
dominant in a social order that can be perpetuated
only through women, but they intricately veil this
"natural" fact by ritual means. Although the
personhood of women differs markedly in both kind
and degree from that of men, women are endowed with
special valued qualities, mystical powers, and
ritual capacities upon which men ambivalently
depend.

Indeed, the influence of women pervades almost
every realm of community life, shaping the early
years of childhood, tending pigs and gardens,
assisting in the tasks of housebuilding, making cord
and weaving, foraging for food and firewood,
mediating affinal relations, providing special magic
and curative substances and techniques, supporting
political and ritual activities, and ensuring
significant ancestral intervention in everyday
affairs. Men tend to claim, in different contexts,
that women are nurturant and supportive, unruly and
perverse, polluting and mystically dangerous,
sensual and erotic, dumb and passive, wise and

active, strong and forceful, weak and submissive, and often powerful in subtle ways. By male ideological reckoning, the *khaapkhabuurien*, fostered by female influences, bodily substances, foods, and secret rites, is dominant in women, and, thus, they are less attached to and constrained by the socio-moral order and more impulsive or indeterminate in thought, feeling, and behavior. But some women show themselves to be stable and judicious, exhibiting ideal male virtues beyond those demonstrated by particular men. Often feeling especially ambivalent about their changing relations with women, newly initiated boys sometimes long to retreat into their recent, affectionate domination by women, yet they may also assert in exaggerated fashion their newfound superiority over women as a result of their initiation as "becoming new men." For them, *kamdaak waneng* provides an example of the complexity of women, and in *gabruurian* they may find a glimpse of something in themselves.

The immature *gabruurian* is utterly dominated by his impulsive *khaakhabuurien*, like the archetypal woman, despite his claim to ritual manhood. Physically dirty, ill, disfigured, and uncontrolled as signs of his impaired and undeveloped personhood and flawed moral character, his claim to ritual power is unfounded and doomed to failure. In his blind determination and boyish ignorance, he easily dismisses the repeated attempts of *kamdaak waneng* to warn him of danger, strengthen his *finiik* spirit, control his bodily urges, temper his indiscretions, and encompass him morally through the *naa-kunum* relationship. He is oblivious to her careful shielding of her polluting capacities or her insistent, subtle wisdom as Afek. Through courage, compassion, sympathy, entreaty, fear, steadfastness, anger, food, omen, and finally self-sacrifice, she futilely tries to bind him to her and to give moral foundation to his ritual undertakings with respect to the *naa-kunum* relationship. This ambiguous claim of the *naa-kunum* bond, however, marks the boundaries of the widest extent of the moral sphere of

"humanity" encompassing the Bimin-Kuskusmin
community. By her identification with Afek and her
offer of ritual taro, she becomes a kinswoman,
worthy of respect and the full complement of moral
treatment due to a woman. Although, for women,
natal attachments and marital obligations may
complicate the loyalties of kinship, this conflict
of duty does not pertain to the unmarried *kamdaak
waneng*. By her appearance, behavior, and apparent
customs, she shares with *gabruurian* that modicum of
cultural affinity that entitles her to at least
minimal ethical recognition as a person. Although
alien "human" women are often killed in contexts of
warfare and feud, one's treatment of them marks a
situation of moral accountability in which injury
must be justified by particular circumstances and
rape is never condoned. By her judicious and
emotional concern for *gabruurian* despite his
imprudence and ill temper, she demonstrates
friendship, which is ethically ambiguous because of
its ad hoc, tenuous, mutable nature. It is a
relationship that neither requires kinship or
cultural commonality nor denies strangerhood, and it
confounds and extends the normative boundaries of
moral concern and distributive morality. Normally,
friendship overlaps with considerations of kinship,
locality, and ethnicity, yet it is encompassed by
none of these bonds and may extend beyond all of
them under exceptional circumstances. Indeed, the
magical resourcefulness and extraordinary abilities
and powers of *kamdaak waneng* suggest that she may be
a "stranger" (*igaar*), perhaps a spirit messenger
from the ancestral underworld.

The virtuous *kamdaak waneng*, although young,
virginal, uninitiated, and female, displays the
moral qualities of the *naa-kunum* relationship in all
of these several senses. From her example, the boys
can learn that women may combine the traits of
dapsaan and Afek in a manner that exhibits the
fortitude and wisdom and judgemental capacity of
developed persons, and that immature youths,
although initiated in a limited way, are undeveloped

persons who are not yet proper men. With caution, moderation, and attention to advice, as well as further ritual experience in male initiation, the youths may slowly enhance their ritual capacities, but ritual power -- the paramount sign of full manhood -- must be founded upon their maturation as moral persons of wisdom, judgement, control, and carefully considered, forceful action in a community of persons. En route to full male personhood, the "man's path" is marked by *kamdaak waneng* the woman and not by *gabruurian*, the boy who would make a drum.

Kin and Stranger: "Twisted Taro"

Long ago, in the distant forest, strong *gabruurian* of the great cassowary plumes and white cockatoo fan lived alone near the great hamlet and sat by his two hearths chanting 'sacred things' (*aiyem*). At the edge of the forest clearing, large, white taro grew tall and in abundance. Its leaves and stalks shone in the sunlight. The great cassowary came often to the clearing to watch the taro . . . .

One day, a fine, strong woman stood at the edge of the forest and watched the taro . . . Her hair was long and braided with black feathers. She carried a large, flat *guutkha* axe and a *batbat* netbag that bulged. She stood silently for a long time and then retreated into the forest . . . In the dawn light of many mornings, she returned alone to stand and watch the taro . . . Strong *gabruurian* watched her from his hearths . . . When she departed, the great cassowary always came . . . She was *kamdaak waneng* . . . .

One day, *kamdaak waneng* stood in the dawn light at the edge of the forest and beckoned to *gabruurian* . . . He ignored

her . . . She beckoned again and held up
enormous red taro . . . Strong *gabruurian*
asked her to approach as the fires burned
low in his hearths . . . She turned and
then disappeared into the forest . . .
Strong *gabruurian* followed and soon found
her footprints among those of the great
cassowary . . . For many, many days,
gabruurian followed, sometimes seeing her,
sometimes seeing the cassowary through the
trees of the forest . . . .

One day, *gabruurian* came suddenly
upon an overgrown clearing in the forest.
Strange animals and trees were all around
. . . Old *kamdaak waneng* stood by a great,
long house, shining in the early moonlight
. . . He was afraid . . . As he
approached, he saw many men and women
sitting together in the big house . . . He
heard the sounds of children in the
forest, but he saw none anywhere . . .
Many small animals ran among the trees at
the edge of the clearing. The women fed
them . . . Old *kamdaak waneng* gave him red
taro, but there was no fire in the great
house . . . As he ate, he felt dizzy and
ill . . . The men watched him. Then, they
asked him to stay and marry *kamdaak
waneng's* younger sister. She was a fine,
strong woman with many large, round scars
on her belly . . . The men asked for his
fine headdress . . . He saw them harvest
taro nearby . . . They copulated in the
garden . . . The taro was small, black,
and twisted . . . They warmed the taro in
the morning sun and caressed it with their
hands . . . They covered it with red
pigment and sweat . . . They screamed for
his headdress, calling him *naa-kunum* . . .
They kept him in the great house . . .
They took his headdress . . . .

One day, when they were in the garden *gabruurian* crept away with a stalk of the red taro they had given him. He took his fine headdress too . . . For many days, he wandered through the dark forest, and the "red" taro stalk made sores on his back . . . Finally, he came upon his large, white taro and his hearths . . . When he had lit his fires, eaten his taro, sung his chants, and was well, he planted the stalk of "red" taro in the forest . . . In time, it grew straight and tall. The leaves and stalk shone . . . The tubers were large and white . . . The cassowary came again every morning . . . He never saw *kandaak waneng* again . . . At dawn one day, an unknown black bird was killed by an *iintang* hawk in a nearby pandanus grove . . . When *gabruurian* came to look, there was only a single black feather near the new taro plant . . . .

The opening scene of the narrative is both recognizable and ambiguous to the boys. By his elaborate headdress of cassowary and cockatoo feathers, the sacrificial hearths, the chanting of "sacred things," and the nearby ritual taro and pandanus, *gabruurian* is immediately understood by them to be a paramount male ritual elder. They readily identify the great cassowary with the founding ancestor Afek, but they also suspect that *kamdaak waneng* may be Afek the cassowary in one of her many mythic disguises. The youths have already learned to be suspicious of isolated clearings in the forest, which they now also recognize as the predictable haunt of tricksters, but this clearing is apparently sunlit, contains a ritual taro garden and a cult house, and is surrounded by familiar flora and fauna. Yet, they claim that true cult houses are not usually located far from hamlet communities. An isolated clearing is not apparently linked to the concerns of a particular community,

and perhaps the wily *gabruurian* is really a
dangerous forest spirit masquerading as a ritual
elder. They argue that, despite his expected
appearance, behavior, and immediate surroundings in
the clearing, *gabruurian* cannot be a proper ritual
elder because his "great hamlet" is never seen or
identified, and the shining taro stalks and leaves
are a suspicious mystery to them. Familiar with
many tales of wanderers in the forest and knowing
that ritual elders do not casually travel beyond the
pale of Bimin-Kuskusmin territory, the youths are
prepared to discover some critical flaw in the body,
behavior, and moral character of *gabruurian* that
will provide an omen of an unfortunate fate. From
hearing the previous and earlier narrative, they now
expect *kamdaak waneng* to follow the "man's path" and
gabruurian to deviate from it. But they can find
neither a defect in the person of *gabruurian* nor a
clear misfortune at the conclusion of his
adventures. They are confused about the
significance of the many strange scenes, events, and
objects that are to be found as *gabruurian* follows
kamdaak waneng beyond the clearing.

In the context of this story, the men offer
only limited preliminary exegesis on matters of
scene and character. They focus primarily upon what
occurs initially in *gabruurian's* forest clearing,
leaving his more bizarre exploits to later
interpretation. By restricting their commentary to
only the first part of the tale, they actively
encourage the boys to search for clues that will
facilitate making sense out of later narrative
events. Thus, the men note that there are indeed
proper cult houses and ritual taro gardens in the
distant forest near the perimeter of Bimin-Kuskusmin
land. These sacred sites are intended to guard the
integrity of the traditional territory of the
mythically founded, ritually sanctified "center
place" (*abiip mutuuk*) of all Bimin-Kuskusmin. Each
ritual clearing is associated with the "great
hamlet" or cult house center of a particular clan,
and the paramount male ritual elder of the clan is

responsible for the linked cult houses in forest and settlement. Consequently, when a ritual elder tends either cult house, he is said to be near the "great hamlet" or ritual center of his clan. Ritual elders frequently visit such clearings to conduct sacrifices to the great ancestor Afek for the growth of ritual taro and pandanus and for protection against alien intruders. The ritual taro grown there is believed to be a powerful, *finiik*-bearing male food for warriors who must battle against intruders, and the pandanus nuts are reserved for the forest cassowaries, who represent Afek. The double hearth of the cult house, however, is related only to taro rites, with the larger hearth devoted to male ritual taro and the secondary hearth associated with taro's younger sister, the female sweet potato. With a proper cult house, a fine ritual taro garden, stands of pandanus trees, and the regular visits of cassowaries, this isolated forest clearing is, in fact, a focus of the male ritual life of a patriclan community.

Beyond these sacred clearings and the boundaries of traditional Bimin-Kuskusmin land, however, dwell various kinds of beings in the farflung mountain valleys beyond normal travel, and the most distant of these beings are not endowed with any significant attributes of moral personhood (Poole 1983). Such creatures engage in outrageous forms of cannibalism and have no fire for sacrifices and feasts. Men and women often live together in a highly polluted state, and no understandings of incest exist. Morally inverted in many ways, these beings may differ little from insignificant forest animals in most respects. Lost in the far forests, unwary travellers may encounter at their peril beings who are not *naa-kunum*, for there is no vestige of shared moral understandings upon which to rely in such confrontations. Legends tell of occasional wayfarers who have been lost forever to these humanoid creatures, but a few strong, powerful men have escaped and returned to the "center place" to tell of their bestial horrors. Such men have

almost always been possessed of high moral
principles and great ritual power.

The men maintain that in this trickster tale
gabruurian is a strong and powerful ritual elder.
The stalks and leaves of his fine ritual taro shine
from being anointed with boar and human semen,
indicating that they bear strong *finiik* spirit. His
tall pandanus groves stand near and are protected by
Afek's spirit messenger, the *iintang* hawk, who is a
warrior of the high forest. His cult house is
active, and his sacred chants are powerful. Thus,
Afek, in the form of the great cassowary, comes
often to the clearing to admire the strength of his
ritual endeavors, as revealed in the tall and
glistening stalks and leaves and large, white tubers
of the taro. Strong, wise *gabruurian* wears the
honored headdress of cassowary and white cockatoo
plumes, which signifies his paramount ritual status.
In his ritual seclusion, he eats only the strong,
finiik-bearing taro and pandanus from the clearing,
and, thus, he has prepared himself against many
dangers.

Initially, *kamdaak waneng* appears as a strong,
proper woman, but she is also seen immediately to be
ambiguous. No proper woman should approach a ritual
clearing of this kind under normal circumstances.
She remains silent, coming to the edge of the
clearing at dawn to watch the magnificent taro. The
men claim that, fearing the powerful ritual *sacrae*,
she cannot enter the clearing. Is her fear as a
woman or as a stranger from afar? In the manner of
a female ritual elder, who would be entitled to
approach the sacred site, she wears male ritual
regalia, but her adornment is bizarre. She carries
the recognizable *batbat* netbag of male ritual
elders, yet her long, braided hair, interwoven with
black feathers, makes her an anomaly. Female ritual
elders wear only separable headdresses, and male
ritual elders alone are entitled to grow long and
unbraided hair decorated with white and red
feathers. She bears the *guutkha* axe of barbarous
peoples to the far southwest that are renown in

legend for their perverted customs and lack of ritual power. But *gabruurian* notes that *kamdaak waneng* seems to be associated with the great cassowary, and he knows that Afek takes many other guises in her effort to watch over the Bimin-Kuskusmin community. As an innovator in ritual matters, he is intrigued by the red taro, for ritual elders are eager to incorporate cautiously new *sacrae* into their cult houses to enhance the power of their clans. Nevertheless, uncertain about her true identity, he invites her into the clearing only after his ritual fires have burned down. When she refuses to enter and turns to leave, *gabruurian* follows her through the forest. He observes that her footprints are intermingled with the tracks of a cassowary, and he recognizes that this sign may indicate that she is the great ancestor Afek or perhaps a dangerous *tamam* witch (Poole 1981a). Immune to witchcraft and a devotee of Afek, the ritual elder *gabruurian* cautiously pursues the mysterious woman and the unknown red taro as a proper part of his ritual undertakings.

After this initial commentary, the men and boys together begin their collective interpretation of the story and focus their attention on the central theme of the "man's path." Strong *gabruurian* is conducting sacrifices that have made the ritual taro tall, large, strong, and straight. The characterization of the taro as straight suggests that it is endowed with *finiik* spirit and, therefore, with important aspects of personhood. Indeed, ritual taro is believed to possess various human capacities, to be a sentient being, to be related to other human and nonhuman persons in mythic genealogies, and to provide male food that strengthens the most valued attributes of male and sometimes female persons. Powerful *gabruurian* has enhanced the strength of his ritual taro by ritual means in anointing its leaves and stalks with human and boar semen. The taro garden is fertile as a consequence of not only the ritual applications of semen and *finiik*, but also the powerful sacrifices

that have attracted the regular visits of Afek the
cassowary, the mother of taro who first created it
in her womb from her purified menstrual blood and
the semen of her consort and brother, the great
ancestor Yomnok. The taro encircles the forest
clearing, forming a ritual barrier between the
dangerous, spirit-ridden forest and the cult house
devoted to the two hearths of proper taro rites. At
this ritual center, *gabruurian* appropriately eats
only the sacred taro and pandanus from the clearing.
His splendid headdress is made of the cassowary
plumes of taro rites and the white cockatoo feathers
of pandanus rituals. He is the great ritual elder
of Afek's taro.

The strange, deceptive *kamdaak waneng* appears
at dawn at the edge of the clearing. Wary of
entering the ritual center, she stands silently and
observes the fine taro. She comes from far away,
bearing the *guutkha* axe of mysterious beings near
the edge of the sky canopy beyond which there are no
living creatures. She seems to wear *sacrae* of
ritual importance in a strange assemblage that is
unknown to *gabruurian*. Her black feathers come from
no known bird of the "center place," and her braids
belong to a custom abandoned by ritual elders long
ago after the great darkness of the sun when animals
came to the hamlets and people fled to the forest.
Yet, she wears the long hair of Afek and the most
powerful ritual elders. She appears in the shadow
of the cassowary at the forest's edge, and both she
and Afek watch the taro. She carries an unknown red
taro, which suggests the ritual strength of male
blood as a complement to the semen and *finiik* of
white taro. The true red taro of the ancestors
disappeared from the "center place" after the great
eclipse, and now taro rites are not as strong as
they once were. Perhaps *kamdaak waneng* is a
powerful ancestor from the time of immortality when
red taro grew, now returning with ritual secrets
from the ancestral underworld. Perhaps she is the
great Afek, who still grows the true red taro. The
strong *kamdaak waneng* beckons to him from the edge

of the clearing. When the sacrificial fires are
finished, *gabruurian* summons the silent *kamdaak
waneng*, but she turns and fades into the dark forest
of spirits and evil creatures.

Girded with great ritual power and wearing his
sacred headdress, *gabruurian* follows the track of
kamdaak waneng and the track of the cassowary into
the forest. He notes the confounded tracks and
wonders if her bizarre ritual adornment signifies
that she is a witch or another highly polluted
woman-being. Unknown to him, Afek watches over his
journey and protects him. Indeed, he glimpses both
kamdaak waneng and the cassowary through the trees.
For a very long time, he travels through the forest
beyond all that he knows. Among the strange flora
and fauna, he comes upon a clearing that is
overgrown, which suggests a lack of order and pride
among its inhabitants. In the clearing stands a
single longhouse of a kind known only among very
distant peoples who are not *naa-kunum*. The strange
kandaak waneng, now an old woman and no longer
strong, stands in the moonlight. Strong *gabruurian*
becomes fearful, for he knows that there is danger
here, which the moonlight of menstrual power may
obscure. His suspicions are confirmed when he sees
that men and women dwell together in the longhouse
and there are no children to be seen. In horror, he
realizes that their rampant pollution has given them
animal children whom they feed at the edge of the
forest. They have no fire, which is a minimal sign
of recognizable humanity in all trickster tales.

Strong *gabruurian* accepts warily a presumed
offer of hospitality from *kamdaak waneng* in the form
of red taro. He eats it in a raw state, which
indicates that there is a lack of true food-sharing.
The red taro makes him ill and dizzy, which are
signs of either ritual hallucinogenic substances of
great power or dangerous menstrual pollution that
can destroy the power of male rites and men.
Severely weakened, he soon discovers that he is
indeed polluted. The strange men and women have
sexual intercourse in their taro garden and, as a

consequence of the horrifying pollution of this act, harvest small, black, twisted taro without *finiik* spirit. The apparently red taro is a sham, for ordinary red ochre hides its true and hideous nature. It is also covered with the polluting sweat of sex, rather than the boar and human semen that strengthens the *finiik* of taro. In an especially strange act, the men and women warm and shape the taro tubers as proper men do with newborn infants. Indeed, the polluted taro tubers, grown in their sexual fluids, are their children, but these children possess no *finiik* spirit.

In another feigned act of moral relationship, the strange men offer *gabruurian* in marriage the younger sister of *kamdaak waneng*. He now understands that they seek to create strong taro and children through the union of himself, the ritual expert in taro, and the younger sister, the female sweet potato. In this way, they wish to imitate the power of the two sacred hearths of his taro cult house. At first, the younger sister of *kamdaak waneng* appears to be a fine, strong, initiated woman, but then he sees that the large, round scars on her belly are not the marks of proper female initiation. They are the marks of old sores caused by great pollution. For bridewealth, the men demand and finally seize his magnificent ritual headdress in their futile desperation for proper ritual taro to give them the *finiik* of true persons. Deceitfully, they call *gabruurian* by the basic term of moral relationship, *naa-kunum*. But they hold him captive in the polluted longhouse.

Finally, *gabruurian* finds his ritual headdress and escapes. In order to purify himself and his headdress later, he brings a stalk of the "red" taro with him. But, carried in his netbag, the "red" taro seriously contaminates his skin and causes great sores to form. The loss of pus weakens his *finiik* spirit. But Afek is guiding and protecting him. After a long trek through the forest, he comes at last upon his ritual clearing. After he makes sacrifices, warms himself, and eats roasted ritual

taro, he regains his strength; and then he plants
the dangerous "red" taro stalk in the forest where
it will not contaminate the clearing. In time, the
"red" taro grows tall, strong, white, shiny,
finiik-bearing, and straight as a consequence of his
ritual "work," and then he can purify himself and
his great headdress. When he has done so, the
cassowary returns to watch the taro. Old *kamdaak
waneng* is not seen again near the clearing, but one
day a strange black bird is found and killed by
Afek's messenger, the warrior *iintang* hawk, among
the ritual pandanus trees. With both the taro and
the pandanus now safe from *kamdaak waneng*, strong
gabruurian finds a black feather -- the sign of
kamdaak waneng -- near what was once the polluting
"red" taro.

The interpretation of the "man's path" of this
tale attends to the triumph of full personhood and
ritual manhood over immoral beings who exist beyond
the pale of the socio-moral order of the human
community, and who are not encompassed by the
furthest extension of the Bimin-Kuskusmin ethical
category of the person. As a paramount male ritual
elder, *gabruurian* seems to represent the ideal
values of full personhood in almost all respects.
Beyond the immediate constraints of community life,
he toils alone for the welfare and protection of his
clan and his people. By emphasizing his solitary
conduct outside of the moral order, the story
stresses how much he is embedded in it. In
strengthening the ritual taro and pandanus of his
clan, *gabruurian* acknowledges the moral bonds of
kinship that are expressed in the idiom of semen and
finiik spirit. By attempting to reclaim the true
ancestral red taro, he marks the importance of those
moral bonds of kinship that are cast in the idiom of
male blood. Male blood, semen, and *finiik* spirit
not only represent moral and jural attachments to
social persons of lineage, clan, ritual moiety, and
initiation age group, but also are the male
procreative foundation of personhood. The strength
of the developed moral personhood of men -- of the

finiik spirit -- depends upon proper experience of
male ritual and consumption of *finiik*-bearing male
food, and *gabruurian*, as a paramount ritual elder,
performs powerful male rites that are devoted to
finiik-bearing ritual taro and pandanus. In league
with Afek and the *iintang* hawk, he guards the
Bimin-Kuskusmin community against intrusions and
moral and ritual defilements of many kinds. More
generally, he upholds, guards, and strengthens the
ancestral ritual traditions that are the foundation
of the socio-moral order of all *naa-kunum*. He
deflects the danger of *kamdaak waneng* at great risk
to himself and through admirable strength, courage,
wisdom, and proper judgement. He does not succumb
to the illusions and the deceits of *kamdaak waneng*,
and he fully comprehends the perils that he
confronts. No form of seduction, threat, pollution,
or fear can overcome his power and resolve. Yet,
although he soon recognizes the strange men and
women of *kamdaak waneng's* longhouse to be what they
are, he never treats them as less then *naa-kunum* in
his own behavior. A lesser person would have
succumbed to a different fate, as other stories,
with which the boys are familiar, recount in detail.

In contrast, *kamdaak waneng* represents the
utter lack of moral personhood beyond the pale of
naa-kunum relationships. She and her "community"
are strangers *par excellence*, spatially and morally
at or beyond the margins of human communities. They
do not recognize the most basic moral
discriminations and understandings, and all manner
of perversions, pollutions, and abominations are
rampant among them. The essential differences
between human persons of moral value and ethically
insignificant animals are blurred or confounded.
Dominated by only the *khaapkhabuurien* spirit, they
cannot be predicted or encompassed by any tacitly
understood senses of socio-moral order. Indeed,
possessing virtually no *finiik* spirit, they are
denied the very foundation of moral personhood.
Consequently, such socially and morally distant
beings are both unknown and unknowable in many

senses, but the exaggerated immorality of their behavior and the defects in their nature set in relief the ethical premises of the known socio-moral order. In this narrative, the boys encounter the ideals of that order in the person and action of *gabruurian* and the denial of morality in the figure of *kamdaak waneng*. The men emphasize that, in the early years of their development as men, they must follow a "man's path that travels the way of the tracks of *gabruurian* and the great cassowary," which may sometimes be confused with the tracks of *kamdaak waneng* or the *tamam* witch. As one ritual elder noted, "it is the strength of your *finiik* that will make you see what tracks you follow."

Elder and Younger: "Boy Who became a Cassowary"

In a long abandoned hamlet, the young *gabruurian* lived alone with his old father *tuguur* ("fat one"). Many times, his father went alone into the forest and returned with mud on his arms . . . His father said that he went to trap the *duboor* marsupial in a clearing near his garden . . . Young *gabruurian* knew that his father did not do what he said . . . He knew that his father had ritual secrets . . . He did not ask his father what he did in the forest . . . .

Not long ago, young *gabruurian*'s mother died, and he was very sad. Often, he went to the forest to find the *kasoor* bird, who wailed in mourning for his mother . . . He played alone and was sad . . . The *kasoor* was his only friend . . . Young *gabruurian* was now a strong "becoming new man." He was proud . . . His father took him to learn of hunting in the forest . . . His father took him to the new taro garden through the forest.

His father took him to the shrine in the
forest clearing . . . Many times, they
went to the clearing . . . His father was
proud . . . He was strong. He learned the
ways of men . . . .

One day, *gabruurian's* father took him
to the great cave and showed him the skull
of his dead mother . . . He looked at her
skull for a long time. The *kasoor* was
silent nearby . . . Later, near the fire,
he spoke to his father about his dead
mother . . . He said that he remembered
how she had cooked food for him . . . He
recalled how she had touched his face of
tears when he was still only a "person of
a woman's house." He spoke of her hard
work in her sweet potato garden as he
watched . . . His father was silent and
then went to trap the *duboor* . . . .

In the morning, *gabruurian* went again
to find the *kasoor* bird. He had not gone
to the forest alone for a long time . . .
Later, he went to his dead mother's garden
and dug up a fine sweet potato . . . At
night, he roasted the sweet potato at the
men's house hearth and watched it near the
embers . . . His father came, and his skin
glistened with boar fat . . . Young
gabruurian told his father of his visit to
his mother's garden . . . His father was
very angry and hurled the sweet potato
into the forest . . . His father told him
never to cook women's food in the men's
house. He told *gabruurian* that he must be
a man and men do not do such things . . .
His father struck him with a firebrand . .
. .

In the morning, *gabruurian* again went
into the forest to find the sweet potato
and the *kasoor* . . . The sweet potato had
grown into a large pandanus tree near the
great cave . . . The *kasoor* bird pecked at

the large pandanus, and nuts fell to the
ground. Young *gabruurian* ate the pandanus
and went to the great cave to sit by his
mother's skull . . . After many days, he
came out at dusk and went into the high
forest near the "spirit path holes."
Young *gabruurian* was now a cassowary . . .
Often, he ate the pandanus and returned to
the cave. He no longer saw the *kasoor*
bird nearby . . . At dusk, he went to the
high forest near a large "spirit path
hole." Always, there were cooked sweet
potatoes in the forest for him to eat . .
. .

In this particularly poignant story, the newly
initiated youths immediately identify with the young
gabruurian, who, like themselves, is a "becoming new
man" between the first and second stages of male
initiation. Several boys have experienced the loss
of a mother, and all of them know about the tragedy
of a death of close kin among their acquaintances.
Most boys have also experienced some sense of
discomfort in adjusting to new relationships with
their fathers and in leaving behind them the
emotional nurturance and warmth they have known as
"people of women's houses" before initiation. Thus,
with respect to this tale, the men offer little
preliminary exegesis, for they maintain that there
are few esoteric details of scene and character that
need to be explained. It is expected that the
youths are familiar with most of the tacit contexts
of the narrative, as well as the subtle allusions
that are bound up with an appropriate interpretation
for purposes of "moral instruction." Three specific
details, however, are explained. The *kasoor* bird is
a spirit of the ancestral abode, who is said to bear
messages between the realms of the living and the
dead. With its keening cry, the *kasoor* is known as
one of the birds of mourning. Endowed with *finiik*
spirit and, thus, certain attributes of personhood,
the *kasoor* is believed to understand the sadness of

death, loss, and grief. The sweet potato garden of a recently deceased woman is placed under a special taboo forbidding trespass until the pandanus trees ripen after the formal conclusion of public mourning, and it is strictly forbidden to her descendants until, after several years, it has been ritually reconsecrated and then replanted with new sweet potato cuttings. For her descendants before that time, the garden may be dangerous because her *khaapkhabuurien* spirit may linger there and attack intruders who are close kin. When the garden is safe, the *kasoor* is said to cry no more in its vicinity. For the husband of a deceased woman, the sign of the conclusion of formal mourning is the removal of all traces of funerary mud and the anointing of the skin with boar fat. Then, the *kasoor* disappears into the deep forest. After these brief remarks, the men and boys begin the interpretive task of unravelling the "man's path" of the tale.

Young *gabruurian* and his old father dwell alone in an abandoned hamlet. Sometimes hamlets are deserted after an especially inauspicious omen has appeared, such as a peculiar kind of death or some other odd and major tragedy. On occasion, older men may remain alone or with a son in the hamlet for a time on account of their nostalgia for the community life they remember there. Widowers often may stay in the decaying hamlet where they have lived for the last years of their marriage, and this manner of seclusion is taken to be a sign of deep grief. Being a widower still in mourning, the old father is somehow flawed in body and in moral character, for his name *tuguur* ("fat one") is unbefitting for a fully initiated man. At the beginning of male initiation, enforced fasting strips away boyish fat, and men are expected to remain lean for the rest of their lives. Bodily fat is produced by the female procreative contribution, and, in excess, it is said to indicate the weakened state of the *finiik* spirit and the dominance of the *khaapkhabuurien* spirit. Under the pretence of trapping the *duboor* marsupial,

the father disappears into the solitary forest. The
young *gabruurian* understands that his father's
explanation is deceitful, for the *duboor* is neither
found near gardens nor trapped. He attributes no
significance, however, to the strange yellow mud on
his father's skin, which is the funerary mud of
mourning. He knows that fully initiated men often
cannot reveal secret knowledge about their ritual
activities, which frequently take place in the
forest. With proper respect, he does not challenge
the apparent deceits of an older and ritually more
powerful man.

As a "person of a woman's house" before
initiation, *gabruurian* has suffered the loss of his
mother. Apparently an only or lastborn child, he
experiences great sadness over the death of his
mother, for the lastborn child is the "mother's
child." In childish, private mourning, he retreats
to the forest away from the hamlet community. He
finds the *kasoor* bird, who understands his grief and
has known his mother's spirit in the ancestral
underworld, to which it often travels. The *kasoor*
becomes his friend and, with its cry of mourning,
helps him to acknowledge his mother's death in a way
denied to him in the keening of mortuary rites, from
which children are often excluded. He wants only to
mourn his mother and to be alone with the *kasoor*.
The cry of the *kasoor* also represents his own
weeping.

Now, *gabruurian* is a strong "becoming new man."
According to custom, his father teaches him the
manly skills of bow hunting and taro gardening and
shows him the sacred lineage shrine, which contains
"bones" of all members and wives of his
patrilineage, living and dead. Again and again,
they visit the shrine in a forest clearing, but he
does not know that his mother's bones are contained
within the shrine. As *gabruurian* learns these male
traditions, he is proud, and his father too takes
pride in his developing manhood. One day, his
father shows him the secret ossuary cave of their
clan and points out the skull of his mother. He

knows that his father has honored his mother as a
fine woman for whom he has much respect, for his
father must have given many pigs and strings of
shells to her natal clan in order to have her skull
placed in his own clan's ossuary. Young *gabruurian*
gazes at her skull for a long time. That night, he
speaks of his memories of his mother's gentleness,
kindness, and domestic labors. His father says
nothing and then again departs for the forest
clearing, where he claims to trap the *duboor*
marsupial but where, in fact, he visits the lineage
shrine to mourn his wife alone and to rub himself
with funerary mud.

Young *gabruurian* again experiences the sadness
of his boyhood. After a long absence, he returns to
his old haunt in the forest to seek the sympathetic
company of the *kasoor* bird and to weep alone in a
manner no longer proper for a "becoming new man."
Then, he goes to his mother's abandoned garden as he
has done so often as a child, for he does not fear
the *khaapkhabuurien* spirit of the mother whom he
misses and who has cared for him so well. He knows
that, as a "becoming new man," he should no longer
enter a woman's sweet potato garden, but, in his
grief, he remembers only the times of his childhood
with his mother. He takes a sweet potato from the
garden and roasts it in the hearth of the men's
house, watching the tuber that has been tended by
his mother. Wanting the female food of his mother
and his boyhood, he ignores the fact that female
foods must never be cooked in a men's house. His
old father returns, and his once dull, mud-caked
skin glistens with boar fat, indicating the end of
his ritual mourning for his wife. Young *gabruurian*
tells his father of his day's experiences in the
forest with the *kasoor* bird and in his mother's
garden. His father becomes very angry over his
son's several violations of the proper customs of
manhood, which often must be emphasized repeatedly
to "becoming new men." He throws the cherished
sweet potato into the forest and strikes the boy
with a hot firebrand, which is an especially

inappropriate and harsh punishment under these circumstances.

Young *gabruurian* retreats to the secluded forest to find comfort in his mother's sweet potato and in his boyhood friend, the *kasoor* bird. The sweet potato has taken root and grown into a large pandanus tree near the sacred ossuary cave, and the *kasoor* knocks the pandanus nuts to the ground for him. After he eats the strong pandanus male food, *gabruurian* enters the cave and stays by his mother's skull for many days. In his memories of childhood, the pandanus is still his mother's sweet potato. As a "becoming new man," he knows that he must eat strong, *finiik*-bearing male pandanus nuts before entering the clan ossuary. When *gabruurian* emerges from the great cave, he has become a cassowary. He travels to the "spirit path holes" in the karst of the high forest. Once his mother's sweet potato, the pandanus nuts strengthen his *finiik* spirit, and he often visits the sacred cave to be near his mother's skull. The *kasoor* disappears, for he no longer needs its comfort, cry of mourning, and tales of his mother's spirit in the ancestral underworld. In the evenings, he returns to a large "spirit path hole" in the high forest, where he always finds a mysterious meal of cooked sweet potatoes. Young *gabruurian*, the spirit cassowary, has joined the ancestral spirit of his dead mother, who now cares for him as she once did for her young son before her death.

This renown trickster tale explores some of the characteristic ambivalences and discomforts of young boys, accustomed to the expressive, nurturant domain of women, who must confront the more stoic and demanding standards of expected male behavior upon first initiation. Within this acutely recognizable context, the story examines the constant struggle of "becoming new men" to follow the prescribed "man's path" and the occasional and understandable lapses to which still young, immature boys are prone, as well as the insensitivities of adult men to the difficulties that young boys experience at this

time. The narrative presents to the youths an image
of themselves that takes into moral account their
often deeply felt anxieties about being no longer
children and yet not fully men. The "man's path" of
the tale focuses these themes upon ambiguities in
the expectations about the personhood of elder and
younger. Despite his indiscretions as a "becoming
new man," *gabruurian* emerges as the hero of the
story, for he deals with a real personal dilemma
that strikes a balance between his memories and
feelings about his mother and the comforts of
childhood and his allegiance to his father and the
ideals of manhood. Often implicitly, this sense of
balance is embedded in the notions of
khaapkhabuurien and *finiik* spirit. His ultimate
moral triumph over his old father is suggested in
his being transformed into a cassowary, which, as a
symbol of the great ancestor Afek, is often endowed
with most complete moral personhood known to
Bimin-Kuskusmin ethics.

The flaw of moral character that is suggested
by the bodily fatness of the old father *tuguur* is a
subtle one, for it involves a lack of understanding,
empathy, and compassion of a kind rarely mentioned
with respect to cultural images of manhood and manly
behavior. Although his obesity is a sign of the
dominance of the often unruly *khaapkhabuurien*
spirit, he neglects a more valued aspect of this
spirit force within him -- the personal memories and
feelings about the experiences of a lifetime. In
effect, the force of his *finiik* spirit allows no
sanctuary for some sense of his experiential self,
and, thus, he cannot empathically and
compassionately comprehend or tolerate the
expression of that facet of others. It is said that
the strong and forceful dominance of the *finiik* in
proper men should not obliterate the more positive
characteristics of the *khaapkhabuurien*. Indeed, the
admired traits of male curers, diviners, and ritual
and political elders, who must assess and judge the
behavior of others in many contexts, are believed to
be dependent upon a powerful *finiik* in control of an

experienced *khaapkhabuurien*. Bimin-Kuskusmin moral philosophy gives recognition and value to both the person and the individual-in-society and focuses upon the nature and quality of the always delicate relationship between the *finiik* and the *khaapkhabuurien*. For *gabruurian's* father, however, there is no sense of himself -- or of his son -- beyond a rigid image of proper manhood and prescribed male behavior, as though there was nothing of significance and value in community life and in personal experience beyond "pure" *finiik* spirit. Interestingly, his distorted perspective, which only emphasizes the *finiik* and the publicly accessible actor, is seen as the dominance of the *khaapkhabuurien*, the perversion and weakening of the *finiik*, and the denial of proper moral personhood.

Old *tuguur's* considerable and understandable grief is apparent throughout the tale in his prolonged formal mourning, isolated dwelling in the abandoned hamlet, long procrastination in reconsecrating the wife's garden, constant visits to the lineage shrine, excessive and compulsive applications of funerary mud, periodic visits to the clan ossuary where the wife's skull has been placed by special arrangement, total silence when his son recalls his mother, and exaggerated anger at his son's attempts to mourn in a personal way. Yet, all of the father's grief is encompassed by the mask of stoicism, force, and anger of the stereotypic adult man and is expressed in proper male ritual forms. The more individually expressive nuances of the personal dimensions of grief and mourning are veiled and suppressed in the narrative image of *tuguur*. In turn, he expresses pride in his son's accomplishments as a "becoming new man," but he has no understanding of the predictable fragilities of a young boy during this transitional phase of the social life-cycle, much less of the emotional needs of a boy who suffers deeply from the recent loss of his mother and mourns that loss in a different, more personally expressive manner. The two emotions of

tuguur, pride and anger, express what he comprehends
and what he does not.

In contrast, young *gabruurian* follows the
"man's path" as best he can in his perceptive
acknowledgement of his father's legitimate ritual
superiority and right to maintain ritual secrets and
the necessity of eating *finiik*-bearing pandanus
before entering the sacred ossuary. Adhering to the
expectations of adult men with respect to "becoming
new men," he learns the manly skills of hunting and
gardening and witnesses the shrine and ossuary. He
is properly proud of his accomplishments. Even when
he longs for his mother and childhood, weeps with
the *kasoor* bird, visits his mother's garden, and
roasts the sweet potato in the men's house, he
understands the implications of these feelings and
actions for a "becoming new man." Yet, he also
tends to understand the full dimensions of loss,
grief, and mourning more sensitively than his
father, and he imaginatively creates -- in the
forest, in the garden, and in the men's house -- a
highly personal rite of death. Powerful spirits of
the ancestral underworld, which take the forms of
the *kasoor* bird and the cassowary and are endowed
with strong *finiik* spirit, assist him in his
endeavors and comprehend his grief as old *tuguur*
cannot do. Remaining a boy in need of motherly
compassion and nurturance to the end, he becomes,
nevertheless, the most powerful of Bimin-Kuskusmin
spirits, the cassowary. The great creature is
endowed with all the features of human personhood.

From this tale, the newly initiated boys learn
that their often confused sense of themselves is
recognized and taken into moral account, that their
occasional longings for nurturant mothers and
childhood pleasures are predictable, and that
personal expressions of loss and grief and sadness
are understood under certain kinds of circumstances.
Their view of the delicate relationship between
finiik and the *khaapkhabuurien* becomes more subtle
and complex. They also come to realize that the
expected alignment of moral personhood with age and

social status is never certain in community life and
that proper manhood is far more than the awesome,
rigid masks of public stoicism and ritual power
which they have seen as "people of women's houses"
and then as novices before they were recognized as
"becoming new men."[21] The men emphasize that
gabruurian, as a "becoming new man," was able to
establish a new kind of relationship with his
mother. The men also make allusion, however, to an
unexamined implication of this story, which will be
taken up and explored in another narrative
incorporated in the second stage of male initiation.
They claim that *gabruurian*, as a "becoming new man,"
must come to see that once he has established a new
relationship with his mother, he must undertake
another personal mortuary rite for his longing
memories of childhood.

Ritual Adept and Novice: "Track of the Echidna"

Long ago, in the bright sunlight, old
kamdaak waneng stood in the smooth forest
clearing near a great house. She wore the
fine cassowary headdress and a shining
stone in her septum . . . As she chanted
"sacred things" (*aiyem*), a marsupial came
to the clearing . . . .
Old *kamdaak waneng* killed the
marsupial with her decorated,
bamboo-bladed arrow and hung it above the
fire in the great house . . . Its head was
singed by the fire . . . She told the
ancestral skulls of the great size of the
marsupial . . . She told the ancestral
skulls of its beautiful white fur, . . .
its fine red fur, . . . its big tail . . .
The ancestral skulls made no sound . . .
She spoke to them again and then chanted .
. . The skulls whistled . . . .

Young *gabruurian* of the bloody nose
stood and watched *kamdaak waneng* in the
great house . . . He saw the black fur of
the small marsupial . . . It was the
dapsaan marsupial . . . He carried the
great ancestral skulls to the forest and
hid them in a cave there. He covered them
with pandanus fronds . . . He waited
nearby . . . Later, a large, strong man
with the headdress of white cockatoo and
red parrot feathers brought them back to
the clearing . . . The great *duboor*
marsupial hung above the fire by its great
tail . . . The ancestral skulls hummed . .
. A large cassowary came into the great
house . . . Young *gabruurian* became strong
. . . .

When the great house was burned,
gabruurian set out through the forest to
find old *kamdaak waneng* . . . For many
days, he travelled in the forest until he
became lost . . . He came upon a strange
forest clearing full of bones . . . As he
rested in the sunlight, he felt a great
pain and dizziness . . . Suddenly, the
great echidna came to the clearing, and
gabruurian saw *kamdaak waneng* run into the
forest . . . He followed the track of the
echidna . . . He was no longer lost . . .
He came upon another clearing where
kamdaak waneng sat on her moss. The
echidna helped him to chase her away . . .
Strong, courageous *gabruurian* followed the
track of the great echidna and returned to
his hamlet . . . .

This trickster story depicts an initial scene
that is vividly familiar to the newly initiated
youths, for it resembles in many ways a central
segment of the "great ancestor cassowary/spiny
anteater rite" phase of the first stage of male
initiation. The smooth forest clearing suggests the

massive effort by initiators to provide a physically and ritually clean arena for the "work" of the "forest house" (*ais am*) stage. The great house is similar to the "forest house" itself in its size, its apparent hearth, and in the positioning of the sacrificial marsupial. The fire in the great house, which transforms it into the "fire house" (*weng am*), indicates that it is the appropriate context for the focal events of the central phase of this stage of initiation. In turn, the initial appearance of *kamdaak waneng* is similar to that of the paramount female ritual elders who participate in this stage of male initiation, although the boys do not yet know them as the ritual impersonators of Afek and Yomnok who appear in the "great ancestor cassowary/spiny anteater rite" phase (Poole 1981b, 1982b). Appropriately, *kamdaak waneng* is an old woman who wears the cassowary-plume *siriik* headdress of the *ning siir ben* stage of the male initiation cycle and a *kondus* nasal ornament similar to that of men in the *kidikairiin ben* stage (Poole 1981b:153). The young *gabruurian* has the bloody nose of a novice who has just experienced some of the ordeals of the central phase of the "forest house" stage of initiation, and the presence of the ancestral skulls in the "fire house" is indicative of the focal ritual power of that phase.

Assuming that the "becoming new men" are familiar with most relevant details of this aspect of the narrative setting, the men's commentary takes a different tack than usual. They provide no specific preliminary explanations beyond identifying the echidna as the great ancestor Yomnok, and then they focus upon key features of the tale without explanation or elaboration. Thus, they suggest that the boys should attend carefully to the minute details of setting, dress, paraphernalia, and action which are associated with the figure of *kamdaak waneng*. In so doing, they deflect the youths' attention away from *gabruurian*, with whom they readily identify, and encourage the boys to begin a more or less haphazard hunt for clues to the

character of *kamdaak waneng*, to which the men listen
without comment. When the boys have quite exhausted
their powers of interpretation, they join with the
men in the collective task of comprehending the
"man's path" of the narrative.

The trickster *kamdaak waneng* stands upon the
cleared site of the "forest house" initiation
ritual. With a sacrificial marsupial hanging above
the hearth fire and ancestral skulls nearby, the
"fire house" phase is active, and the "great
ancestor cassowary/spiny anteater rite" is in
progress. Perceptively, young *gabruurian*, the
novice, watches the ritual activities of *kamdaak
waneng* and notes that all is not well. The central
phase of the first stage of initiation should take
place at night when the ancestral underworld is
active, and not in the glare of sunlight. As an
apparently proper female ritual elder, *kamdaak
waneng* is old and wears the *siriik* headdress, but
the ornament in her septum is not a proper *kondus*
limestone carving. As it shines in the sunlight, it
is seen to be a sacred crystal, which only the
paramount male ritual elders are entitled to
possess. Perhaps it has been stolen! Her "sacred
chants" are mumbled in the manner of male ritual
elders who wish to preserve the secrecy of their
content, but female ritual elders are forbidden to
know the chants of male initiation. Her mysterious
chants, nevertheless, entice a marsupial to the
clearing, but this curious event does not occur in
the "forest house" or any other stage of male
initiation. She kills the marsupial with a
decorated, bamboo-bladed sacrificial pig arrow,
which is inappropriate for this intended sacrifice
and may not be touched by a female elder. She
addresses the ancestral skulls as she describes the
red and white fur and long tail of what she implies
to be the large *duboor* marsupial, which she has hung
by its tail over the ritual fire. Although a *duboor*
is hung in this way during this ritual phase, this
marsupial, as *gabruurian* recognizes, is the small,
black-furred *dapsaan*; and female elders may not

speak to the sacred skulls. The *dapsaan* is the only nonhuman creature to menstruate and is sometimes the spirit familiar of the polluting *tamam* witch, who menstruates continuously. Discerning the present dangers, the skulls are reflectively silent and then emit the characteristic whistle of *tamam* witchcraft as an omen. The ritual is severely contaminated, and its efficacy is destroyed. Old *kamdaak waneng*, in the guise of a powerful female ritual elder, is a *tamam* witch (Poole 1981a).

The *tamam* witch is known to steal proper male ritual paraphernalia and to use them perversely to confound the traditional sacred discriminations and patterns that are believed to lend power to male ritual "work." She is said to attack male rites in the light of the sun, which she uses to blind and stun the unwary. Assisted by the polluting *dapsaan* marsupial, she has damaged the "forest house" in its most central phase. The *tamam* witch and her familiars are lethally dangerous to male interests and to men, whose bodily substances, procreative powers, foods, and ritual secrets they crave and pervert. Courageously, young *gabruurian* recognizes the disaster that has befallen the "forest house" and hides the sacred ancestral skulls in the forest, properly protecting them with *finiik*-bearing pandanus leaves. He watches over them until a paramount male ritual elder, wearing the revered headdress of white cockatoo and red parrot feathers, returns them to the purified ritual clearing. With a true *duboor* marsupial now installed above the sacrificial fire, the "forest house" stage of initiation proceeds. The ancestral spirits within the skulls hum in approval, and the true ritual impersonators of the cassowary, who, unbeknownst to the boys then and now, are female ritual elders, enter the "fire house." Young *gabruurian* becomes strong from his experience of the powerful rite.

When the great house is destroyed at the conclusion of this stage of initiation, brave *gabruurian*, now a "becoming new man," seeks to destroy the danger of *kamdaak waneng*. Losing

himself in the forest during a long and arduous
trek, he encounters a clearing filled with human
bones, which are signs of a witch's lair strewn with
relics of her victims. As he rests, the unseen
kamdaak waneng attacks him through the rays of the
sun, making him feel pain and dizziness. She is
attempting to cut and devour his male organs,
weakening his *finiik* spirit. Before he succumbs to
her sudden assault, the great echidna Yomnok appears
and chases her away. Young *gabruurian* is guided
through the forest by Yomnok to another clearing
where they find *kamdaak waneng* menstruating on the
moss, which is a characteristic position for the
witch at rest. Together, *gabruurian* and Yomnok
drive her away again, and Yomnok guides *gabruurian*
back through the forest to the safety of his hamlet
community. From that time through the second stage
of initiation, *gabruurian* follows the track of
Yomnok the echidna.

This brief story is intended to encourage the
youths to reflect upon certain aspects of their
ritual experience in the first stage of initiation
and of their new obligations as "becoming new men"
toward ensuring the efficacy of male ritual "work."
More generally, they are said to begin to consider
the focal position of ritual endeavors in the male
domain and their own changing relationship to ritual
performances and ritual elders. Accordingly, the
narrative portrays the development of *gabruurian*
from an insightful and wise novice in the context of
"forest house" initiation to a courageous "becoming
new man" who tries to protect the male ritual realm
of which he is now a part. Ever vigilant, the
novice *gabruurian* correctly identifies the fact that
a *tamam* witch, masquerading as *kamdaak waneng* the
ritual elder, has taken control of the initiation
ritual. Defenseless against her power and
pollution, he wisely rescues the central *sacrae* of
the rite and protects them in the forest. When a
paramount male ritual elder has resanctified the
site and retrieved the sacred skulls, *gabruurian*
completes his initiation experience, and his *finiik*

becomes strong. Bravely, he sets forth with his new ritual power to destroy the danger of *kamdaak waneng*. Not yet strong enough to combat the *tamam* witch, who consumes human *finiik* in many forms and transforms it into her terrifying *khaapkhabuurien*, he becomes dangerously lost and weakened until he is rescued by the powerful Yomnok the echidna. Together, they triumph over *kamdaak waneng* for the moment, but male ritual endeavors are always vulnerable to her renewed attacks. Thereafter, *gabruurian* finds the "man's path" in the track of Yomnok the echidna whom he follows into the second stage of initiation, in which the ritual symbols of Yomnok provide the key emphases in continuing the process of ritually making boys into men. The men note that, following the second stage of initiation, *gabruurian* will again battle the witch *kamdaak waneng* in another kind of trickster tale, inflicting more harm but never destroying her.

The youths begin to understand the delicacy and fragility of proper male ritual performance and their growing responsibility to ensure its efficacy and to guard it against harm. As their *finiik* spirit and ritual knowledge develop together, the youths will become more able to perform, judge, criticize, and defend various ritual undertakings. In this story, *kamdaak waneng* represents to the boys not only the more obvious threats of pollution and witchcraft to male ritual "work," but also the uncertainties and contradictions that may mark the subtle qualities of ritual leadership. Their ritual seniors will always be presumed to exceed their own kind and degree of ritual power and moral personhood, but the youths must now begin to assist in evaluating the actual course of ritual endeavors directed by their elders. They must recognize that the office of ritual elder, male or female, is separate from its incumbent, and that the developed moral personhood expected of the office may not be demonstrated in its execution.[22] If ritual comes ultimately to be seen as "what men do" (Tuzin 1980, 1982), it is also fallible human decisions that allocate to sometimes imperceptibly flawed men the enormous authority to govern the ritual "work" to be done. Conversely, the boys must learn that the youth of lower ritual status, largely by virtue of age and lesser ritual experience, may exhibit a more developed moral personhood in some respects than certain ritual experts. A defect of moral character in a ritual elder may erode or pervert the efficacy of ritual undertakings that are the foundation of moral personhood and order for the entire Bimin-Kuskusmin community and beyond, as the extreme case of *kamdaak waneng* as ritual elder and witch suggests. In turn, the community may come to be in the debt of a person whose moral character exceeds the expectations assigned to his position in the ritual system, as the narrative image of the perceptive and courageous novice and "becoming new man" *gabruurian* demonstrates. Yomnok the echidna established the mythic divinatory procedures by which to detect and interpret these contradictions and ambiguities in moral and ritual expectations and realities with respect to the discrepancies between personhood and ritual office. Thus, the "man's path" of this trickster tale is said to follow his tracks.

CONCLUSION

The Bimin-Kuskusmin trickster narratives that are focused upon the themes of a "man's path" effectively perform the didactic function of moral instruction for the "becoming new men" by the ways in which they direct, shape, contextualize, and mediate ethical discussion. In each instance, the scenes, characters, and plots that frame the exploits and forge the fates of *gabruurian* and *kamdaak waneng* create and portray a sense of community, of moral order and personhood, against which are set in narrative relief normative assumptions and less acknowledged ambiguities and contradictions embedded in the ethical foundations of Bimin-Kuskusmin morality. Thus, the tales tend to provide a special cultural lens for perceiving what generally remains tacit in the normative ebb and flow or debate and conflict of community life.

The "becoming new men," who themselves are in a somewhat liminal phase of the social life-cycle, actively and enthusiastically engage in the discussions of ethical problems posed by these tales. Indeed, they often recognize something of themselves, others, and known or imagined social and personal situations in these both near and distant narrative images. Through the provision of esoteric knowledge and both subtle and forceful forms of guidance, their mentors enter into the process of interpretation by directing attention to the ethical questions that a particular story represents. Thus, for both men and boys, the trickster tales promote a playful and a carefully considered reflection upon fundamental ethical reckonings that underlie common and unexamined moral precepts, judgements, and actions.[23]   Most trickster tales are centrally concerned with ritual forms and behaviors, which are of paramount interest to men and which, in turn, provide another prominent lens for viewing ethical issues among Bimin-Kuskusmin. Yet, cultural explorations of ethics in either ritual or narrative forms are inevitably founded upon notions of personhood, of the person and the individual-in-society, cast in the complex idioms of *finiik* and *khaapkhabuurien*.

These folk concepts, as they are incorporated, implicitly or explicitly, in different narrative contexts, permit a subtle exploration of how an actor develops and is identified in a moral career. These polysemic notions allow an examination of how an actor comes to possess various capacities of discrimination, recognition, interpretation, intentionality, responsibility, and judgement; to be linked to a physical body, a set of social categories, and a natural and supernatural realm; to be related to an experiential self and its territorial extensions, and to social statuses and roles; to be propelled or constrained in thought, feeling, and action; and, consequently, to be taken into moral account.

This analytic concern with personhood and its implications for the study of ethical systems has been limited in this essay to several selected and condensed narratives, yet it is significantly informed by Read's (1955) early analysis of Gahuku-Gama notions of the person in relation to a distributive form of morality. Of course, my formulation of personhood includes recognition of the variable individual-in-society in problematic relationship to the socially constituted person, and my sense of the distributive form of morality has attended more to categorical distinctions of gender, age ritual status, and differences between kinship and strangerhood, than to Read's concern with distinctions built on kinship, descent, marriage, and ethnicity. While I have placed much value on Read's remarkable insights into the analysis of the person, morality, and ethics, I have attempted to complement and elaborate them in certain ways. First, I have suggested that some theoretical development of the analytic concept of personhood, which formally implicates the relationship between the social person and the individual-in-society, allows a greater range of systematically linked questions to be asked about the alignment of persons, individuals, selves, empirical actors, and so forth, with respect to conceptualizations of ethics and formulations of morality. Although the conceptual landscape to be explored in this regard remains complex and messy in many respects, it has the potential of enriching the comparative study of ethics that Read so elegantly launched. Indeed, the pervasive Bimin-Kuskusmin concern about discrepancies between individual propensities and attributes of the person requires an analytic framework of this kind if such folk reckonings are to be interpreted comparatively.

Second, I have been concerned to explore folk models that focus on the contours of and linkages between various boundaries, features, properties, attributes, signs, and capacities of personhood -- of the person and the individual-in-society -- and cultural constructions of how such boundaries, features, and so on may become critical attributes of actors that are taken into or excluded from moral account. In this regard, my analysis is implicitly comparative with respect to Read's portrayal of the Gahuku-Gama in at least some respects. The exploration of these folk models, however, is structured in a manner that is informed by the analytic notion of personhood presented above.

Third, I have chosen, in a methodologically deliberate fashion, to explore the moral imagination of the Bimin-Kuskusmin in a corpus of narratives of a particular genre which are intended, by Bimin-Kuskusmin themselves, to promote considerations of morality and ethics, and which are both close to and distant from the exigencies of everyday community life in more or less specifiable ways. Thus, although the Bimin-Kuskusmin are no more prone than the Gahuku-Gama, I suspect, to engaging in abstract discourse about ethical philosophy in most contexts, these narratives and their interpretations reveal a privileged context of more elaborated concern with construals of the ethical categories of the person and the individual-in-society than would be found in everyday communal discourse. Although these narratives are concerned to probe the connections between ritual experience and the experience of mundane community life, they are not simply ritual formulations of a special and restricted kind. Rather, they provide a special lens for illuminating more general problems of socio-moral order in a manner that is consistent with the broader foci of Read's analysis. Indeed, the interpretations of these tales by the newly initiated Bimin-Kuskusmin boys are thought to have primary relevance in making sense of their new position as "becoming new men" in the socio-moral order of their communities -- in the ebb and flow of hamlet life perhaps more than in the

more or less tightly prescribed endeavors undertaken
in the cult houses.

In these ways, I have shown how Bimin-Kuskusmin
moral accounts and ethical concerns in narrative
form are predicated on more or less articulated
assumptions about the nature of the *finiik*, the
khaapkhabuurien, and the *naa-kunum* relationship that
variously link the social person, the
individual-in-society, the experiential self, and
the culturally constituted human being. These
linkages intrude upon personal thoughts, feelings,
actions, bodily constitutions, and various
extensions of the boundaries of the self. They
implicate kinship relations, social categories,
ethnic boundaries, and certain contractual
arrangements within and beyond the Bimin-Kuskusmin
community. They extend to a wider sphere of
natural, supernatural, and regional kinds and
degrees of moral personhood that encompasses and
defines what is distinctive about the
Bimin-Kuskusmin moral community of persons. Indeed,
the range of Bimin-Kuskusmin concepts of personhood
and their moral and ethical entailments is
extensive, and the extent of this range is
significantly bound up with the distributive form(s)
of their moral reckonings. One of the contexts that
provides the greatest and most articulate and
imaginative cultural elaborations and extensions of
these concepts of personhood and the moral and
ethical encompassment that they entail is the
special performances of the narrative genre which
portrays the characters and exploits of *gabruurian*
and *kamdaak waneng*, the Bimin-Kuskusmin trickster
spirits. The impetus of the analysis of these tales
and what they imply about the ethical premises of a
moral life, however, remains embedded in Read's
(1955) splendid "Morality and the Concept of the
Person among the Gahuku-Gama," and I have drawn upon
its enduring contribution in a special and limited
way in this essay.

FOOTNOTES

1. Studies of ethics in New Guinea societies are
   rare. Glimpses of such an analytic concern,
   however, are to be found in Barth (1975),
   Burridge (1969), Fortune (1935), Gell (1975),
   Meggitt (1976), Poole (1982b), Schieffelin
   (1976), and Wagner (1972). The most exemplary
   and detailed analysis of religion and ethics is
   unquestionably by Tuzin (1980, 1982), but the
   relationship between personhood and ethics has
   been explored by A. Strathern (1975, 1981) and
   M. Strathern (1968). Nevertheless, few of
   these studies have developed Read's (1955)
   early and prescient ideas. Of particular
   relevance to this essay, images of ethical
   concern in oral narratives have been examined
   by Burridge (1969) and Meggitt (1976).

2. Field research among the Bimin-Kuskusmin
   (1971-1973) was generously supported by the
   National Institutes of Health, the Cornell
   University-Ford Foundation Humanities and
   Social Sciences Program, and the Center for
   South Pacific Studies of the University of
   California, Santa Cruz. The New Guinea
   Research Unit of the Australian National
   University and the Department of Anthropology
   and Sociology of the University of Papua New
   Guinea provided valuable assistance. The
   primary debt of gratitude, however, is owed to
   those Bimin-Kuskusmin who were concerned that I
   should understand the moral precepts and
   ethical contours of their world. For
   thoughtful criticisms of an earlier version of
   this essay, I am especially grateful to Terence
   E. Hays, L. L. Langness, and Michael E. Meeker.

3. The Bimin-Kuskusmin rarely venture far from
   their traditional territory of the "center
   place" (*abiip mutuuk*). Yet, the wanderings of

persons beyond the protective sphere of
community life hold special fascination for
them. Often, it is the aggressive man --
sometimes in the image of *gabruurian* and in
search of adventure, war, wealth, game,
mystical secrets, or solitude -- who pushes
beyond the security of the community as a
solitary wanderer, depending on his own
resources. In contrast, it is often the woman
-- perhaps in the image of *kamdaak waneng*, a
spirit or witch, or an inmarrying, alien woman
-- who comes from abroad, seeking refuge in and
bringing danger to the community. This
complementarity and contrast in the images of
men and women crossing the borders of the
community is transformed in various and
unexpected ways in the category of "trickster
tales" to be examined in this essay.

4.   Although many genres of Bimin-Kuskusmin tales
     contain accounts of both *gabruurian* and *kamdaak
     waneng*, they are the central *dramatis personae*
     of only the category of "trickster tales," many
     of which are told to audiences of men, women,
     and children on numerous occasions. Indeed, on
     the eve of the first stage of male initiation,
     boys are already very familiar with many of the
     exploits of these narrative figures, but not
     with the particular shape that is given to
     their characters in the particular selection of
     tales identified with the "man's path."
     Implicitly, the larger class of ordinary
     "trickster tales," which exhibit more affinity
     with typical analytic portrayals of the central
     characteristics of the "trickster," are
     intended to be set in contrast with those tales
     that follow the "man's path."

5.   Those "trickster tales" that are marked by the
     theme of a "man's path," however, are narrated
     only before audiences of at least partially
     initiated males in men's houses, and are

associated only with the important interludes between formal stages of male initiation. Indeed, this particular selection of tales -- a covert category -- is told only in the interval between the first and second stages of initiation. At subsequent points in the initiation cycle, nevertheless, these tales may become an implicit or explicit background or point of reference when ritual elders elaborate upon particular ethical themes through other narrative genres.

6.   The "trickster" narratives that contain the "man's path" are said to forge a significant link between the ritual and the secular socialization experiences of the boys, forcing them to consider the relevance of ritual knowledge and experience to the concerns of everyday life. Indeed, the linkage between initiation rites and this genre of narrative is highly complex. In both cases, the cultural construction and location of the person in a social and moral order is a central concern. In both instances, "natural" processes and individual propensities are more or less brought under imaginative control and made to appear to conform to cultural attributions of personhood. In these special tales, however, the conformity itself is brought into question and rendered problematic in certain ways.

7.   Folk models of the complex, hierarchically organized, ritual sociology of knowledge that is elaborately aligned with successive stages of male initiation are paralleled by cultural conceptions of the structured progression of understandings that are wrought in the intervals *between* the stages of initiation (Poole 1982b; Barth 1975). Indeed, the progression of secular socialization within the temporal frame of the male initiation cycle is marked by shifts in the genres of narratives

that are incorporated in the corpus of "moral
instruction," and by elaborations of the
accompanying exegeses that are offered in the
narrations. The culmination of this parallel
progression tends to merge both ritual and
secular experience in the telling of the highly
sacred genre of "Afek myths" (*afek aiyem sang*)
both in cult and initiation houses and in men's
houses.

8. Prior to the inception of the male initiation
    cycle, the boys are classified as *wanengamariin*
    ("people of women's houses") who have been
    nurtured and reared almost exclusively in the
    female realm of social life; and their
    perceptions of themselves, society, socio-moral
    order, and the "culturally constituted
    behavioral environment" (Hallowell 1955) are
    believed to be significantly different from
    those of initiated men (Poole 1982a, 1982b).

9. The juxtaposition of similar and dissimilar
    traits in constructing the narrative character
    of tricksters creates ambiguous or
    contradictory frames of reference throughout
    the course of the stories.

10. Exemplary discussions of the epistemological
    problems of cultural and ethical relativism and
    comparative ethics may be found in Brandt
    (1954, 1959) Downie (1971), Foot (1979), Hanson
    (1975), Hare (1952), Hartung (1954), Hatch
    (1983), Kluckhohn (1955), Ladd (1957, 1973),
    Little and Twiss (1978), Norton (1976), Rudolph
    (1968), Taylor (1958), and Tennekes (1971).

11. See Norton (1976) and Lukes (1973) for
    anthropologically useful examinations of the
    logic and history, respectively, of ethical
    individualism. See Macfarlane (1979) for an
    excellent historical analysis of the

development of English individualism and its ethical significance.

12. See Downie (1971) for a particularly insightful exploration of interconnections between values, persons, and roles in the construction of a distinctively social theory of ethics.

13. For an elaboration of this view of personhood, see Fortes (1973), Harris (1978, 1980), Mauss (1968, 1969), and Poole (1982a, 1982b).

14. Harris (1980), in an exceptionally clear discussion of the conceptual landscape of personhood and related ideas, has clarified these features of judgemental capacity admirably, and I draw on her insights in this regard.

15. See Poole (1981b, 1982a, 1982b) for a detailed analysis of the grounding of personhood and gender in bodily capacities and limitations among the Bimin-Kuskusmin.

16. Following Dumont (1965), Carter (1982) has usefully developed the notion of the empirical actor and the human actor as identified in social life.

17. See Fortes (1973) and Poole (1981b, 1982b) for ethnographic instances among the Tallensi and the Bimin-Kuskusmin, respectively, of nonhuman entities endowed with aspects of personhood.

18. Male blood, in turn, is the idiom of substantial connection between a person and his cognatic kindred and agnatic lineage (Poole 1981b).

19. In their full versions, these tales involve about twenty to fifty minutes in the telling. With deliberate dramatic gestures, chanting,

drumming, commentaries, pauses, and the like, a
given performance may take up to twice as long.
The subtle cadences, paralinguistic features,
and linguistic turns of these performances are
ignored in this essay for reasons of brevity
and interest in only certain thematic features
of the tales for the present purposes.

20. One of the most notable features of these tales
is the elaborate interweaving of metaphorical
constructions that cross-reference allusions
throughout this bounded and special corpus of
trickster stories.

21. This narrative vividly demonstrates a pervasive
assumption about this genre of tale:
narratives promote a self-understanding of
involvement in social life beyond the
prescriptions of rules and norms that cannot be
learned directly in either community life or
ritual experience. Thus, by binding together
phases of intensive ritual experience and
reflective narrative experience, the elders
recognize that social and moral wisdom demands
a kind of detached, imaginative endeavor that
is not ascribed or achieved in the endurance of
ritual performances.

22. Once again, the pervasive problem of the
linkage between the individual-in-society and
the social person is explicitly recognized in
the problematic "fit" between the prescriptions
of office (the attributes of the person) and
the incumbent (the individual-in-society who
may not conform to the expected attributes of
the person demanded by the office).

23. It should be noted, however, that this
sustained and elaborate attention to
ambiguities, margins, mysteries, appearances,
and so on in Bimin-Kuskusmin ethical concerns

is not characteristic of "ethics" in the Judeo-Christian tradition.

REFERENCES

BABCOCK-ABRAHAMS, B. 1975. "A Tolerated Margin of
Mess": The Trickster and His Tales Reconsidered.
Journal of the Folklore Institute 11:147-186.
BARTH, F. 1975. *Ritual and Knowledge among the
Baktaman of New Guinea.* New Haven: Yale
University Press.
BEIDELMAN, T.O. 1980. The Moral Imagination of the
Kaguru: Some Thoughts on Tricksters, Translation
and Comparative Analysis. *American Ethnologist*
7:27-42.
BETTELHEIM, B. 1978. *The Uses of Enchantment.*
Harmondsworth: Penguin Books.
BRANDT, R. B. 1954. *Hopi Ethics.* Chicago: The
University of Chicago Press.
BRANDT, R. B. 1959. *Ethical Theory.* Englewood
Cliffs: Prentice-Hall.
BURRIDGE, K. O. L. 1969. *Tangu Traditions.*
London: Oxford University Press.
CARTER, A. T. 1982. Hierarchy and the Concept of
the Person in Western India. *Concepts of Person.*
(A. Ostor, L. Fruzzetti and S. Barnett, eds.),
pp. 118-142. Cambridge: Harvard University
Press.
DOWNIE, R. S. 1971. *Roles and Values.* London:
Methuen.
DUMONT, L. 1965. The Modern Conception of the
Individual: Notes on its Genesis. *Contributions
to Indian Sociology* 8:13-61.
DURKHEIM, E. 1974. *Sociology and Philosophy.* (D.
F. Pocock, trans.). New York: Free Press.
FOOT, P. 1979. *Moral Relativism.* Lawrence:
University of Kansas Press.
FORTES, M. 1973. On the Concept of the Person
among the Tallensi. *La notion de personne en
Afrique noire.* (G. Dieterlen, ed.), pp. 283-319.
Paris: Editions du C.N.R.S.
FORTUNE, R. F. 1935. *Manus Religion.* Lincoln:
University of Nebraska Press.
FREUD, S. 1962. *Civilization and its Discontents.*
(J. Strachey, trans.). New York: W.W. Norton.

GEERTZ, C. 1976. "From the Native's Point of View": On the Nature of Anthropological Understanding. *Meaning in Anthropology.* (K. H. Basso and H. A. Selby, eds.), pp. 221-237. Albuquerque: University of New Mexico Press.

GELL, A. 1975. *Metamorphosis of the Cassowaries.* London: Athlone Press.

GINSBERG, M. 1968. On the Diversity of Morals. *Essays in Sociology and Social Philosophy.* (M. Ginsberg, ed.), pp. 235-270. Baltimore: Penguin Books.

HANSON, F. A. 1975. *Meaning in Culture.* London: Routledge and Kegan Paul.

HARE, R. M. 1952. *The Language of Morals.* Oxford: Clarendon Press.

HARRIS, G. G. 1978. *Casting out Anger.* Cambridge: Cambridge University Press.

HARRIS, G. G. 1980. Universal Elements in Concepts of the Person: The Taita Case. Paper presented at the 79th Annual Meeting of the American Anthropological Association, Washington D.C.

HARTUNG, F. 1954. Cultural Relativity and Moral Judgements. *Philosophy of Science* 21:118-126.

HATCH, E. 1983. *Culture and Morality.* New York: Columbia University Press.

KANT, I. 1959. *Foundations of the Metaphysics of Morals.* (L. W. Beck, trans.). Indianapolis: Library of Liberal Arts Press.

KLUCKHOHN, C. 1955. Ethical Relativity: Sic et Non. *Journal of Philosophy* 52:663-677.

LADD, J. 1957. *The Structure of a Moral Code.* Cambridge: Harvard University Press.

LADD, J. 1973. *Ethical Relativism.* Belmont: Wadsworth.

LANGNESS, L. L. 1976. Discussion. *Man and Woman in the New Guinea Highlands.* (P. Brown and G. Buchbinder, eds.), pp. 96-106. Washington D.C.: American Anthropological Association.

LITTLE, D. AND S. B. TWISS 1978. *Comparative Religious Ethics.* New York: Harper and Row.

LUKES, S. 1973. *Individualism.* Oxford: Basil Blackwell.

MACFARLANE, A. 1979. *The Origins of English Individualism*. Cambridge: Cambridge University Press.

MAUSS, M. 1968. Une categorie de l'esprit humain: la notion de personne, celle de "moi". *Sociologie et anthropologie*. (M. Mauss, ed.), pp. 331-362. Paris: Presses Universitaires de France.

MAUSS, M. 1969. L'ame, le nom, et la personne. *Oeuvres II*. (M. Mauss, ed.), pp. 131-135. Paris: Editions de Minuit.

MEGGITT, M. J. 1976. A Duplicity of Demons: Sexual and Familial Roles in Western Enga Stories. *Man and Woman in the New Guinea Highlands*. (P. Brown and G. Buchbinder, eds.), pp. 63-85. Washington, D.C.: American Anthropological Association.

MUCH, N. C. and R. A. SHWEDER. 1978. Speaking of Rules: The Analysis of Culture in the Breach. *New Directions for Child Development* 2:19-39.

NADEL, S. F. 1964. Morality and Language among the Nupe. *Language in Culture and Society*. (D. Hymes, ed.), pp. 264-266. New York: Harper and Row.

NORTON, D. L. 1976. *Personal Destinies*. Princeton: Princeton University Press.

NOZICK, R. 1981. *Philosophical Explanations*. Cambridge: Belknap Press of Harvard University Press.

PELTON, R. D. 1980. *The Trickster in West Africa*. Berkeley: University of California Press.

POOLE, F. J. P. 1981a. *TAMAM*: Ideological and Sociological Configurations of "Witchcraft" among Bimin-Kuskusmin. *Social Analysis* 8:58-76.

POOLE, F. J. P. 1981b. Transforming "Natural" Woman: Female Ritual Leaders and Gender Ideology among Bimin-Kuskusmin. *Sexual Meanings*. (S. B. Ortner and H. Whitehead, eds.), pp. 116-165. Cambridge: Cambridge University Press.

POOLE, F. J. P.   1982a.   Coming   into Social Being: Cultural Images   of   Children   in   Bimin-Kuskusmin Folk Psychology.   Paper   presented   at   the   11th Annual   Meeting   of   the   Association   for Social Anthropology in Oceania, Hilton Head.

POOLE, F. J. P.   1982b.   The   Ritual   Forging   of Identity: Aspects   of   Person   and   Self   in Bimin-Kuskusmin   Male   Initiation.   *Rituals   of Manhood*.   (G. H. Herdt, ed.),   pp.   99-154. Berkeley: University of California Press.

POOLE, F. J. P.   1983.   Cannibals,   Tricksters, and Witches: Anthropophagic   Images   among Bimin-Kuskusmin.   *The Ethnography of Cannibalism*. (P.   Brown   and D.   Tuzin,   eds.),   pp.   6-32. Washington D.C.:   Society   for   Psychological Anthropology.

READ, K. E.   1955.   Morality   and the Concept of the Person   Among   the   Gahuku-Gama.   *Oceania* 25:233-282.

RICHARDS, A.   1969.   Characteristics   of   Ethical Systems in Primitive Human   Society.   *Biology and Ethics*.   (F. J.   Ebling, ed.),   pp.   23-32.   New York: Academic Press.

RUDOLPH, W.   1968.   *Der   Kulturelle   Relativismus*. Berlin: Duncker und Humblot.

SCHIEFFELIN, E. L.   1976.   *The Sorrow   of the Lonely and the Burning   of   the   Dancers*.   New York: St. Martin's Press.

SHWEDER, R. A.   and E. J. BOURNE.   1982.   Does   the Concept   of   the   Person   Vary   Cross-Culturally? *Cultural Conceptions   of   Mental   Health Therapy*. (A. J.   Marsella   and G. M.   White,   eds.),   pp. 97-137 Dordrecht: D. Reidel.

STRATHERN, A. J.   1975.   Why   is   Shame on the Skin? *Ethnology* 14:347-356.

STRATHERN, A. J.   1981.   *"NOMAN"*:   Representations of Identity in Mount   Hagen.   *The   Structure   of Folk   Models*.   (L.   Holy   and M. Stuchlik, eds.), pp. 281-303.   London: Academic Press.

STRATHERN, M.   1968.   *Popokl*:   The   Question   of Morality.   *Mankind* 6:553-562.

TAYLOR, P. W. 1958.   Social Science and Ethical
    Relativism. *Journal of Philosophy* 55:32-44.
TENNEKES, J.   1971.   *Anthropology, Relativism, and
    Method.* Assen: Koninklijke Van Gorcum.
TUZIN, D. F.   1980.   *The Voice of the Tambaran.*
    Berkeley: University of California Press.
TUZIN, D. F.   1982.   Ritual Violence   Among   the
    Ilahita Arapesh: The Dynamics of Moral   and
    Religious Uncertainty. *Rituals of Manhood.* (G.
    H.   Herdt,   ed.),   pp.   321-355.   Berkeley:
    University of California Press.
WAGNER, R.   1972.   *Habu.*   Chicago: The University of
    Chicago Press.

About the Contributors

Terence E. Hays received his Ph.D. in Anthropology from the University of Washington in 1974, following fieldwork in the Eastern Highlands of Papua New Guinea. He is the author of numerous scholarly articles on the Ndumba Tairora and compiled *Anthropology in the New Guinea Highlands: An Annotated Bibliography*, published in 1976. Since 1973, he has been with the Department of Anthropology and Geography at Rhode Island College, where he is currently Associate Professor, specializing in Oceania, ethnobiology, and linguistic, medical, and psychological anthropology.

Gilbert Herdt is Associate Professor, Committee for Human Development, University of Chicago. He studied with K. E. Read at the University of Washington, where he did graduate work in 1972-1974. Herdt was awarded a Fulbright Scholarship to Australia, from which he conducted fieldwork among the Sambia of the Eastern Highlands, Papua New Guinea (1974-1976). For this research on individual identity and ritual initiation, Herdt was awarded a Ph.D. from the Institute of Advanced Studies, The Australian National University, in 1978. Herdt was a Postdoctoral Fellow in Psychiatry at UCLA between 1978-1979. He taught at Stanford prior to Chicago. Herdt's publications include *Guardians of the Flutes* (1981), *Rituals of Manhood* (1982), *Ritualized Homosexuality in Melanesia* (1984), and other papers. He wishes here to acknowledge -- again -- his great professional debt to Mick Read, and to pay tribute to his continuing friendship with him through this essay.

L. L. Langness received his Ph.D. from the University
of Washington in 1964. He has done fieldwork in the
New Guinea Highlands and also on the Northwest Coast.
He has taught at the University of Washington,
Northwestern University and at UCLA where he is
currently Professor of Psychiatry and Anthropology.
He has authored and edited a number of books
including *The Study of Culture* and (with Gelya Frank)
Lives: An Anthropological Approach to Biography.

Harold G. Levine is Associate Professor of Education
at the Graduate School of Education, University of
California at Los Angeles. Trained as an
anthropologist at the University of Pennsylvania he
spent 19 months among the Kafe of the Eastern
Highlands Province, Papua New Guinea. His primary
research interests are in the area of cognition and
culture.

Anna S. Meigs is Assistant Professor of Anthropology
at Macalester College, St. Paul, Minnesota. A
graduate of Wellesley College, she received her
doctorate from the University of Pennsylvania. Her
fieldwork among the Hua of the Eastern Highlands
focused on an extensive set of food rules which she
analyzed as a system of symbols for talking about the
body and sex. Her New Guinea data has been published
in several articles and in a book *Food, Sex, and
Pollution: A New Guinea Religion* (Rutgers University
Press, 1983).

K. J. Pataki-Schweizer was educated at Cornell
University, the University of Chicago, and the
University of Washington where he did graduate
studies. He has done field research in the United
States, British Columbia, Malaysia, Papua New Guinea

and Irian Jaya. His publications include the monograph *A New Guinea Landscape: Community, Space and Time in the Eastern Highlands*. He has taught at Reed College, the University of Colorado, San Jose University, and the University of California, San Francisco where he is a Research Associate. He is Associate Professor of Behavioural Science and Medical Anthropology in the Department of Community Medicine, Faculty of Medicine, University of Papua New Guinea.

Fitz John Porter Poole is Associate Professor of Anthropology and Co-Director of the Melanesian Studies Resource Center at the University of California, San Diego. Educated in the United States and Europe, he received his doctorate in Anthropology and in Social Psychology from Cornell University in 1976. His field research among the Bimin-Kuskusmin of the West Sepik Province, Papua New Guinea, has yielded a number of studies of male initiation, ritual symbolism and experience, gender idealogy, and indigenous epistemology that have appeared in numerous edited volumes and such journals as *Ethos*, *Mankind*, and *Social Analysis*. He is now completing a monograph on *The Rites of Childhood: Images of the Child as Person in Bimin-Kuskusmin Society* and is beginning another study on the Bimin-Kuskusmin male initiation cycle.

Marie Reay is senior lecturer in Anthropology at the Australian National University in Canberra. She was one of the pioneer anthropologists in the New Guinea Highlands where she continues to do research. She is the author of *The Kuma: Freedom and Conformity in the New Guinea Highlands* and editor of *Aborigines Now: New Perspective in the Study of Aboriginal Communities*.

Roy Wagner (also Sogang, Unakulis Clan, central New Ireland) is Professor and Chairman, Department of Anthropology, at the University of Virginia. His first fieldwork among the Daribi of Mt. Karimui was carried out under the direction of Kenneth E. Read and James B. Watson, as part of the New Guinea Native Religions Project, funded by the Bollingen Foundation and the University of Washington. He has since conducted additional fieldwork among the Daribi and also among the Usen Barok, of New Ireland, and has published three monographs on the Daribi, as well as a more general book, *The Invention of Culture*.

George D. Westermark is Associate Professor of Anthropology at the University of Santa Clara. He was born in California in 1950 and received his secondary and undergraduate schooling there. His graduate studies were pursued at the University of Washington where he worked under the supervision of K. E. Read and James B. Watson. In 1977-78, he conducted research concerning legal and political development among the Agarabi of the Eastern Highlands. He was awarded the Ph.D. in 1981 for the resulting dissertation.

Bibliography of Kenneth E. Read
Compiled by Terence E. Hays

1946. Social Organization in the Markham Valley, New Guinea. *Oceania* 17(2):93-118.

1947. Effects of the Pacific War in the Markham Valley. *Oceania* 18(2):95-116.

1949-50. Notes on Some Problems of Political Confederation. *South Pacific* 3(12): 229-234; 4(1):5-10.

1950. The Political System of the Ngarawapum. *Oceania* 20(3):185-223.

1951a. The Gahuku-Gama of the Central Highlands. *South Pacific* 5(8):154-164.

1951b. Developmental Projects in the Central Highlands of New Guinea. *South Pacific* 5(10):202-207.

1952a. Missionary Activities and Social Change in the Central Highlands. *South Pacific* 5(11):229-238.

1952b. Land in the Central Highlands. *South Pacific* 6(7):440-449, 465.

1952c. Nama Cult of the Central Highlands, New Guinea. *Oceania* 23(1):1-25. (Reprinted 1971 in *Melanesia: Readings on a Culture Area.* [L. L. Langness and John C. Weschler, eds.], pp. 214-239, Scranton, Pa.: Chandler.)

1954a. Cultures of the Central Highlands, New Guinea. *Southwestern Journal of Anthropology* 10(1):1-43. (Reprinted in 1954 with abridgements in *South Pacific*, 7(9):840-852.)

1954b. Marriage among the Gahuku-Gama of the Eastern Central Highlands, New Guinea. *South Pacific* 7(10):864-871.

1955. Morality and the Concept of Person Among the Gahuku-Gama, Eastern Highlands, New

Guinea. *Oceania* 25(4):233-282. (Reprinted 1967 with abridgements in *Myth and Cosmos: Readings in Mythology and Symbolism.* [John Middleton, ed.], pp. 185-229, Garden City: Natural History Press.)

1957.   Review: J. D. Legge, Australian Colonial Policy. *Pacific Historical Review* 26:307

1958a.   A "Cargo" Situation in the Markham Valley, New Guinea. *Southwestern Journal of Anthropology* 14(3):273-294.

1958b.   Review: Peter Worsley, The Trumpet Shall Sound. *American Sociological Review* 23:345-346.

1959.   Leadership and Consensus in a New Guinea Society. *American Anthropologist* 61(3):425-436. (Reprinted 1964 in *Cultural and Social Anthropology: Selected Readings.* [Peter B. Hammond, ed.], pp.239-249, New York: Macmillan.)

1961.   Review: Robert H. Lowie, Robert H. Lowie, Ethnologist: A Personal Record. *Pacific Northwest Quarterly* 52:36.

1965.   *The High Valley.* New York: Charles Scribner's Sons. British Edition: London: Allen and Unwin, 1966.
           Lyceum Edition: New York: Scribner's, 1968.
           Russian Edition: Moscow: Nauka, 1969. Special American Museum of Natural History Edition: Garden City: Doubleday, 1970.
           Reprinted, with a new Preface: New York: Columbia University Press, 1980.

1967a.   Review: Maslyn Williams, The Far Side of the Sky. *Book Week*, 28 May, 4:11.

1967b.   Review: Louis Giddings, Ancient Men of the Arctic. Book World, 10 September, 1:14.

1971.   *The Human Aviary.* Photographs by George Holton; Text by Kenneth E. Read.) New York: Charles Scribner's Sons.

1980.   *Other Voices: The Style of a Male Homosexual Tavern.* Novato, CA.: Chandler and Sharp.

1986.   *Return to the High Valley.* Berkeley: University of California Press.

ahead or out of his time — ex: High V + "Sch
for those who didn't study w/ him,
he still had a large impact
bec. of his prescience —
eg. — "Lead + Consensus" — etc.
By far the most influential essay in the
volume — Read's "Morality..."